Praise for *The Richest Man*

"Fugger was the first modern plutocrat. Like his contemporaries Machiavelli and Cesare Borgia, he knew the world as it was, not how he wanted it to be. This is the absorbing story of how, by being indispensable to customers and ruthless with enemies, Fugger wrote the playbook for everyone who keeps score with money. A must for anyone interested in history or wealth creation."

—Bryan Burrough, author of *Days of Rage* and co-author of
Barbarians at the Gate

"Greg Steinmetz has unearthed the improbable yet true story of the world's first modern capitalist. . . . Fugger, a wily lender and capitalist who courted risk, defied potential bankruptcy, and made kings his virtual dependents . . . emerges from this solidly researched and briskly narrated biography as surprisingly recognizable—a moneymaker from a distant time who, one suspects, would be thoroughly at home with the Midases of today."

—Roger Lowenstein, author of *When Genius Failed* and
Buffett: The Making of an American Capitalist

"Jacob Fugger was the Rockefeller of the Renaissance. He was a capitalist genius who, in Greg Steinmetz, has finally found the English-language biographer he deserves. Steinmetz's fast-moving tale—of money-making, religious tumult, political chicanery, and violent clashes between the disciples of capitalism and communism—is one for all time, but especially for our time."

—James Grant, author of *The Forgotten Depression: 1921,
the Crash That Cured Itself*

"Greg Steinmetz has rescued from the footnotes of history the Renaissance equivalent of a modern-day Zelig. Master moneyman Jacob Fugger pops up at virtually every critical moment of his era. Kings, emperors, and popes all knew him. Now, thanks to this remarkably researched and fascinating book, we do, too."

—Steve Stecklow, Pulitzer Prize–winning journalist

"A colorful introduction to one of the most influential businessmen in history."

—*The New York Times Book Review*

"Enjoyable . . . readable and fast-paced."

—*The Wall Street Journal*

"The tale of Fugger's aspiration, ruthlessness and greed is riveting."

—*The Economist*

"Steinmetz lays out the fascinating story of a man who shaped modern business practices and the borders of Europe."

—*The New Yorker*

"Provides a fascinating and useful cautionary tale of the dangers of unbridled capitalism, particularly in economies dominated by autocratic rulers."

—*The New York Times*

"Who says the biography of a German Renaissance banker has to be as dense and as dull as the Fed's latest annual report? . . . In his first full-length history, a biography of a Renaissance industrialist and financier named Jacob Fugger, Steinmetz is witty, highly knowledgeable and always entertaining. . . . Pure reading pleasure."

—*The Buffalo News*

"Makes a persuasive case that Fugger was 'the most influential businessman of all time.' "

—*New York Post*

"Steinmetz makes a convincing case for the value of studying enigmatic banker Jacob Fugger. . . . A straightforward, engaging look at this 'German Rockefeller.' "

—*Kirkus Reviews*

THE
RICHEST
✦ MAN ✦
WHO EVER LIVED

The Life and Times of Jacob Fugger

GREG STEINMETZ

SIMON & SCHUSTER PAPERBACKS

New York   London   Toronto   Sydney   New Delhi

Simon & Schuster Paperbacks
An Imprint of Simon & Schuster, Inc.
1230 Avenue of the Americas
New York, NY 10020

First Simon & Schuster trade paperback edition August 2016

SIMON & SCHUSTER PAPERBACKS and colophon are
registered trademarks of Simon & Schuster, Inc.

For information about special discounts for bulk purchases,
please contact Simon & Schuster Special Sales at
1-866-506-1949 or business@simonandschuster.com.

The Simon & Schuster Speakers Bureau can bring authors to your live event.
For more information or to book an event, contact the
Simon & Schuster Speakers Bureau at 1-866-248-3049 or
visit our website at www.simonspeakers.com.

Interior design by Ruth Lee-Mui

Manufactured in the United States of America

9   10   8

The Library of Congress has cataloged the hardcover edition as follows:

Steinmetz, Greg.
  The richest man who ever lived : the life and times
of Jacob Fugger / Greg Steinmetz.
    pages cm
    1. Fugger, Jakob, 1459–1525. 2. Bankers—Germany—Biography.
3. Moneylenders—Germany—Biography. 4. Businessmen—Germany—
Biography. 5. Germany—History—1273–1517. I. Title.
  HG1552.F795S74 2015
  332.092—dc23
  [B]

                                    2014047507

ISBN 978-1-4516-8855-9
ISBN 978-1-4516-8856-6 (pbk)
ISBN 978-1-4516-8857-3 (ebook)

To my parents, Art and Thea Steinmetz, two Swabians who, like Fugger, know the value of hard work and thrift.

Contents

THE
RICHEST
❖ MAN ❖
WHO EVER LIVED

Introduction

On a spring day in 1523, Jacob Fugger, a banker from the German city of Augsburg, summoned a scribe and dictated a collection notice. A customer was behind on a loan payment. After years of leniency, Fugger had finally lost patience.

Fugger wrote collection letters all the time. But the 1523 letter was remarkable because he addressed it not to a struggling fur trader or a cash-strapped spice importer but to Charles V, the most powerful man on earth. Charles had eighty-one titles, including Holy Roman emperor, king of Spain, king of Naples, king of Jerusalem, duke of Burgundy and lord of Asia and Africa. He ruled an empire that was the biggest since the days of ancient Rome, and would not be matched until the days of Napoleon and Hitler. It stretched across Europe and over the Atlantic to Mexico and Peru, thus becoming the first in history where the sun never set. When the pope defied Charles, he sacked Rome. When France fought him, he captured its king. The people regarded Charles as divine and tried to touch him for his supposed power to heal. "He is himself a living law and above all other law," said an imperial councilor. "His Majesty is as God on earth."

Fugger was the grandson of a peasant and a man Charles could have easily strapped to the rack for impertinence. So it must have surprised him that Fugger not only addressed him as an equal but furthered the affront by reminding him to whom he owed his success. "It is well known that without me your majesty might not have acquired the imperial crown," Fugger wrote. "You will order that the money which I have paid out, together with the interest upon it, shall be reckoned up and paid without further delay."

People become rich by spotting opportunities, pioneering new technologies or besting opponents in negotiations. Fugger (rhymes with *cougar*) did all that but had an extra quality that lifted him to a higher orbit. As the letter to Charles indicates, he had nerve. In a rare moment of reflection, Fugger said he had no trouble sleeping because he put aside daily affairs as easily as he shed his clothing before going to bed. Fugger stood three inches taller than average and his most famous portrait, the one by Dürer, shows a man with a calm, steady gaze loaded with conviction. His coolness and self-assurance allowed him to stare down sovereigns, endure crushing amounts of debt and bubble confidence and joviality when faced with ruin. Nerve was essential because business was never more dangerous than in the sixteenth century. Cheats got their hands cut off or a hot poker through the cheek. Deadbeats rotted in debtor's prison. Bakers caught adulterating the bread received a public dunking or got dragged through town to the taunts of mobs.

Moneylenders faced the cruelest fate. As priests reminded their parishioners, lenders—what the church called usurers—roasted in purgatory. To prove it, the church dug up graves of suspected usurers and pointed to the worms, maggots and beetles that gorged on the decaying flesh. As everyone knew, the creatures were confederates of Satan. What better proof that the corpses belonged to usurers?

Given the consequences of failure, it's a wonder Fugger strove to rise as high as he did. He could have retired to the country and, like some of his customers, lived a life of stag hunting, womanizing and feasts where, for entertainment, dwarfs popped out of pies. Some of his heirs did just that. But he wanted to see how far he could go even if it meant risking his freedom and his soul. A gift for rationalization soothed his conscience. He understood that people considered him "unchristian and unbrotherly." He knew that enemies called him a usurer and a Jew, and said he was damned. But he waved off the attacks with logic. The Lord must have wanted him to make money, otherwise he wouldn't have given him such a talent for it. "Many in the world are hostile to me," Fugger wrote. "They say I am rich. I am rich by God's grace without injury to any man."

When Fugger said Charles would not have become emperor without him, he wasn't exaggerating. Not only did Fugger pay the bribes that secured his elevation, but Fugger had also financed Charles's grandfather and taken his family, the Habsburgs, from the wings of European politics to center stage. Fugger made his mark in other ways, too. He roused commerce from its medieval slumber by persuading the pope to lift the ban on moneylending. He helped save free enterprise from an early grave by financing the army that won the German Peasants' War, the first great clash between capitalism and communism. He broke the back of the Hanseatic League,

Europe's most powerful commercial organization before Fugger. He engineered a shady financial scheme that unintentionally provoked Luther to write his Ninety-five Theses, the document that triggered the Reformation, the earth-shattering event that cleaved European Christianity in two. He most likely funded Magellan's circumnavigation of the globe. On a more mundane note, he was among the first businessmen north of the Alps to use double-entry bookkeeping and the first anywhere to consolidate the results of multiple operations in a single financial statement—a breakthrough that let him survey his financial empire with a single glance and always know where his finances stood. He was the first to send auditors to check up on branch offices. And his creation of a news service, which gave him an information edge over his rivals and customers, earned him a footnote in the history of journalism. For all these reasons, it is fair to call Fugger the most influential businessman of all time.

Fugger changed history because he lived in an age when, for the first time, money made all the difference in war and, hence, politics. And Fugger had money. He lived in palaces and owned a collection of castles. After buying his way into the nobility, he lorded over enough fiefdoms to get his name on the map. He owned a breathtaking necklace later worn by Queen Elizabeth I. When he died in 1525, his fortune came to just under 2 percent of European economic output. Not even John D. Rockefeller could claim that kind of wealth. Fugger was the first documented millionaire. In the generation preceding him, the Medici had a lot of money but their ledgers only report sums up to five digits, even though they traded in currencies of roughly equal value to Fugger's. Fugger was the first to show seven digits.

Fugger made his fortune in mining and banking, but he also

sold textiles, spices, jewels and holy relics such as bones of martyrs and splinters of the cross. For a time, he held a monopoly on guaiacum, a Brazilian tree bark believed to cure syphilis. He minted papal coins and funded the first regiment of Swiss papal guards. Others tried to play the same game as Fugger, most notably his Augsburg neighbor Ambrose Hochstetter. While Fugger was never richer or more solvent than at the time of his death, Hochstetter, the pioneer of banking for the masses, went bust and died in a prison.

Fugger began his career as a commoner, the lowest rung in the European caste system. If he failed to bow before a baron or clear the way for a knight on a busy street, he risked getting skewered with a sword. But his mean origins posed no obstacle; all businesspeople were commoners and the Fugger family was rich enough to buy him every advantage. The Fuggers had a knack for textile trading and records show they were among the biggest taxpayers in town. There were nevertheless challenges. Fugger's father died when he was ten. If not for a strong and resourceful mother, he might have gotten nowhere. Another handicap was his place in the birth order. He was the seventh of seven boys, a spot in the lineup that should have landed him in a monastery rather than in business. He had character flaws like anyone else. He was headstrong, selfish, deceitful and sometimes cruel. He once sent the family of a top lieutenant to the poor house after the aide died and he refused to forgive a loan. But he turned at least one of those flaws—a tendency to trumpet his own achievements—into an asset. His boasts were good advertising; by letting visitors know what he paid for a diamond or how much money he could conjure for a loan, he broadcast his ability to do more for clients than other bankers.

The downside of notoriety was resentment. Enemies pursued

Fugger most of his working life and his career unfolded like a video game. They attacked him both head-on and from surprising angles, throwing him progressively more difficult challenges as he rose in wealth and power. Luther wanted to bankrupt him and his family, declaring he wanted to "put a bit in the mouths of the Fuggers." Ulrich von Hutten, a knight who was the most famous German writer of his time, wanted to kill him. But he survived every assault and accumulated more points in the form of money and power.

Did success make Fugger happy? Probably not, at least not by conventional terms. He had few friends, only business associates. His only child was illegitimate. His nephews, to whom he relinquished his empire, disappointed him. While on his deathbed, with no one at his side other than paid assistants, his wife was with her lover. But he succeeded on his own terms. His objective was neither comfort nor happiness. It was to stack up money until the end. Before he died, he composed his own epitaph. It was an unabashed statement of ego that would have been impossible a generation earlier, before the Renaissance philosophy of individualism swept Germany, when even a self-portrait—a form of art Dürer created during Fugger's lifetime— would have been regarded as hopelessly egotistical and contrary to social norms.

TO GOD, ALL-POWERFUL AND GOOD! Jacob Fugger, of Augsburg, ornament to his class and to his country, Imperial Councilor under Maximilian I and Charles V, second to none in the acquisition of extraordinary wealth, in liberality, in purity of life, and in the greatness of soul, as he was comparable to none in life, so after death is not to be numbered among the mortal.

Today Fugger is more known for philanthropic works, notably the Fuggerei public housing project in Augsburg, than for being "second to none in the acquisition of extraordinary wealth." The Fuggerei remains in operation and attracts thousands of foreign visitors a year thanks to investments Fugger made five centuries ago. But Fugger's legacy is even more enduring. His deeds changed history more than those of most monarchs, revolutionaries, prophets and poets ever did, and his methods blazed the path for five centuries of capitalists. We can easily see in Fugger a modern figure. He was at his core an aggressive businessman trying to make as much money as possible and doing whatever it took to achieve his ends. He chased the biggest opportunities. He won favors from politicians. He used his money to rewrite the rules to his advantage. He surrounded himself with lawyers and accountants. He fed on information. These days, billionaires with the same voracious instincts as Fugger fill the pages of the financial press. But Fugger blazed the trail. He was the first modern businessman in that he was the first to pursue wealth for its own sake and without fear of damnation. To understand our financial system and how we got it, it pays to understand him.

1

※

SOVEREIGN DEBT

In Renaissance Germany, few cities matched the energy and excitement of Augsburg. Markets overflowed with everything from ostrich eggs to the skulls of saints. Ladies brought falcons to church. Hungarian cowboys drove cattle through the streets. If the emperor came to town, knights jousted in the squares. If a murderer was caught in the morning, a hanging followed in the afternoon for all to see. Augsburg had a high tolerance for sin. Beer flowed in the bathhouses as freely as in the taverns. The city not only allowed prostitution but maintained the brothel.

Jacob Fugger was born here in 1459. Augsburg was a textile town and Fugger's family had grown rich buying cloth made by local weavers and selling it at fairs in Frankfurt, Cologne and over the Alps, in Venice. Fugger was youngest of seven boys. His father died when he was ten and his mother took over the business. She had enough sons to work the fairs, bribe highway robbers, and inspect cloth in the bleaching fields, so she decided to take him away from the jousts and bathhouses and put him on a different course. She decided he should be a priest.

It's hard to imagine that Fugger was happy about it. If his mother got her way and he went to the seminary, he would have to shave his head and surrender his cloak for the black robes of the Benedictines. He would have to learn Latin, read Aquinas and say prayers eight times a day, beginning with matins at two in the morning. The monks fended for themselves, so Fugger, as a monk, would have to do the same. He would have to thatch roofs and boil soap. Much of the work was drudgery, but if he wanted to become a parish priest or, better yet, a secretary in Rome, he had to pay his dues and do his chores.

The school was in a tenth-century monastery in the village of Herrieden. Near Nuremburg, Herrieden was a four-day walk from Augsburg or two days for those lucky enough to have a horse. Nothing ever happened in Herrieden and, even if it did, Fugger wouldn't be seeing it. Benedictines were an austere bunch and seminarians stayed behind the walls. While there, Fugger would have to do something even more difficult than getting a haircut or comb wool. He would have to swear to a life of celibacy, obedience and, in the ultimate irony considering his future, poverty.

There were two types of clerics. There were the conservatives, who blindly followed Rome, and reformers like Erasmus of Rotterdam, the greatest intellectual of the age, who sought to eradicate what had become an epidemic of corruption. We will never know what sort of priest Fugger would become because just before it was time for him to join the monks, Fugger's mother reconsidered. Fugger was now fourteen and she decided she could use him after all. She asked the church to let Fugger out of his contract, freeing him for an apprenticeship and a life in trade. Years later, when Fugger was already rich, someone asked how long he planned to keep working. Fugger said no amount of money would satisfy him. No matter how much he had, he intended "to make profits as long as he could."

In doing so, he followed a family tradition of piling up riches. In an age when the elite considered commerce beneath them and most people had no ambitions beyond feeding themselves and surviving the winter, all of Fugger's ancestors—men and women alike—were strivers. In those days, no one went from nothing to superrich overnight. A person had to come from money—several generations of it. Each generation had to be richer than the one before. But the Fuggers were a remarkably successful and driven bunch. One after the other added to the family fortune.

Jacob's grandfather, Hans Fugger, was a peasant who lived in the Swabian village of Graben. In 1373, exactly a century before Jacob started in business, Hans abandoned his safe but unchanging life in the village for the big city. The urban population in Europe was growing and the new city dwellers needed clothing. Augsburg weavers filled the demand with fustian, a blend of domestic flax and cotton imported from Egypt. Hans wanted to be one of them. It's hard to imagine from our perspective, but his decision to leave the village took incredible courage. Most men stayed put and earned their living doing the exact same job as their father and grandfather. Once a miller, always a miller. Once a smith, always a smith. But Hans couldn't help himself. He was a young man with a Rumpelstiltskin fantasy of spinning gold from a loom. Dressed in a gray doublet, hose and laced boots, he made his way to the city, twenty miles down the Lech River, on foot.

Augsburg is now a pleasant but small city fabled for its puppet theater. A long but doable commute to Munich, it is no more significant in world affairs than, say, Dayton, Ohio. Its factories, staffed by the sort of world-class engineers that keep Germany competitive, make trucks and robots. If not for a university and the attendant bars, coffeehouses and bookstores, Augsburg would risk obscurity as a prosperous but dull backwater. But when Hans arrived it was on its way to becoming the money center of Europe, the London of its day, the place where borrowers looking for big money came to press their case. Founded by the Romans in AD 14 in the time of Augustus, from whom it takes its name, it sits on the ancient road from Venice to Cologne. In AD 98, Tacitus described the Germans as combative, filthy and often drunk, and remarked on their "fierce blue eyes, tawny hair and huge bodies." But he praised Augsburgers and declared their city "*splendidissima.*"

A bishop controlled the city when, in the eleventh century, the European economy rose from the Dark Ages and merchants set up stalls near his palace. As their numbers grew, they bristled at the bishop telling them what to do and they chased him to a nearby castle. Augsburg became a free city where the citizens arranged their own affairs and reported to no authority other than the remote and distracted emperor. In 1348, the Black Death hit Europe and killed at least one in three Europeans but miraculously spared Augsburg. This enormous stroke of good fortune allowed Augsburg and other cities of southern Germany to replace ravaged Italy as the focal point of European textile production.

As Hans Fugger approached the city gates and first saw the

turrets of the fortification wall, he could be forgiven if he thought Augsburgers did nothing but make fabrics. Bleaching racks covered with cloth spread in every direction. Once inside the gates, he would have been struck by all the priests. The bishop was gone, but Augsburg still had nine churches. Franciscans, Benedictines, Augustinians and Carmelites were everywhere, including the bars and brothels. Hans would also have noticed swarms of beggars. The rich, living in gilded town houses on the high ground of the city's center, had nine tenths of Augsburg's wealth and all the political power. They found the beggars unsightly—if not menacing—and passed laws to keep them out. But when the gates opened in the morning and peasants from the countryside streamed in to earn a few pennies sweeping streets or plucking chickens, the guards failed to sort out who was who. The beggars darted by.

Hans registered at City Hall. When he got there, he told the scribe his name. Germans used Latin for official documents and the scribe thought for a moment before coming up with the proper translation for Fugger. He wrote down the letters as they came to him: *F-u-c-k-e-r*. The registration, now in the city archives, reads *Fucker Advenit* or Fugger arrives. Fugger historians have enjoyed the laugh ever since.

Hans prospered and soon had enough money to leave the spinning to others. He became a wholesaler, buying cloth from other weavers and selling it at trade fairs. He began a family tradition of advantageous matches by marrying Clara Widolf, the daughter of the head of the weaver's guild. The weavers were the most powerful commercial group in town. They showed their teeth in 1478 when they forced the execution of a mayor sympathetic to the poor. After Clara died, Hans married the daughter of another guild boss. This woman, Elizabeth Gfatterman, had an astonishing head for trade. She took over the family business after Hans died and ran it for twenty-eight years. It's interesting to think how far she might have gone if society had given her a fair chance. Women had no political rights and were considered the legal subjects of their parents or husbands. If they engaged in business without a husband, they had to work through front men. As difficult as it was, Gfatterman still managed to bargain with suppliers, negotiate with customers and invest in real estate while, at the same time, raising her children. She made sure her two boys, Andreas and Jacob the Elder, received the training to take her place. Not wanting to dilute the inheritance, she never remarried. She was one of the largest taxpayers in Augsburg when she died.

Augsburg minted its own coins and Fugger's other grandfather, Franz Basinger, ran the mint. He grew rich watching workers pour molten silver into molds and cast coins one at a time. Jacob the Elder married Basinger's daughter Barbara. Just months after the wedding, authorities caught Basinger diluting the silver coins—a capital offense in some places—and threw him in jail. Jacob helped pay his debts and get him out. It all worked out for Basinger. Sprung from jail, he fled to Austria and, despite his criminal past, became master of the mint in a city outside the Tyrolean capital of Innsbruck.

Barbara had the same gift for business as her mother-in-law Elizabeth. She and Elizabeth were so remarkable that one can easily argue that they, more than the Fuggers' male ancestors, gave him his talents. Like Elizabeth, Barbara outlived her husband by nearly thirty years and took the challenging course of remaining a widow. Like Elizabeth, she took the Fugger business to the next level by reinvesting the profits and buying and selling even more cloth than her husband. This would come later. Her immediate job after getting married was to have children.

The Fuggers lived in a three-story town house at the corner where the old Jewish quarter met the commercial center. It stood across from the hall of the weavers' guild. A street called Jew Hill sloped down behind the house, ending at a canal. The Romans had dug the canals and lined them with wooden beams. At night, when all was quiet, one could hear water running through.

Barbara gave birth to Fugger on March 6, 1459. Jacob the Elder had resisted naming any of his other sons after himself. He yielded with number seven. He didn't spend much time with his namesake; he died when young Jacob was ten. By then, some of the boys—Ulrich, Peter and George—were already working in the business. Another brother, Markus, was a priest climbing the ranks of the Vatican bureaucracy. Two other brothers had died young. As for the girls—Jacob had three sisters—Barbara was preparing them for good matches.

Fugger looked up to his brothers and envied them and their adventures on the road. His own chance for his adventure came soon enough. After dropping the idea of the church for Fugger, Barbara secured him an apprenticeship in Venice. Venice was the most commercially minded city on earth. It was the way station that linked the Silk Road with the Rhine, where French wine found its way onto boats to Alexandria and Constantinople and where traders swapped pepper, ginger and cotton from the East for horn, fur and metal from the West. Venice was founded on commerce and businessmen ran the place. Money was all anyone talked about. Venetians, wrote the banker and diarist Girolamo Pruili, "have concentrated all their force for trading." Venice made Augsburg look like a village. Hot, loud and crowded, its population of 200,000 made it one of the largest cities in Europe. Traders shouted at each other from the warehouses that lined the canals. "Who could count the many shops, so well furnished that they look like warehouses," the priest Pietro Casola wrote in his travel journal. "They stupefy the beholder." Everyone in Venice prospered. The chronicler Sansovino described how the locals slept on walnut beds behind silk curtains. They ate with silver. Added Casola: "Here wealth flows like water in a fountain."

The spice trade made it happen. Europeans loved spices, especially pepper, to liven up bland meals and mask the taste of rotten meat. Arabs bought it in India and hauled it to Levantine ports by camel. Venice monopolized the business. Owing to its fortunate location far up the Adriatic coast, it offered the most economical way to reach the rest of the continent. Venice grew wealthy as a middleman. Fugger had no way of knowing it, but he would one day play a role in the system's destruction.

Naturally enough, Venice became the place where young men went to learn about trade. Well-to-do families sent their children there to discover the secrets of commerce and to make contacts. Fugger said good-bye to his family and set off over the Alps, probably through the Brenner Pass. It took him about two weeks to reach Mestre. From there, he boarded a boat and crossed the lagoon to the main island. After the crossing, Fugger headed to the Fondaco dei Tedeschi, a warehouse where Venetians insisted all the Germans conduct their affairs. They wanted them under one roof to more easily hit them for taxes.

Located smack on the Rialto, the Fondaco was a crowded bazaar with goods piled to the ceilings. "I saw there merchandise of all kind," wrote the visiting knight Arnold von Hanff. Wrote Casola: "The Fondaco at Venice is so rich in merchandise that it might supply the whole of Italy." In 1505, well after Fugger's time in Venice, a fire destroyed the building. When the city rebuilt it, Titian and Giorgione painted murals on the wall facing the Grand Canal and made the Fondaco a destination for art lovers. But in Fugger's time, the Germans not only worked there but lived there, too. Fugger slept beside his countrymen on a straw-covered floor in the attic. In addition to learning about importing and exporting, he might have made himself useful by packing crates, making deliveries and copying letters. Approaching St. Mark's from the Ponte della Paglia, Fugger could watch the galleys sailing in from the Bosporus and the Holy Land. He could wonder about the African slaves—the household servants of the rich—in the squares or join other Germans as they hawked pearls and stones at astronomical markups along the Riva degli Schiavoni, the city's famous promenade. He could hear the trumpets that announced the arrival of every foreign ship.

We know little of Fugger's years in Venice other than the marks they left. The marks were few but profound. Some were stylistic. Here Fugger picked up a love for the gold beret that became his signature. And it was in Venice that he began to sign letters in the Latin way. He went to Italy as Jacob, knowing only how to read and write. He came back as Jacobo, an international businessman intent on making a splash.

More importantly, it was during this time that he learned about banking. Fugger was to become many things in the ensuing years—an industrialist, a trader and at times a speculator—but he was foremost a banker. He learned everything he needed to know about banking in Venice. The Italians invented it, as shown by our borrowing of the words *credito, debito* and even *banca*. Venice also exposed him to the advantageous craft of accounting. Most of the merchants back in Germany were still jotting down numbers on paper scraps that were never organized. Italians had moved beyond that. Needing more robust methods to handle large, multinational enterprises, Italians developed double-entry bookkeeping, so named because each entry had a corresponding entry to make the books balance. It let them understand a complex business in a quick glance by summarizing the highlights and condensing the value of an enterprise to a single figure, its net worth. Years after Fugger left Venice, the mathematician friar Luca Pacioli wrote the first accounting textbook. Fugger knew all the tricks before Pacioli's book went to press. He converted his brothers to the system and brought a new level of sophistication to the family business. He gave the rest of Augsburg no choice but to follow. The fact that Fugger, as a teenager, already understood the importance of bookkeeping and how it gave him an edge says something about his intuitive grasp of business. He knew that those who kept sloppy books and overlooked details left money on the table, something he considered unconscionable.

A Venetian ambassador, years later, heard that Fugger had learned his craft in Venice. He replied that Fugger had learned more than Venice could teach: "If Augsburg is the daughter of Venice, then the daughter has surpassed her mother."

⚜

In the same year that Fugger left for Venice, something happened in Augsburg that had monumental consequences for him and his family: The family made its first contact with the Habsburgs, the royal house of Austria. In time, the Habsburgs became Fugger's biggest customer and Fugger became their counselor and unrivaled financial backer. The relationship was never easy and it almost collapsed several times. But the bond held and became the greatest private-public partnership the world had ever known.

That spring, just after the snow in the Alpine passes melted, the emperor Frederick III left Innsbruck for an important diplomatic mission to Trier on the French border. Frederick rode to meet Charles the Bold, the fantastically rich archduke of Burgundy, and stopped in Augsburg on the way. In addition to serving as emperor, Frederick was the archduke of Austria and the Habsburg family patriarch. The Habsburgs had their roots in Switzerland where, in the eleventh century, a warlord named Radbot of Klettgau built the Castle of the Hawk—"Habsburg" in German—on the road from Zurich to Basel. Europe had dozens of royal families and the Habsburgs were minor leaguers until 1273, when one of their number, Rudolf, became king of the Germans and the inevitable pick to become Holy Roman emperor. Three years later, the family took Vienna, giving them a more pleasant address than the lonely castle in Switzerland. But even then, the family remained weak compared to the great houses of Europe. Rudolf died before becoming emperor, but, truth be told, "emperor" was a grand title that meant little.

Napoleon was supposedly the one who said the Holy Roman Empire was none of the three. It was too debauched to be holy, too German to be Roman and too weak to be an empire. But to make sense of Fugger's life, it helps to understand how he could exploit this odd creation and why the emperor needed a banker. On paper, the empire united Christian Europe along the lines of the Roman

Empire with the emperor serving as the secular equivalent and partner of the pope. But only Charlemagne, the first emperor, approached mastery of Europe. After he died, Europe split into kingdoms that further split into principalities, duchies or whatever other entities had enough military power to stay independent.

By the time Frederick was emperor, the boundaries of the Holy Roman Empire had narrowed to just the eastern part of Charlemagne's realm and included little more than Germany. It was still big, but the emperor received no funding except from his own estates and thus could only field a small army. This made him easy to ignore, and most everyone did just that. Even in Germany, where the people called him king of the Germans, he was weak because, unlike in the centralized states of France and England, Germany's provincial lords clung to their independence. The job of emperor was an elected position like the papacy, but the emperor was more of an empty suit than a king. If France or the Turks attacked Germany, the German lords might ask the emperor to lead the defense. But for the most part, they were happy if he did nothing.

Seven princes and bishops—the most powerful of the scores of territorial leaders—played the role of Vatican cardinals and comprised the electoral college that selected the emperor. When they offered Frederick the job, he took it only after deciding he could turn it into the very force of centralization that the electors feared. The great game of the era was what the Germans called *Hausmachtpolitik,* the quest to expand the family power base. The winner? Whoever grabbed the most titles and territories. It was a bloody business that the participants found infinitely absorbing but ordinary people found horribly disruptive. The Habsburgs were losing to the likes of the Valois in France and the Tudors in England.

Even in German-speaking Europe, they lagged behind such houses as the Wettins of Saxony and the Wittelsbachs of Bavaria. Frederick had the fantastic notion that the imperial crown could make his family the most powerful in Europe. He believed it so much that he stamped the initials AEIOU on his tableware. As revealed only after his death, it stood for *Alles Erdisch ist Osterreich Untertan* (All Earth Is Under Austria). He dared to consider himself another Frederick Barbarossa—a ruler who, during another low point for the empire, brought order to Germany and restored imperial authority in Italy with little more than charisma and drive. Others agreed with Frederick about the potential. If nothing else, the formidable title gave the job an aura of divine sanction. "His name is great," said a papal envoy. "In a land of factions he can do much." But Frederick was nothing more than a dreamer. When the electors refused to cede him power, he failed to exploit factions. He retired to a life of gardening and overeating. Detractors, not without some justification, called him Frederick the Fat.

Then came the meeting with Charles the Bold and the chance it offered Frederick to shape history. As duke of Burgundy, Charles had the province of Burgundy as well as what is now the Netherlands, Belgium and Luxembourg. These were the richest, most industrialized parts of Europe, and Burgundy itself set the standard for European luxury and sophistication behind its symbol of the Golden Fleece. Although officially accountable to the French king, Charles did as he pleased and, backed by a magnificent army, he dreamed of conquest and becoming the next Alexander. An English official called Charles "oon of the myghtyest Princez that bereth no crown." More than anything, Charles dreamed of raising Burgundy to a kingdom and formally separating from France. This is why Frederick came to Trier. He could elevate Charles because, as emperor, he had an ancient power that required neither money nor an army to exercise. On a whim, with the stroke of his pen, he could create kingdoms and monarchs. In return for that, Charles offered to wed his only child, fifteen-year-old Mary of Burgundy, to Frederick's thirteen-year-old son Maximilian. This was a fantastic offer. Maximilian and his children would eventually become kings of Burgundy if all went well. The Habsburgs would be second-tier sovereigns no more.

Frederick stopped in Augsburg on his way to Trier to buy clothes. Charles was the dandiest prince in Europe. The Habsburgs could not match his gold, diamonds and ostrich plumes but they had to try. The problem was that Frederick, unable to fund an imperial lifestyle on a ducal income, was broke and the Augsburg merchants, stiffed by Frederick in the past, refused him credit. That led Frederick to Ulrich Fugger, the oldest of the Fugger brothers, to help. Ulrich gave Frederick silk and wool for his tailors to stitch into imperial robes.

Marketing is an ancient craft. Roman promoters hung posters to advertise chariot races and the hookers of Ephesus carved their addresses into marble slabs near the Temple of Artemis. By lending a hand to Frederick, Ulrich saw a chance to sell himself. He wasn't stupid; he knew the emperor was broke and would never repay. But he received something of intangible yet undeniable value—a coat of arms. The crests weren't just for knights in battle. Monarchs gave them to anyone they favored including businessmen. Displayed outside a shop, a warehouse or trade fair stall, the arms proclaimed the bearer's products fit for a king. The royal endorsement was well worth a few bolts of cloth for the Fuggers. Ulrich had a petty motive, too. He wanted the coat of arms to settle a score. Eleven years before, Frederick had given one to the other line of the Fugger family, the descendants of Andreas Fugger, Hans Fugger's other son. The heirs of Andreas, dubbed the Fuggers of the Roe for the deer head on their crest, held it over Ulrich as a mark of superiority. Ulrich hated being the lesser Fugger. So did his little brother Jacob. Eager to catch up, Ulrich gave Frederick what he wanted. A letter for Ulrich arrived one day with a picture of three lilies on a piece of parchment. It was from the emperor. A note explained that this was a coat of arms awarded for the family's "respectability, truthfulness and rationality." The letter named each of Ulrich's brothers, including Jacob, as recipients. They were now the Fuggers of the Lily and so were their descendants.

The spectacle of the emperor begging for help must have startled Jacob. Any belief he may have had in the emperor's superhuman qualities could not have survived the fact that mere shopkeepers—ordinary people that he saw on the street every day—had denied credit to the supposedly most powerful secular figure in Europe. Whether Fugger actually witnessed the snubs didn't matter. The lesson was the same: Money was an equalizer. It made no difference that someone was an emperor and another a commoner. If a commoner had money, he could make anyone, even an emperor, grovel.

Fugger received greater honors over his long career, but the coat of arms pleased him most. Years later, he offered to renovate the members-only tavern where Augsburg's leading merchants went to socialize, talk shop and drink. Called the *Heerentrinkstube* or Gentlemen's Drinking Room, it sat across from City Hall. Fugger demanded that three lilies appear on the facade as a condition of the renovation. It was a reasonable request; the Medici put their crest on everything, even churches. But the members of the drinking club had more pride than the priests of Florence. They turned him down. A Fugger family chronicle commissioned by one of Fugger's nephews in 1545 claimed the club came to regret the decision.

❧

Just as Fugger was finishing his Italian education, he received some bad news. His older brother Markus was dead. Markus, who was thirty when he died, had taken the path that Fugger had avoided. He had taken his priestly vows, received a university education and worked in Rome as an overseer of the pope's affairs in Germany. A plague hit Rome in 1478 and took him just as he was becoming influential. The family sent Fugger, then nineteen, to Rome to settle his brother's affairs. The visit was presumably formative. Sixtus IV, the pope who built the Sistine Chapel, was in his prime. If nothing else, Fugger saw the splendor of the papal court and the riches available to those who served it. From there, Fugger returned to Augsburg and began his work at the firm of Ulrich Fugger & Brothers. He traveled extensively, visiting trade fairs and inspecting the branch offices. Travel was punishing. Erasmus, another frequent traveler, complained about filthy inns, rude hosts and wretched food. But face-to-face communications was about the only way to get anything done. Ambitious people like Erasmus and Fugger had to hit the road.

After Fugger finished in Rome, the family sent him to Austria, in the footsteps of his shifty grandfather, Franz, to get in on a mining boom. This was a big step for Fugger, but one has to wonder why the family didn't send him to an established and important outpost like Nuremberg. Fugger was now twenty-six and the fact that his brothers sent him to explore a new industry in a place that didn't matter to their current business suggests they had doubts about his ability. In any case, he went to Austria not as an apprentice or a junior associate but as a full-fledged businessman with authority to make decisions. He made the most of it. Austria was where Fugger first emerged as a business genius. His Austrian deals reveal a gift for handling customers, a willingness to take enormous risk and an extraordinary talent for negotiations.

Until this point, the family had concentrated on buying and selling textiles. But mining was beckoning as a new business line because it offered better profits. The lure of fat paydays took Fugger to the village of Schwaz. Schwaz is twenty miles down the Inn River from Innsbruck. For most of its history, Schwaz was a community of poor farmers. Because of its elevation, the weather was cool and the growing season short. Worse, the river flooded every few years, destroying the crop. The luck of Schwaz changed in 1409, when a farm girl, out in the fields with her cow, stumbled on a patch of shiny metal that others soon identified as silver. The timing was fortunate. Owing to scarcity, the price of silver reached its peak in the fifteenth century when it traded as close to the price of gold as it ever came. Mints needed silver for coins. The rich wanted it for silver plate—dishes and other place settings—that they bought as a form of savings.

Fortune hunters mobbed Schwaz and made it the Spindletop of its day. At its height, the population reached forty thousand, making it bigger than Augsburg and the second-biggest city in Austria after Vienna. Taverns and inns sprung up overnight. Miners from Bohemia came in such numbers that they built their own church. The mines provided for all. Schwaz was the largest silver mine on earth and occupied that spot until the New World discoveries of Potosi and Zacatecas a century later. In its prime, Schwaz produced four of every five tons of European silver.

The local ruler, Archduke Sigmund, owned the mines. A jowly sovereign with bulging eyes and a hooked nose, he was another Habsburg. He and Emperor Frederick were cousins. If Fugger wanted to participate in Tyrolean mining, he had to go through Sigmund. Sigmund controlled a patchwork of territories that included the Tyrol, the Black Forest, Alsace and part of Bavaria. Schwaz should have freed Sigmund of money troubles. But moderation wasn't his style. He loved luxury and spent beyond his means. He rejected his father's palaces as too drafty and built new ones that were just as drafty but looked better. He built a series of grand hunting lodges—Sigmund's Joy, Sigmund's Peace, Sigmund's Corner—where he could unwind after a day of chasing stags. With a vast staff of chefs, valets and butlers, he tried to copy the splendor of the Burgundian court and hosted parties where a dwarf jumped out of a pie to wrestle a giant. Sigmund got the trappings of Burgundian culture right but was too much of a slob to master the nuances. An ambassador from Burgundy once dined with Sigmund and expressed horror at the table manners in a memo to Charles the Bold. "It is noteworthy," he wrote, "that as soon as the dishes were placed on the table everyone grabbed with their hands." Although Sigmund married twice, his only children were the fifty from his girlfriends. He paid to support them lest the mothers embarrass him with claims.

The only ones who received no support were his subjects. Other sovereigns shared their wealth by building roads, draining swamps and creating universities. Sigmund spent only on himself. When money ran out, he borrowed against the output of his mines by selling silver to a group of bankers at a discount. Fugger wanted to be one of the bankers and, remarkably, he got in on a deal in December 1485, not long after arriving in Austria. A day after hearing the Advent mass and smack in the middle of a witch-hunting affair that competed for Sigmund's attention, Fugger advanced the duke 3,000 florins. The amount was small; it took only a fraction of the Fugger family's capital and paled compared to what other bankers had loaned the duke. But it made Fugger a banker, the profession that over the next forty years he would take to new heights. In return for the money, Sigmund delivered a thousand pounds of silver in installments. Fugger paid eight florins a pound and sold it in Venice for as much as twelve florins.

It was a great deal but it looked for a while like this was the only one Fugger would ever get. For four years he kept trying to land another one and for four years he failed. The duke continued to borrow from the same Italians he had known for years. Then came a border skirmish between Sigmund and Venice that changed everything.

Venice's hinterland reached the Tyrolean frontier. Sigmund and the doge had been bickering over some of the border towns. After a flare-up over trading privileges, Sigmund's advisors encouraged the duke to send troops and take the villages in Venetian hands. Tyrol was a backwater, and Sigmund had to rely on mercenaries because he had no standing army. Compared to Venice he was a pipsqueak. Venice had military power to match its wealth. Behind the high brick walls of the Arsenal shipyard, where Venetian shipwrights pioneered the system of mass production, the Republic had built one of the largest naval fleets on earth to protect a string of trading posts that stretched down the Dalmatian coast, along the shores of Macedonia and to the most distant islands of Greece. Its ground forces were just as formidable. If sufficiently riled, Venice could march on Tyrol, lay waste to Innsbruck and put Sigmund in chains.

But Venice had concerns besides little villages in the Alps. The Turks had taken Constantinople in 1453 and were now making trouble in Venetian waters off Greece. If Venice lost the Greek coast, the Turks could block its trade with the East and bring the republic to its knees. Sigmund gambled that Venice was sufficiently distracted to let the towns go without a fight. After the astrologer gave the all clear, Sigmund sent thousands of mercenaries to the Rovereto and captured it after weeks of firing flaming bombs of tar over the city walls. The victory elated Sigmund. He talked of marching his troops into St. Mark's Square.

He assumed his bankers would support him. But when he asked for more money, they offered only excuses. They knew that Venice considered Rovereto and its neighbors as a first line of defense. They refused to get involved in a tangle with the region's largest power. Broke and fearful of a Venetian counter attack, Sigmund sued for peace. Venice hit him with tough terms. It promised not to invade only if Sigmund surrendered Rovereto, abandoned his other claims and paid 100,000 florins in reparations. That was a lot of money and Sigmund tried his bankers one more time. But by now Sigmund's years of unchecked spending and mounting debt had caught up with him. No matter what he promised, the bankers refused to help. Then a young German whose grandfather once ran the mint came forward with an offer. Fugger combined his family's money with money raised from friends back in Augsburg and agreed to loan Sigmund the full amount. It was a whale of a deal for

Fugger, coming in at more than ten times the size of his earlier loan with the duke.

The other bankers laughed. They couldn't believe Fugger was willing to give Sigmund anything, let alone a bigger loan than any they had ever made. If Sigmund repaid, Fugger would make a fortune because the contract entitled him to all the output from Schwaz, at a discount, until the loan was repaid.

But if Sigmund welched—and, given his record, it seemed likely—Fugger would be finished.

To prevent ruin, Fugger filled the loan agreement with safeguards. He barred Sigmund from touching the silver, he made the mine operators cosign the loan and he insisted on forwarding the money to the duke in installments rather than as a lump sum. That way, he could keep the loan balance reasonable. Before signing the agreement, Fugger made a final demand: He insisted on control over the state treasury. Fugger wanted stability and, by controlling the Tyrol's purse strings, he could act as a one-man International Monetary Fund and keep the state afloat by paying its bills when due. Sigmund agreed to all of Fugger's terms. He had no choice. But the agreement was only words on paper. Sigmund was the law of the land. Like all royals, he could renege without consequences. Debtor's prison was for little people, not archdukes. The only things that kept him honest were his honor and his desire to borrow again in the future.

The loan marked a pivotal moment in the ascent of Fugger. It was not only the biggest piece of business he ever conducted. It was also the biggest for his family. But there was nothing pioneering or innovative about the loan, and his competitors could have made it as easily as Fugger. All Fugger did was put up his money when no one else had the guts. Such out-of-favor investments became a hallmark of his investing career.

When the other bankers saw wagons loaded with Sigmund's silver roll up to Fugger's warehouses, it became clear that Fugger had struck a winning deal. It drove them crazy. They complained of unfair treatment and accused Fugger of cheating the duke. They encouraged him to dissolve the agreement and renegotiate. But by this time Fugger had made friends with Sigmund. Knowing the duke was vulnerable to flattery, Fugger had won a spot in Sigmund's heart by celebrating the greatest achievement in the duke's otherwise disastrous reign. The achievement involved coins. At a time when other monarchs—or their minters—watered down coins to make them stretch further, the vast output of the Schwaz mine allowed Sigmund to mint a silver coin of unsurpassed purity. The coin featured an image of him holding a scepter and wearing a jaunty, oversized crown. The coins were a hit and earned him the name Sigmund Rich in Coins. When a merchant received one of Sigmund's silver guldiners, he knew he could trust it. The popularity of the coin—weighing the same as six quarters—attracted imitators across Europe, including the German city of Joachimsthal. Joachimsthal introduced a coin of identical size and silver content, and called it the thaler. The Danes called their version the dollar. Three centuries later, Americans gave a nod to the Danes and ran with it. Sigmund loved his guldiners and Fugger gave him bags of the coins as gifts. Sigmund appreciated Fugger's thoughtfulness. He stayed true to his banker. But his loyalty was one-sided. Soon enough, Fugger would return the duke's loyalty by turning on him.

Nothing boosted a city's economy in Fugger's time like a trade fair and no city in Germany got a bigger boost than Frankfurt. The population swelled by half during its fall fair. By renting out their floors for sleeping, homeowners made more money in a week than their regular jobs paid all year. An innkeeper made enough in three weeks to cover the costs of building the inn. The city had no bigger source of revenue. It collected money on everything from tolls to taxes to the fees for weighing goods on the public scales.

Frankfurt was well situated. Located along the Main River, the biggest tributary of the Rhine, Frankfurt is in the middle of Germany. It is an easy boat trip from Cologne and Antwerp, and was only a few days from Augsburg even in that era of slow travel. Frankfurt began preparing for the fair months in advance. Soldiers swept the roads of highway robbers. Barges packed with beer and herring arrived from the Baltic. Apprentices unpacked boxes, sorted goods and stocked the shelves. Country girls came to town to compete with the full-time prostitutes. Authorities barricaded the brothels to corral the expected throngs. Acrobats, dancers and singers readied their acts. Jugglers polished their pins.

Fugger considered Frankfurt the ideal spot to network. He was a regular visitor and when the fair came together for the 339th time in 1489, he was there as usual. This may have been the most important fair of his life because it was where historians believe Fugger first met Maximilian of Habsburg, Emperor Frederick's son—the man who, with Fugger's help, would take the Habsburgs to greatness. No one recorded their first impressions as the two of them, born sixteen days apart in 1459, considered each other for the first time. Maximilian knew other bankers and probably saw Fugger as just another one. Fugger must have wondered if Maximilian was a safe bet.

They may have talked about the time, six years earlier, when Maximilian and his father had passed through Augsburg on the way to meet Charles the Bold in Trier. That visit ended disastrously. Frederick refused to trust Charles and, just days before the wedding, he and Maximilian snuck across the Mosel back to Germany. Maximilian eventually married the duchess, but only after Charles had died and Burgundy went back to France. Maximilian only got Flanders and some neighboring areas, and he had a weak hold on these places. After he tried to raise taxes in Ghent, angry taxpayers threw him in jail and beheaded some of his staff, including his court jester, before his eyes. They released Maximilian after limiting how he could spend Flemish tax revenue. This was just the latest setback for the Habsburgs. A few years earlier, the Hungarian king Matthew Corvinus had chased them from Vienna after a long siege. While the sultan of Turkey congratulated Corvinus with a gift of two dozen camels, Maximilian's father, Frederick, who was still alive, fled to Salzburg and resigned himself to the loss. "Happiness is to forget what cannot be recovered," he said.

About the only things Maximilian had left were his titles. He was still a duke and, while he was in the Netherlands, the electors, not caring who became emperor as long as he left them alone, had made him king of the Germans with the promise of making him emperor after Frederick died. But what did "king of the Germans" even mean? And what did emperor even mean? It certainly didn't make him a real sovereign like Henry VII of England and Charles VIII of France. They had armies, tax revenues and authority. Maximilian served at the pleasure of seven men uninterested in sharing power.

What saved Maximilian from irrelevance was a winning collection of personal attributes. Charming and athletic, admirers called him the Last Knight. He was never happier than when in his armor, jousting in a tournament or fighting the enemy. He was a hard worker. After a day in the field, when his captains relaxed with beer around a campfire, Maximilian retired to his tent to address official correspondence. He had plenty of faults. He was moody, easily distracted and prone to get ahead of himself. But he had intelligence, determination, physical courage and a desire to do whatever it took to advance his family. Maximilian believed in AEIOU as much as Frederick and took it upon himself to make it happen.

Fugger correctly grasped that Maximilian, who had the Tyrolean nobility in his corner, would outmaneuver the dull-witted Sigmund. Maximilian did it with a ploy that Fugger himself could have devised given its ingenuity. Maximilian loaned money to Sigmund backed by a mortgage on the duchy. If Sigmund failed to repay in three years, Maximilian would take over. Sure enough, Sigmund defaulted. He could have repaid if Fugger had loaned him the money. But Fugger, who preferred the ambitious Maximilian as a customer to Sigmund, did nothing. One could argue that Fugger behaved dishonorably. But he knew Sigmund had no chance against the young and talented Maximilian. To back Sigmund would have been a pointless act of loyalty.

After a legislative session where the nobility accused Sigmund of treason for his earlier flirtations with the Bavarians, Sigmund, rattled and exhausted, signed his holdings over to Maximilian. Maximilian wasn't vindictive. He made Sigmund's final years happy by giving him a castle, a staff and unlimited hunting and fishing privileges. Fugger might have done his part, too. Legend has it that as Sigmund was dying, he asked for a bag of silver coins, the ones with his likeness. He wanted to again feel the cool metal against his skin. Fugger delivered a bag in person.

2

✠

PARTNERS

Dobratsch Mountain climbs 5,700 feet above sea level, a snowy lump imposed on the high meadows of southeast Austria and a soaring boundary at the intersection of Austria, Italy and Slovenia. The village of Arnoldstein sits at the base. Monks looking for solitude built a monastery there in the twelfth century. Apart from a bad year in 1348—the Black Death and an earthquake that buried the village—they got what they were looking for. Trouble came later. In 1478, Turkish adventurers attacked Arnoldstein and killed monks and anyone else they could find. In 1494, the Turks came back and captured ten thousand people in a neighboring province to use as slaves. The monks feared more killing. Then, just a year later, the stillness that once reigned over Dobratsch vanished amid a riot of saws, axes and falling timber. Fugger had come to

Arnoldstein. He broke ground on the biggest factory Europe had ever seen.

The commercial potential of the area had always been there. An old Roman road crossed the Drau River in neighboring Villach. Traders worked the territory in the Middle Ages before earthquakes and Turks made them reconsider. Fugger liked the idea of being close to his Italian customers. Using his Tyrolean profits, he bought land near the monastery. The acquisition marked the first step in an eastern expansion that underlined his willingness to bet big, defy conventional wisdom and go anywhere for a deal. It was a sensational move, one that to outsiders looked as crazy as Fugger's giant loan to Sigmund. It again showed his striking independence of thought.

Called the Common Hungarian Trade on his books, the effort that began in Arnoldstein became his most profitable investment. It took all his political cunning to make it work, but nothing contributed more to his fortune. He remained consumed by the Hungarian Trade on his deathbed decades later.

The story began when Maximilian, just after taking Tyrol, came to Fugger with a plan to reclaim Vienna. Even then, Vienna was a jewel. A university gave it a lively cultural life. St. Stephen's Cathedral, begun in the massive Romanesque style and completed with airy Gothic flourishes, gave the city a stunning centerpiece. "It cost more than could be got for our whole kingdom," said a Bosnian ambassador. Corvinus liked Vienna better than his own dreary capital city of Buda and had moved there. After he died, the students of Vienna rose against the Hungarians and begged Maximilian to free them. Fugger was Maximilian's favorite banker, at least at the moment. He saw advantages of a Habsburg return to Vienna and gave

Maximilian what he needed. Approaching Vienna at the head of a large, Fugger-financed army, Maximilian took the city without a fight. Then he marched into Hungary in search of more conquest. Hungary couldn't battle Maximilian and the Turks at once. It signed a peace treaty that opened Hungary to German merchants. Fugger was the first who came.

At the time, Fugger needed another deal. He was suffering from the high-class problem of having too much money. His silver profits generated more cash than he could invest in Tyrol and he was already loaning Maximilian as much as he reasonably could. The easy option would have been putting more money into textiles. It was a huge industry that could absorb his capital. The drawback was competition. Nothing much had changed since Hans Fugger left his village. Augsburgers and everyone else in southern Germany made or sold cloth. As an asset class, textiles were overbought and margins were thin. Land was another investment possibility. But land suffered from even lower returns than textiles. Fugger wanted an investment as lucrative as his silver deal in Schwaz.

It spoke to his ambition that he turned to the wild East. The opportunity was in copper. A copper belt ran along the Carpathian Mountains from Slovakia to Romania. Hungary controlled it all. Like silver, copper was in high demand. Copper is infinitely useful. A low melting point makes it easier to shape than iron and, when mixed with tin to form bronze, it is unlikely to shatter. This made it ideal for cannons and muskets—the weapons that swung the balance in Renaissance warfare. The *Hausmachtpolitik* crowd paid dearly for them.

Private operators owned the mines in Hungary. Fugger wanted to buy them and process the copper across the border in

Arnoldstein. He could make more money as a mine owner than as a lender, but only after investing scary amounts of money up front. He needed to clear the land, dig the mines and install roof supports. At Arnoldstein, he would have to build a smelter to refine the ore and a factory to turn it into cannons. He needed to build roads to connect the mines with the smelter. These were huge investments. It was risky enough with the Turks at the door. The long payback period on the capital improvements made it even riskier. It would take years before he could turn a profit even under good conditions. If conditions turned on him, he could lose everything. He knew the perils and observed that most who tried mining met their demise. "No business can fall apart more quickly than mining," he said. "Most of the time, ten perish before one gets rich." Then there was the political risk. Maximilian's peace treaty offered protection, but treaties were not guarantees. Official protection could turn to hostility in an instant. The Hungarians had let Germans invest in their country. But they never promised to like them.

To cover himself, Fugger made an inspired decision. He agreed to take on a partner named Johannes Thurzo. Germany's vaunted reputation for engineering began with men like him. By the time Thurzo met Fugger, he was already famous among German miners for restoring a flooded mine in Saxony. His method seemed simple. Workers in the mines filled sacks with water and a wheel, propelled by a stream, pulled a rope to bring them to the surface. Workers dumped the sacks and sent the empties back down the shaft. The complexity came in getting the system to function.

Thurzo had talents besides pumping. He knew all about metallurgy and was an expert in a new process called liquidation, used to separate copper from silver. Even more important to Fugger was

Thurzo's heritage. Thurzo was Austrian and spoke German, but his ancestors came from Hungary, making him tolerable to the locals. There was one more thing. He was a citizen of Cracow, making him tolerable to Hungary's King Ladislaus, who took over for Corvinus and was part of the same family, the Jagiellons, who ruled Poland. King Ladislaus controlled the mining rights. He was more likely to grant rights to one of his own than to a German like Fugger.

Thurzo already had a few contracts in Hungary to save flooded mines. But the mine operators were too poor to pay him. Here they were, with rights to exploit some of the richest mines in Europe, but unable to bring them into service. The ore might as well have been at the bottom of the ocean. This was a problem made for Fugger because it could be solved with money. Fugger traveled to Vienna in the summer of 1495 to sign the deal with Thurzo. The terms spoke to Thurzo's significance. Although Fugger put up all the cash, he agreed to give Thurzo half the profits. The deal pleased both sides. Three years after it began, Fugger and Thurzo solidified the arrangement when Fugger's niece married Thurzo's son, George. This was the first of two Fugger-Thurzo marriages. Another came sixteen years later. A Fugger family chronicle makes no mention of romance. The marriages, it says, were "for the furtherance of the Fugger trade."

With Fugger's money, Thurzo bought up leases. He struck good deals because he and Fugger were the only ones in Hungary with the capital and know-how to restore them. While Thurzo collected mines, Fugger built the operation in Arnoldstein. He built a fortress as much as he built a factory. Mindful of the Turks and the murderous licking they gave the monks, Fugger built high, crenelated walls into the mountainside. His men could look over the river and roads from the turrets and spot attackers before they got close. They could open fire from on high. Behind the walls, workers installed furnaces, vats and molds to smelt copper and cast cannons. The structure was ugly but functional. The locals called it Fuggerau or the place of Fugger.

Fuggerau loomed over the village. The monks suddenly found themselves in a factory town. Fellers cleared timber for miles around to fire the furnaces and left the hillsides barren and pockmarked. To get water for the production process, Fugger diverted the nearby rivers and dumped the factory's waste back in. The monks complained about the noise and filth. Fugger took a modern approach to stifling dissent by paying them a modest sum of ten florins a year to shut up.

Here is a good place to mention that Fugger's far-flung experiences put him in the path of many of the era's most interesting figures. Even in Arnoldstein, on the fringes of civilized Europe, Fugger may have had such an encounter. The factory complex doubled as a research center. Fugger hired alchemists to find him the next metallurgical breakthrough and hired teachers to train mining engineers. One was a Swiss doctor, William von Hohenheim, whose son Philip attended the Latin school in Villach and later learned chemistry from Fuggerau instructors. Under the name Paracelsus, he became a father of modern medicine. He ridiculed the Greek notions about medicine then in vogue, with all their talk about balancing humors and biles, in favor of observation and scientific analysis. He coined the word "zinc" and inspired the fictional Dr. Frankenstein. Fugger may or may not have met Paracelsus. If he did, he might have lost interest in him once he realized Paracelsus cared more about disease than about mixing chemicals to create gold.

❧

Paracelsus got a lot of things wrong. He believed in astrology and witches, and billed his book *Nymphs, Gnomes and Vulcans* as a non-fiction field guide. But he was right about mining. It was a brutish occupation, particularly in his time. Using only picks and hammers, Fugger's miners scraped the walls in low-ceiling tunnels 500 feet beneath the surface. Roofs collapsed. Shafts flooded without warning. Even under the best circumstances, the work was punishing. Ventilation was a few holes punched into the mountain or whatever fresh air made it through the mine entrance. Water dripped from the ceiling and leached through the walls. In the Schwaz mine, the temperature was a constant 54 degrees. Humidity was 99 percent. Lamps fueled by foul-smelling animal fat lit the way. Miners choked on the smoke. The result, as Paracelsus noted in *On Miners' Sickness and Other Miners' Diseases*, the first book on occupational health, was lung disease and stomach ulcers. High pay made up for the health risks. A miner earned a third more than a farmer and, if he was smart and worked hard, he moved up. The peasant Hans Luther began in the pits of Saxony, rose to foreman and eventually owned a mine. He earned enough money to send his son to university and rejoiced when his boy studied law. Then came the thunderbolt that struck young Martin Luther in a field and his promise to become a monk. His law career was finished and so were his father's dreams.

Miners also had to endure harsh bosses. Duke Sigmund was an exception. When Sigmund controlled Schwaz, he took a conciliatory approach to labor relations. In 1485, the same year that Fugger made his first loan to him, miners marched on Innsbruck to demand better treatment. Horrified by confrontation, Sigmund agreed to radical concessions. He gave them five weeks of paid vacation and an eight-hour day. The concessions, made in a moment of desperation, swept the European mining business, traveled to America a century later and became routine practices across industry. But Maximilian was less accommodating. His Gossensass mine near the Brenner Pass was among those supplying Fugger. Miners barricaded the shaft in 1493 and demanded better treatment. Rather than negotiate, Maximilian sent in troops, arrested the ringleaders and chased their sympathizers from the area. At Fuggerau and in Hungary, Fugger drove his workers as hard as Maximilian, and his operators in Hungary once executed an agitator. Fugger might have looked like a benevolent employer when he petitioned the church to give his miners relief from fasting. But this was self-interest—he wanted his miners strong enough to work a full shift. Miners often accused him of chiseling them on wages. His rough treatment of workers came back to haunt him.

❧

Information is everything on a modern trading desk. The first to get important data has an edge he can exploit for millions. In the name of fair play, the government now mandates that everyone get market-moving information at the same time. But that doesn't stop traders from cheating. That's because the slightest head start— whether it's minutes, seconds or even microseconds—can make all the difference.

It was the same in Fugger's time only with longer transmission times and no laws to control the flow. Fugger's competitors knew the advantages of being first as well as Fugger did. But Fugger craved market-sensitive information so much that he created a system to get it first. His creation? A news service, the world's first. He set up a network of couriers who raced to Augsburg with market information, political updates and the latest gossip—anything that would give him an edge. A postal service had been running between Augsburg and Venice since the fourteenth century. A similar network linked Augsburg with Innsbruck and other imperial cities. But the networks, staffed by city-appointed "post boys," were too incomplete and slow for Fugger. He wanted a system tailored just for him. In the years ahead, he learned about important deaths and battle outcomes before Maximilian, the electors and his competitors. Historians dubbed the updates the Fugger News Letters. The letters became more sophisticated under Fugger's heirs. Although content continued to come from Fugger agents, they eventually looked more like newspapers than anything else. Fugger's letters preceded the *Notizie Scritte* of Venice, the first newspaper, by half a century and earned Fugger a footnote in the history of journalism. He had staggering courier bills but he happily paid.

His first recorded use of the news service came just after Maximilian took back Vienna. With that out of the way, the emperor was ready for a new war and turned his thoughts to Burgundy, his inheritance from Charles the Bold. The French had stolen it from him after Mary's death, and he wanted it back. He had no army, and he needed mercenaries and money to fight. He asked Fugger for a loan and offered what he considered the best collateral imaginable: a pledge from Henry VII, the king of England, who hated the French as much as Maximilian. Henry offered Maximilian 200,000 florins. Maximilian asked Fugger to front the money so he could start immediately. He promised to pay him back after he got the money from Henry. Fugger understood that Henry collected a lot of tax money and managed his finances as well as any king in Europe. But he knew better than to trust a promise and dragged his feet.

Fugger was waiting for information. He had spies in England who could tell him if any boats with gold had left English ports. Soon enough, word came back that no boats were coming. Fugger refused to make the loan.

Maximilian was furious with Fugger and refused to believe that Henry had stiffed him. Assuming that the English money was still coming, he threw a small force into Burgundy. The French outnumbered Maximilian, but he had more cannons and defeated the French at Dournon. He came within striking distance of Dijon when he learned that Fugger was right. Henry had dropped him. He later discovered the French had bribed Henry to stay neutral. Fugger played a part in the truce. To keep Maximilian from destroying himself by overreaching, Fugger bribed the French to sign a treaty that let Maximilian lock in his gains.

⚜

In the summer of 1495, Maximilian journeyed to the Rhineland city of Worms to participate in one of the grandest ceremonies of the age: The installation of the emperor. After a joust that he won, rituals in place for six centuries took over. He took his place on a throne and the electors came to his side. Maximilian would have stuck out under any circumstance. He stood over six feet tall and had flowing locks that hung over his broad shoulders. For the ceremony, he wore a cloak held together with a jeweled clasp the size of a dinner plate.

He held a sword in his lap. One elector, on bended knee, brought him an orb, another brought him a scepter and another his crown. Forty princes and seventy counts pledged their loyalty. Everyone called him *Kaiser*, the German word for Caesar. He promised to be a just ruler. The people gave him their adulation. Years earlier, when he became Duke of Flanders, one observer could barely contain himself. "I know not which to admire most—the beauty of his youth, the bravery of his manhood or the promise of his future." Maximilian made a similar impression in Worms. "Not even Alexander the Great heard such praise," remarked a contemporary. For the thirty-six-year-old Austrian, who only a few years earlier was captive in a Flemish jail, it must have seemed like a dream.

Once the ceremony finished, Maximilian presided over his first imperial diet. These assemblies, known as *Reichstags* in German, rotated among cities and resembled meetings of Congress or Parliament except they met less frequently and the participants had more fun. Tournaments preceded the diets and the dignitaries hosted dances and banquets. The electors made Maximilian emperor upon the death of Frederick. They assumed Maximilian would be weak like his father, Frederick the Fat, who barely troubled them during his fifty-three years as emperor. But the ceremony went to the new emperor's head and he believed himself all-powerful. In his first speech to the diet, he all but ordered the electors to hand over enough gold to put him back on the battlefield against the French. The French king Charles VIII was in Italy grabbing territory that Maximilian said belonged to the empire. But what really motivated Maximilian was a desire to get to Rome. Under imperial rules, only a papal coronation could seal his election. He feared that Charles plotted to beat him to Rome and grab the imperial crown for himself.

Word got back to him that, only recently, Charles had appeared at a feast dressed in imperial robes and holding his own orb and scepter. His people called him emperor and astrologers told him his own coronation was written in the stars. The reality was Maximilian had nothing to fear from the French. The electors would never have accepted the French king as emperor, especially not when they had already elected a man they assumed was an unthreatening and impoverished weakling.

Maximilian believed the crown was magical, as magical as King Arthur's sword. If presented to him by the pope, he would possess all the power of Charlemagne and Europe would bow at his feet. With the crown, the people would acknowledge his legitimacy. Without it, they would dismiss him as a phony. Maximilian's great dream was to mount a crusade, slay the Turks and save Christendom. He believed this was his destiny. But first he needed the crown. He wanted it more than he wanted Burgundy, Hungary or anything else. His obsession with the crown cannot be overstated. It dominated his reign and created one opportunity after another for Fugger. If not for the obsession, Fugger might have remained, like his brothers, a rag dealer.

In the Federalist Papers, James Madison needed a phrase to describe a legislative body's ability to control policy by supplying or denying funds. He came up with the "power of the purse." To Maximilian's horror and surprise, the electors used that power unabashedly. Maximilian got a reality check when they locked him out of meetings. Then the electors bogged him down in negotiations and hit him with impossible conditions. He became sullen and moody, and complained of being treated like a "small town mayor."

The emperor only got some money after handing over most of

the little power he had to the electors. He hated giving in, but at least he won some cash. To pay for their promises, the electors introduced a tax called the Common Penny. All imperial citizens had to pay. It was the first federal tax in Germany and mirrored schemes in France and England. The Common Penny was trouble for Fugger because it led Maximilian to believe that he no longer needed bankers. He fired Fugger and terminated the silver contracts. There were millions of Germans. Once they paid the tax, he would have all he needed to beat the French and make it to Rome, or so he thought.

Fugger was furious. What about their deal? What about gratitude? Hadn't he supported Maximilian in the ouster of Sigmund? Hadn't his brother Ulrich come through for Maximilian's father, Frederick, when Frederick needed a wardrobe? Did all this count for nothing? Fugger also worried about his survival. He was in a perilous financial state because he had borrowed money to pay for Fuggerau and a second smelter in Hohenkirchen in eastern Germany. He needed the silver profits to stay afloat and would be bankrupt if the money didn't come through. But not for the last time, he understood the electors better than the man they elected. Fugger's informants told him what he already suspected, that the German lords would forget their promises. Maximilian may have felt threatened by King Charles and his designs on Italy, but the electors, sitting in grand palaces far away from the Italian border, were indifferent. Sure enough, the Common Penny produced only a fraction of the expected revenue and Maximilian remained destitute. He then did the only thing he could do if he wanted to invade Italy and get to Rome: He limped back to Fugger, pledged more of his silver production and signed for another loan.

With money from Fugger, plus promises of support from Venice and Milan, Maximilian headed over the Alps to Genoa and, from there, hired a ship to take him to Pisa on Italy's west coast. Fugger's Genoese branch paid the fare. Maximilian aimed for Florence where the charismatic priest Savonarola had taken control after the death of Lorenzo de Medici. Savonarola promised that God would come to kill the rich. Maximilian cared nothing about that. He only cared that Savonarola supported the French. To make it to Rome and maintain his supply lines, he and his small army needed to take Florence. He got stuck outside the city because Milan and Venice failed to come through with the promised support. Even worse, Maximilian's son Philip, who ruled Flanders as an archduke and had pledged to distract Charles in France, had fallen under the spell of French advisors and did nothing. Disgusted, Maximilian left Italy and returned to Tyrol. He fought depression by engaging in his favorite pastime: hunting goats in the jagged mountains above Innsbruck.

The disappointment shattered Maximilian's innocence. Henry VII, the German electors, the duke of Milan, the doge of Venice, his own son—all had let him down. Maybe he had his epiphany while chasing goats but, somewhere, it dawned on him that he could only trust Schwaz and its silver. As long as he had Schwaz, bankers like Fugger would be there for him. After getting off the rocks, a rejuvenated Maximilian ordered all his bankers to Füssen, in the foothills of the Alps, to ask for money.

❧

Fugger went to church on Sunday, endorsed family values and loved his king and country. But make no mistake: He was a radical. He refused to believe that noble birth made someone better than anyone else. For him, intelligence, talent and effort made the man. His view is now mainstream. But it was subversive at the time. Europe operated according to a caste system as rigid as in India. Three groups comprised society: nobles, priests and commoners. Each group had its own pecking order. Among commoners, patricians stood on top followed by rich merchants like Fugger. Then came artisans, peasants and beggars. Each subset had its own dress code. They had different privileges and obligations. Upward flexibility was limited.

Fugger wasn't buying it. While society as a whole remained glued to the medieval notion of every man in his place, he shared his grandfather's belief that man made his own luck. Albrecht Dürer and the great Renaissance artists of Italy saw it that way. So did the humanists, the writers and philosophers who broke with tradition and celebrated man instead of God. In 1486, when Fugger was twenty-seven, Giovanni Pico della Mirandola delivered his *Oration on the Dignity of Man*. The speech became the manifesto of humanism and landed Pico in jail as a heretic. In the speech, he declared that man was unique among God's creatures because he had free will, and that free will allowed an individual to determine his own course. Fugger was no philosopher and might never have heard of Pico. But he was a product of his times, and the times were changing. By following the dictates of his will, he showed sympathy, unwittingly perhaps, for heretical views.

Fugger's worldview let him recognize his relationship with the emperor in its true form. It wasn't one of master and servant. It wasn't one of lord and serf. It was a relationship of creditor and debtor. In that sort of relationship, he, as the creditor, had the power. Maximilian's titles meant little to Fugger. Yes, Maximilian was a king. The electors gave him an orb and scepter, and peasants trembled in his presence. Noble ladies hid his boots and spurs to keep him longer at their parties. But Fugger knew that as long as he had cash, Maximilian would need him and would have to accept his terms.

While the other bankers answered Maximilian's call to the meeting, Fugger stayed away. It was a deliberate snub. He let the other bankers negotiate with Maximilian while he stayed home. He kept the emperor hanging for ten days. Approached by Maximilian's tailor, of all people, to explain himself, Fugger said he had renounced banking. Still fuming over Maximilian's earlier decision to fire him after the Common Penny, Fugger wanted out. He wrote to Maximilian to explain his decision. Lending, he said, "achieved nothing but trouble, effort and ingratitude."

One could hardly blame him. He didn't want to be at the mercy of a capricious borrower like Maximilian who was above the law and long on questionable promises. Fugger didn't have to look far to see what could go wrong. Lucas Fugger was the son of Fugger's uncle and the patriarch of the Fuggers of the Roe, the other branch of the family. He had been the most celebrated businessman in Augsburg. He had trading operations in Frankfurt, Nuremberg, Venice, Milan, Bruges and Antwerp. When not on the road, he served as an Augsburg town councillor as well as a judge and a guild master. More than anything, Lucas loved deal making and rubbing shoulders with his betters. In 1489, he made his own loan to Maximilian. Maximilian pledged the tax revenue of the Flemish city of Leuven to pay it back. The gentlemen of Leuven were as unwilling to pay as gentlemen of Ghent were five years before when they jailed Maximilian and made him watch as they killed his jester. Although the loan was small, the default busted the thinly stretched Lucas. Fugger and his brothers could have bailed him out but sat idly by as Lucas and his family lost everything. In a fit of rage, Lucas's son attacked him with a knife. Lucas, once the envy of all and holder of many offices, fled to a hut that had once belonged to his grandfather in their ancestral village of Graben. Fugger later gave him a few florins for it.

But fear didn't keep Fugger away from Fussen. He stayed away for tactical reasons. As his early deals with Sigmund showed, Fugger was a crafty negotiator. He knew Maximilian would want him even more if he played hard to get. The other bankers could loan only a fraction of what Fugger could and Maximilian would need him regardless of what the others did. With that in mind, he may have expected Maximilian to come groveling. But this time he miscalculated. With Maximilian all to themselves, the other bankers schemed to ruin Fugger, whom they considered an upstart. Maximilian didn't come groveling to Fugger. Instead, he listened to the bankers who plotted to destroy Fugger.

The rivals had names out of a fairy tale—Herwart, Baumgarten and the Brothers Gossembrot. Maximilian had given them some mining concessions, just not as many as he had given to Fugger. The Gossembrots were the most powerful of the group. Sigmund Gossembrot was the mayor of Augsburg and his brother George was Maximilian's treasury secretary. They came from an old family and hated Fugger for coming into their territory. They wanted his silver contracts and urged Maximilian to confiscate Fuggerau—moves that could have bankrupted Fugger. Maximilian took their advice. He once again issued orders to sever ties to Fugger.

Germans say that to be successful, you need Vitamin B. The B stands for *Beziehungen,* or connections. Fugger had an abundance of Vitamin B and Fugger called on those reserves to secure his assets.

The first to get a call was the bishop of Bamberg. He was the same bishop who had sold him the land that became Fuggerau. He still controlled that part of Austria. Fugger told him about Maximilian's plan to meddle in his territory and seize Fuggerau. Next, Fugger traveled to Saxony to tell the region's duke that once Maximilian took Fuggerau, he would surely go to Saxony and take Fugger's other smelter, Hohenkirchen, in the duke's territory. Horrified by intrusions on their sovereignty, the bishop and the duke sent ambassadors to Innsbruck and ordered Maximilian to back off.

The decisive blow came when Fugger asked another of the emperor's lenders, Melchior von Meckau, to call in a loan and put a cash squeeze on the emperor. Meckau served as bishop of Brixen, south of Innsbruck. He had his own silver mines and dabbled as a lender. He often traded favors with Fugger. When Meckau asked Maximilian for his money back, the emperor discovered Fugger was the only banker who could supply the money in a hurry. Fugger made the loan to Maximilian. Maximilian forgot about Fuggerau.

It might have been difficult to recognize at the time, but Fugger was making himself indispensable. Maximilian felt frustrated by Fugger's methods and demands, but he couldn't deny that Fugger was the only banker he could count on in a pinch. Indispensability helped drive Fugger's success and repeatedly won him special treatment. Fugger knew that the emperor couldn't live without him and made sure it stayed that way.

❧

It goes without saying that monopolists make the biggest fortunes. By controlling supply, they can charge whatever they want and flow the outrageous profits back into other schemes that make even more money. That's why Vanderbilt wanted to dominate the rails and Rockefeller wanted to dominate oil. And that's why Fugger wanted to dominate metals. He would never have become the richest person on earth by sharing a market with others. He had to have it all.

He already had it all in Hungary. Hungary was one of few copper-producing regions in Eastern Europe, which made Fugger just about the only supplier to Danzig and the other markets up north. But it was different in Venice where other Germans—those with their own contracts with Maximilian—competed for every sale.

The competitors were the same gentlemen who had conspired in Fussen to bury Fugger. Baumgartner, Herwart and the Gossembrots hated competition as much as Fugger did. To put a stop to it, they invited Fugger into a cartel to fix prices. They explained how they would make a fortune because customers would have nowhere to go but to them.

Fugger was as greedy as the rest of them, if not even greedier. But he wasn't crazy about partnerships. Unlike the Medici and other Italian banking houses that routinely took in others to spread risk and increase capital, Fugger wanted every penny for himself, and the idea of splitting profits and decision-making repulsed him. His brothers were a special case. Fugger owned 29 percent of Ulrich Fugger & Brothers and he was happy with that as long as Ulrich and George left him alone. As for the partnership with Thurzo, Fugger needed Thurzo for protection in Hungary. But the proposed copper cartel fired his imagination.

Nowadays, such an arrangement would be illegal; authorities long ago prohibited price fixing in the name of consumer protection. But there were no such laws in 1498, only a blanket understanding that businessmen should treat customers in a fair and "Christian" manner. To get around that, the group asked Maximilian for his blessing and explained that they could lend him even more money if he let them make bigger profits. They clinched the deal by bribing him with a loan.

At this point, the story took a surprising turn. It turns out that the cartel had an enemy within in the form of Fugger. Yes, Fugger could sell his copper for high prices if he participated in the cartel. But he wanted more than a quick profit. He saw the cartel agreement as a way to destroy his rivals, run off with their business and create the same kind of monopoly in Austria as he had in Hungary. He had a simple plan: Rather than ship his Hungarian copper to Danzig, he would send it to Venice and flood the market, drive down copper prices and obliterate those too weak to hold on. This sounded great but was a dangerous scheme for Fugger because the other men had the ear of the emperor. The emperor might punish Fugger for attacking them. And there was also no guarantee that Fugger could outlast the others once he slashed the price. Maybe their pockets were deeper than he thought. He could end up bankrupting himself if he wasn't careful. But he had a stomach for this sort of thing. Without fear, he sprung the trap. He would see the game to its brutal conclusion one way or another.

After the cartel's first shipments left Austria for Venice, wagons from Hungary followed. Once the copper arrived, Fugger ordered his Venetian agent to dump everything on the market at once regardless of the price. Take whatever was offered. Just get rid of it, he ordered. Venice was instantly oversupplied. It had never seen so much copper. Prices tanked. Stunned by the sudden collapse of the market, the others let their copper pile up in warehouses. They didn't want to sell into a falling market. But they had bills to pay and could not hold out forever. When Fugger continued to sell and prices kept falling, they ditched everything at a loss.

Bruised and struggling to hang on, the victims accused Fugger of acting in an "unbrotherly and unchristian" way, a characterization that would follow him for the rest of his life. They asked Maximilian to punish Fugger, but the emperor was embroiled in a flare-up in Switzerland and did nothing. Fugger didn't get his monopoly but he did end up with more mining assets than ever.

3

❦

THE THREE BROTHERS

On a January morning in the middle of the copper battle, Fugger shaved, put on his best suit and went to church. He was still living in the house where he was born—a house he shared with his mother until her death the previous year at the impressive age of seventy-eight. His brothers lived down the street. They were raising their families in a big house across from the church of St. Anne. But Fugger was still single. Most men in Renaissance Germany married in their early twenties. His brothers had held on longer. Ulrich made it to thirty-eight and George to thirty-six. Fugger had them beat. He was now thirty-nine. But his status was about to change. He took a spot before the altar and waited for his bride.

The Renaissance marked a turning point for marriage. Couples began marrying for love. Arranged marriages were still the norm in the countryside, where families tied up land by advantageous matches. But fortunes could turn quickly in cities and marriages needed stronger glue than certificates. Love provided the bond. In that context, one might imagine love led Fugger to Sybille Artzt, a vivacious blonde of eighteen. Pictures show her at a dance and riding around town in a sled. But love wasn't what Fugger had in mind. Fugger was old school. He saw a chance for social and commercial gain.

Sybille came from one of the most powerful families in the city. Her parents were among Augsburg's biggest landlords. Her uncle was once the mayor. While the old families in Augsburg looked down on the Fuggers as nouveau riche, Sybille's mother, who arranged the match, overcame snobbery and concentrated on Fugger's money. Fugger concentrated on prestige. The Artzt family brought him power, influence and another badge of success. All were good for business. As for political influence, the Artzt family had two seats on the town council. Fugger could work through them as an in-law and influence local affairs from behind the scenes.

A young Augsburg artist named Hans Burgkmair painted the wedding portrait. Burgkmair had just opened his own shop. Considering Augsburg was also home to Hans Holbein the Elder, Germany's best artist before Dürer, Burgkmair was an odd choice. But Burgkmair's painting is luminescent and detailed, unquestionably the work of a master. It shows the couple arm in arm with a kitschy inscription that reads, "In the year 1498 on January nine, we truly came together so fine." Neither is smiling. Fugger, wearing his gold cap, looks eager to get on with it. Sybille looks lost. She wears a laurel wreath on her head to signal her virginity. Her dress is high-waisted to show off the belly and hint at fertility.

There is no record of the festivities. But the January wedding date is telling. The upper class regularly married in winter because the cool air allowed for exotic delicacies like oysters and lobster. Wedding feasts took in hundreds of guests and lasted several days. Princes and bishops came on one day and friends and family came on another. If a dignitary sent a representative, the family treated him with the same reverence as the man himself and put him in the front row. The Augsburg town council limited the number of wedding guests in an effort to contain luxury and maintain the appearance of social equality. Fugger likely ignored the rules and paid the fines. For him, anything less than a grand wedding would have been shameful. Wilhelm Rem, who worked for Fugger, later attended the ceremony for Fugger's niece Ursula. He found it scandalous that Ursula dressed not with the veil of a commoner but was bareheaded like a noble woman. Rem condemned the family's "overweening pride" and fretted about whether other families would follow the Fuggers' lead.

Fugger and Sybille moved in with Sybille's mother. The couple probably spent their first night together at her house. By law, they had to consummate the marriage to make it legal. Fugger's brothers and their friends may have been outside egging them on, as was the custom. Fugger wanted children if for no other reason than succession. Fugger's brothers each had several, including a number of sons, and Thurzo, his partner in Hungary, had so many sons that he gave three to the church. Each of the Thurzo priests, thanks to the influence of Fugger and Thurzo, became a bishop. Fugger began to think about succession early in his career, but his match with Sybille produced no heirs.

Still, Fugger wasn't childless. At some point, he had met a

woman named Mechtild Belz and took her as his mistress. They had a child together. Mechtild, perhaps with Fugger's intervention, married a doctor and together they raised Fugger's daughter, also named Mechtild, as their own. Society attached little shame to illegitimacy and when the girl grew up, she married Gregor Lamparter, the rector of Tübingen University, the oldest and most prestigious university in Germany. There is some doubt about Fugger's paternity, but there is no other way to account for the generous financial assistance Fugger gave Lamparter. When Lamparter served a five-year stint as a counselor to Maximilian, a job Fugger may have secured for him, Fugger paid his annual salary of 8,000 florins. When a knight kidnapped Lamparter, Fugger paid the ransom. The duke of Württemberg also tried to nab Lamparter and use him as a hostage in a dispute with Maximilian. Lamparter eluded the duke, but the mere fact that the duke targeted him suggests an especially close relationship between Lamparter and Fugger. The emperor didn't care about Lamparter, but he did care about Fugger.

We don't know if Fugger took other mistresses, but we know that Sybille took a lover herself. Conrad Rehlinger was an Augsburg merchant, a family friend and a frequent guest in the Fugger home. When Fugger needed a witness to sign a document, he called Rehlinger. A portrait by Bernhard Strigel of Rehlinger and his nine children hangs in the Alte Pinakothek in Munich. Sybille married Rehlinger within weeks of Fugger's death.

❧

Fugger's most notorious contemporary was Cesare Borgia, the bloodthirsty son of Pope Alexander VI. While Fugger was in Augsburg piling up profits, Borgia was in Rome murdering his way up the professional ladder. Borgia was not the only one using assassination as a means of advancement. The practice was widespread in the Renaissance. The death of Pico della Mirandola, the champion of humanism, was also a case of poison. The prevalence of assassination led the great Fugger historian Gottfried (Götz) von Pölnitz, who spent more time in the Fugger Archives than anyone, to ask if Fugger himself was a murderer. In 1502, Sigmund Gossembrot, Fugger's most dangerous rival, died. His death came just a few months after the death of his brother and partner George. Fugger certainly had a motive: The Gossembrots were out to get him. At the time of their deaths, they were proposing a new plan for Maximilian to drop Fugger. But the only evidence for murder von Pölnitz cites is the absence of documentation about either death. This proves nothing. Even leaving aside that murder was a capital offense and carried enormous risk to the killer, murder wasn't Fugger's game. He didn't need to kill people like the Gossembrots to succeed. He could beat them with his intellect. After Sigmund Gossembrot died, Fugger betrayed no joy. He assumed Sigmund's children would continue to fight him, saying, "Although Gossembrot is dead, his envious seeds have been left behind."

⚜

That same year, three salesmen from the Swiss city of Basel came to visit Fugger. They were selling jewelry and their sources told them Fugger was interested. He often bought jewels for Sybille, including, in Frankfurt, a ring big enough that it had all of Augsburg talking. "She had gold jewelry and gem stones to surpass a princess," wrote a friend.

The men visited Fugger in his office. Located in the house of his brothers, the office was in the back of the building and overlooked a quiet alley instead of the busy street where the men presumably entered. The office became legendary as Fugger's influence grew. Visitors called it the Golden Counting Room. Servants showed the men in. They didn't have the actual stones, only sketches. But that was good enough because the salesmen hawked the most spectacular jewels in Europe and the paint-on-parchment drawings they unrolled for Fugger were stunning. One showed the Little Feather, a jeweled hatpin. Another showed the White Rose, a heart-shaped ruby in a circle of diamonds. The third piece was a diamond-studded garter that once belonged to England's Edward III. One can imagine the Swiss saved the best for last and, after they unveiled the final drawing, they said nothing and let it speak for itself. It showed one of the world's largest diamonds. The jeweler had cut it in a rectangular shape, mounted it in a gold setting and surrounded it with three rubies radiating from the center like rays of the sun. They called it the Three Brothers. It later found its way to England where Queen Elizabeth wore it for the Ermine Portrait. Along with her exaggerated lace collar, hooped skirt and frilly sleeves, the Three Brothers advertised her wealth and power.

Before Fugger saw these four pieces, Charles the Bold owned them and had brought them on his ill-fated, do-or-die invasion of Switzerland twenty-six years earlier. Like Maximilian and his faith in the magic of the imperial crown, Charles believed in the power of objects and that the Lord only granted great things to great people. He also believed in the corollary, that the more objects a person accumuluated—and the more value they had—the stronger the possessor. That's why he also brought to Switzerland his silver plate, gold decanters, ivory ornaments, jeweled swords, high-backed thrones, saintly bones, canopied bed, gilded ostrich eggs and his collection of shoes, including the stylish ones with the impossibly long toes. Maybe the sultan of Turkey had more treasures, but no European collection could compare. And if no collection could compare, no owner could compare, not when it came to power and might. As Charles saw it, he was invincible. He had the stuff to prove it.

The Swiss surprised Charles near Lake Geneva at the Battle of Morat and chased him from his camp before he could grab his things. The quality of the items, not to mention the overwhelming quantity, awed the Swiss generals. They ordered death for anyone who took loot for themselves. The order came too late. The most valuable items, particularly the small ones like jewels, had already vanished into pockets. A witness described how a soldier found the largest of the diamonds beneath a wagon wheel in the mud of Morat. The soldier sold it for a florin—about a month's wages for a mercenary—to a Swiss bishop who sold it to the city of Basel.

Jewels like these were in high demand. Monarchs bought them to advertise their power. Businessmen bought them as a form of savings. They could sell them in a pinch or carry them on a flight to safety. And while diamonds generated no income sitting in a chest, they held up against inflation. They also made handy gifts. But the Swiss found the Burgundian loot hard to sell. Ten years after Morat, they tried to sell one of the larger pieces, most likely the Three Brothers, and received an offer of only 4,000 florins, a sliver of its true value. The trouble was that the items were stolen. Or at least that's what Maximilian and the Habsburgs, as inheritors of Burgundy, would have said. If the items turned up, they still had the right to claim the pieces and demand them back.

Charles the Bold had been dead for eighteen years by the time the Swiss approached Fugger but the men still had to operate in secrecy. Their sketches dazzled Fugger. After more than a year of negotiations, he bought the complete set for 40,000 florins, a large amount of his capital at the time. Like the city elders of Basel, he put them in a vault and said nothing about them.

⚜

Fugger was not a wild-eyed speculator. When he advanced money to Sigmund or Maximilian, ore in the ground stood behind the loans. When he built a smelter, the prevailing price of copper supported a winning return. When he bought jewels, a bargain price compensated for the challenges of trying to sell them.

But even the gimlet-eyed Fugger was subject to the passions of his age. Columbus's discovery of America, Vespucci's discovery of the Amazon and Vasco da Gama's voyage to India excited even the landlocked people of Augsburg. A public gripped by exploration fever collected coconuts, parrot feathers and other Asian curios. Even Fugger caught it and, in 1505, he took a flyer on a Portuguese spice voyage to India. Portugal was battling Spain for mastery of the seas. Portugal was a backwater stranded on the edge of western Europe. It was hopelessly poor, but it had big dreams. While the Spanish focused on America, the Portuguese concentrated on rounding Africa and opening a water route to India. They aimed to smash the Venetian lock on the European pepper trade. Following on da Gama's success, King Manuel I sought investors for a return trip to bring back pepper. Fugger joined in. The investment involved him in a violent trade war and benefitted him in ways he could not have foreseen.

Fugger knew that an ocean journey, especially in the lightly charted water around the Cape of Good Hope, was perilous. By jumping in, he weighed the risk against the return. He would lose his entire investment if the ships splintered on the rocks. He would make a killing if they returned to Lisbon, stuffed with pepper.

Negotiations dragged on for months. When the investors finally signed the papers, Fugger's Augsburg neighbor Anton Welser put down 20,000 florins and Fugger a mere 4,000. Maybe Fugger didn't want to risk more than that. But the energy he put into the effort—he replaced his agent after the first agent failed to make progress with the king—suggests he wanted a larger stake. The Germans leased three ships in Antwerp. Two Augsburg scribes boarded the ships to record events for the folks back home. The ships sailed to Lisbon where they joined a fleet of Portuguese gunboats. Augsburg city manager Conrad Peutinger spoke for all when he wished the voyage well: "It gives us Augsburgers a feeling of great pride to be the first Germans to travel to India."

The Portuguese needed guns because they had to fight to get the pepper. Arabs controlled most of the ports along the way. They bought pepper from Indian growers and shipped it up the Red Sea, where porters loaded it on camels for the walk up to Alexandria or Damascus and the Mediterranean voyage to Venice. The Arabs and their Venetian partners had been trading like this for hundreds of years. But if the Portuguese could secure the trade route, they could win it all because they had several advantages. As Fugger knew, their enormous, square-sailed carracks with their large cargo bellies offered efficiencies that camels could not match. By staying on the water all the way to Lisbon, the Portuguese could avoid the punishing tolls that the sultan of Turkey charged to pass through his territory. Then there was the simple fact that Lisbon was closer than Venice to Spain and the markets of northern Europe. Buyers from Germany, France and Spain would buy from Portugal because it could offer lower prices. The Portuguese writer Guido Detti thrilled over the idea of beating the haughty Venetians: "When they lose their commerce in the East, they will have to go back to fishing." Venice itself feared disaster. Wrote the Venetian banker Pruili: "I clearly see in this the ruin of the city of Venice."

King Manuel entrusted the fleet to an ambitious nobleman named Francisco Almeida. The king wanted him to strike deals for safe passage with the cities along the way and seize or even destroy those who refused to agree. The king offered him a staggering incentive. He promised to make Almeida viceroy of India if he succeeded. As viceroy, Almeida would have complete authority. He would rule Portugal's holdings in the region as a dictator.

Almeida and his ships left Lisbon in March. After an easy trip down the west coast of Africa, the ships swung around the cape and ran into a storm that toppled masts and cracked rudders. They survived to face an even more perilous encounter in Mombasa. Mombasa is an island city directly across the Indian Ocean—what the Portuguese called the Barbarian Gulf—from the Indian spice ports. It is now the second biggest city in Kenya. Then it was the largest city in eastern Africa and belonged to Arab traders. The sheik who ran Mombasa had a palace inside the city wall with gardens and fountains. The rest of the city was lined with streets so narrow that only two people could walk abreast. Balconies hung over the streets as a second road system. Pepper was one source of income. The other was slaves. The sheik sent raiding parties to the mainland and captured slaves for the bazaars of Aleppo, Alexandria and Cairo.

Almeida had to have Mombasa to secure the coast. The whole enterprise depended on it. Unless Mombasa could be won over or neutralized, Portuguese ships could look forward to pirate attacks whenever they came near.

Almeida's ships, the king's flag flying from the masts and guns pointing from the decks, made a fearsome sight as they anchored in the harbor and threatened an attack. But the sheik felt safe behind his fortifications and refused to negotiate. Almeida opened fire. Mombasa harbor echoed with the boom of mortar and the shouts of soldiers. The city was soon ablaze. Almeida ordered a landing party to beach and, after surviving an attack by two elephants the sheik let loose to trample them, the men saw that they had weakened the city's defenses enough to justify a full landing. The Portuguese went ashore the next morning. While the main force fought hand to hand in the city, Almeida easily took the palace. The sheik hitched up his robe and fled with his men into the palms. Slaves, women and children were the only ones left to defend the city. The Portuguese killed everyone they captured. Satisfied with a job well done, Almeida raised the king's red-and-white flag over the palace. Balthazar Sprenger, one of the Augsburgers on the trip, thanked the Lord. "What happened could not have been accomplished without a merciful god," he wrote. "Without God, many of us would have fallen. We conquered and kept the city with happiness thanks to the all-powerful." The sheik wrote a warning letter to a neighboring ruler. "A great Lord came with such strength and fury that few escaped with their lives," he wrote. "The smell of bodies in my city is so repulsive that I can't return." The Portuguese lost five men. The sheik lost 1,500. Mombasa never threatened the Portuguese again.

With the east coast of Africa now under his control, Almeida kidnapped an Arab pilot to guide him across the Indian Ocean. Almeida and Fugger's investment faced more danger on the Indian side. By now, the Arabs had a new ally in the Republic of Venice. The pope had long before ordered Venice to do no business with infidels. But while the Muslims might have been heathens to the pope, Venice embraced them as brothers when money was on the line. Venice had a saying for this: "First Venetians, then Christians." Faith in the slogan was never more evident than in its dealings with Arab spice dealers.

Venice considered two options. The first was to copy the ancient Persian king Darius and dredge a canal to connect the Mediterranean with the Red Sea. Once it did that, it could send ships from Venice to fight. But that cost too much so Venice instead sent shipbuilders from the Arsenal to Alexandria to make planks, ribs and masts that the Egyptians could haul, like the blocks of the pyramids, across the desert to assemble into war ships at Suez. Egyptian crews manned the ships and got as far as Diu in Gujarat where they planned to join the Zamorin of Calicut, a powerful Indian king, to attack Almeida. Almeida got to them first. He overwhelmed the Egyptians, firing cannons at point-blank range and collecting Egyptian heads to hurl into other towns as warning shots. After that and a few more altercations, Almeida grabbed as much pepper as he could and charted a course to Lisbon.

The ships returned to Europe with so much pepper that prices crashed before they even docked. Welser and Fugger wanted to sell the haul immediately. They could still earn a huge profit despite the price drop. King Manuel stopped them by confiscating the cargo and putting it in a warehouse. The Germans accused the king of theft and spent three years in court to get it back. But it ended well.

When Welser and Fugger finally got the pepper and sold it, they tripled their money.

The voyage whetted the appetite of the Welsers for more. Although Lucas Rem, their man in Lisbon, found the Portuguese insufferable and thought the spice trade a horrible business, the Welsers funded more voyages and made so much money on it that, despite being commoners, one of their own married an archduke. But as far as Fugger was concerned, the Welsers could have it all. King Manuel's double cross spoiled his appetite for shipping. He preferred doing business close to home. Besides, he had another way to profit on spices. He could make just as much money as a middleman, buying pepper from the Portuguese and selling it in Germany.

Anyone could be a wholesaler but Fugger had an edge because he had something the Portuguese needed to stay in business: metal. The Portuguese got a lesson in the importance of metal when da Gama went to India in 1498 and tried to entice the Zamorin to trade pepper for European honey and fashionable hats. Arab traders laughed when they saw the wares and the Zamorin seethed at the perceived insult. A friendly Tunisian trader warned da Gama to bring gold next time or else. "If the captains went ashore, their heads would be cut off," he said. "This was the way the king dealt with those who came to his country without gold." Alemeida ran into the same hurdle. No one wanted his honey and hats. The Portuguese realized they needed more than guns if they wanted pepper. Fugger's silver and copper weren't gold, but India wanted these metals, too. Soon, Portugal became Fugger's best customer for metal. He sent wagons full of the ores of silver and copper from Hungary to Antwerp where porters loaded it on ships for Lisbon. Portugal paid him with pepper, making him one of Europe's largest spice wholesalers.

Detractors called Fugger a profiteer, a monopolist and a Jew among other things. The spice voyage earned him another name: Pepper Sack. His pepper deals were more visible than his mining activities. Many assumed pepper was his main business.

As the chronicler Pruili feared, Portugal's success devastated Venice. The city went from exporting pepper to becoming an importer. In 1512, a Venetian diplomat was complaining to the sultan of Egypt about money problems. In 1514, Venice suffered the ultimate humiliation by becoming a Portuguese customer. It was over for the republic. In a last gasp to hold on, it shifted its economy from trade to industry. Glass, soap, silk and wool makers surpassed the Arsenal shipyard as the city's leading manufacturer. But the old spark and work ethic disappeared, and Venice began its decline. Changing with the times, Fugger shifted the center of his foreign activities to Antwerp. As for Portugal, it dominated the spice business until the next century when the Dutch broke its grip.

❧

One of Fugger's tricks was keeping public officials on his payroll, including several who worked for Maximilian. The funny thing is, Maximilian not only knew that Fugger paid his men but tolerated it because it saved him money. He didn't have to pay them himself. Lucas Rem, the Welser agent in Lisbon, found Maximilian's financial naïveté beyond belief. He somehow missed that they might not have his best interests at heart. In his diary, Rem praised Maximilian as pious and honorable but blasted him for financial stupidity. "He has advisors who are parasites that control him completely," he wrote. "They are almost all rich but the emperor is poor." Machiavelli, then a city official in Florence, had a similar take. He called Maximilian a "great general" who was patient and gracious with his subjects but a disaster with money. "His easy nature causes him to be deceived," he said. "A friend of the emperor told me that anyone could cheat him without his knowing it."

The benefits of the bribes became evident after an otherwise forgettable dustup called the War of Landshut Succession. In September 1504, Maximilian put on a suit of armor to fight not the French, the Italians nor the Swiss but one of his bosses: Philip of Wittelsbach, the elector of the Palatinate. Philip had declared war against the Munich branch of his own family over some territory in Bavaria. The other electors asked Maximilian to mediate and he took it as a call to arms. The fight riveted the Augsburg financial community because it featured their customers fighting to the death only miles away. In what would have been a particularly scary moment for Fugger had he known about it, a Bohemian mercenary dragged Maximilian off his horse and came at him with a pike. After a friend beat back the attacker, Maximilian won the battle and, in the peace negotiations, he fought hard and won for himself Kufstein, the textile cities of Kirchberg and Weissenhorn and the silver mine of Rattenberg.

Rattenberg excited the bankers. Maximilian had already pledged every morsel of his silver production. Now, with Rattenberg, he had something new to offer. Fugger wanted it as did every other lender in Germany. But Fugger faced long odds because Maximilian was angry at him. It had dawned on him that Fugger sold him copper—copper from his own mines—at premium prices. "From our treasury to our armory in Innsbruck are perhaps thirty steps," he wrote. "And does the copper in these thirty steps alter its value? We still have to pay for the copper like a stranger, as if the copper did not belong to us, which is unreasonable."

If Sigmund Gossembrot, Maximilian's former financial advisor, had still been alive, he or one of Fugger's competitors might have won Rattenberg. But Gossembrot's replacement, Paul von Liechtenstein, saw things differently. Liechtenstein was a curious figure. Later Liechtensteins served the Habsburgs so skillfully that the Habsburgs gave them a mountainous sliver between Austria and Switzerland that is now the country of Liechtenstein. But Paul von Liechtenstein put his loyalty to Fugger first because Fugger had him on the payroll. Fugger paid Liechtenstein the handsome sum of 2,000 florins a year. Liechtenstein knew better than to cross him. Fugger offered Maximilian 60,000 florins for three years of Rattenberg's production. That sounded good to Liechtenstein. Maximilian accepted.

❧

On a July day in 1509, Fugger took a seat in a coach pulled by twenty-five horses en route to the Swabian village of Schmiechen. As he bounced along the dirt road, he spotted a farmer and ordered the coach to stop. He gave the farmer a coin. His generosity continued once he got to town. He gave money to the peasants and their wives. He gave money to servants and maids. The stable boy got two kreuzers—twice what the farmer got. The bailiff got fifteen kreuzers. Fugger recorded the sums in his ledgers.

A sense of feudal responsibility explained Fugger's largesse. Augsburg had long ago bought its way out of feudal commitments and now reported to no one but the emperor. But Schmiechen still operated under the old feudal contract. The residents weren't freemen like the citizens of Augsburg. They were serfs who bound themselves to a master. They paid the lord tribute and the lord played the part of a tribal chieftain. He protected them from attack. "Thou art our duke," went a Dutch saying. "Fight our battles for us."

The lord during Fugger's visit was Fugger himself. He had become Lord of Schmiechen. In Augsburg, people called him Herr Fugger. But in Schmiechen, the farmer, the stable boy and his other serfs called him by his noble title. To them, this grandson of a village peasant was Count Fugger.

Fugger broke into the nobility after a remarkable string of events that began more than a decade earlier in far-off Spain. Fugger's resources, skill and bravado played a part in the story. But so did the astonishing ups and downs of his clients the Habsburgs. In 1496, when Fugger was busy in Hungary, King Ferdinand of Spain—the same Ferdinand who with Queen Isabella sent Columbus to America—was fighting the French and sought Maximilian's support. To get it, he proposed a marriage between his daughter Joanna and Maximilian's son Philip. Maximilian accepted because it put Philip in line to rule Spain. Her older siblings had to die first for him to become king. But as luck would have it, they died young and, when Queen Isabella died a couple of years later, Philip became king of Castile. He also stood to inherit Ferdinand's Aragon, the other half of Spain, after Ferdinand passed on. This was an incredible turn of fortune. A generation earlier, the Habsburgs had nothing but a few claims. Even Vienna belonged to foreigners. Now, with Philip on the rise in Spain, the Habsburgs had Austria, the Low Countries, Castile and Castile's growing holdings in the New World. Frederick's silly dream of AEIOU—All Earth Is Under Austria—was becoming reality. All the world was coming under control of mountainous, landlocked and hopelessly small Austria.

But just as the Habsburgs and Fugger seemed poised for even bigger things, the skies darkened for them when typhoid fever claimed Philip and imperiled the Habsburg dream. He was twenty-eight when he died and had been king for only three months. Fortunately for the Habsburgs, Joanna was still the queen and her children—Habsburg children—were in line to take over. But Ferdinand, her father, wasn't about to let the Habsburgs take Spain that easily. He was the last of his line, fifty-two years old and impotent. But he was a man possessed. He remarried and took a virility potion with the idea of creating a new set of heirs and taking back Spain for his family. If all went well, his family, the Trastamáras, would inherit Spain, not the Habsburgs.

The possibility of losing Spain threw Maximilian into a panic and offered another opportunity for Fugger. Back in Spain, Joanna tried to shore up Habsburg legitimacy by going on a macabre tour of Castile with her husband's corpse. She aimed to raise awareness and, by doing so, solidify the claims of her sons, ages three and six, to Philip's throne. But the tour did nothing but confirm suspicions of her insanity, earn her the nickname *Juana Loca* and give Ferdinand an excuse to lock her up. Maximilian responded by redoubling efforts to reach Rome and get the imperial crown. He believed more than ever that he needed it for strength.

Liechtenstein outlined the reality to the emperor. To get to Rome, he would need to slip through the French forces in Milan and then fight his way through the Venetians, who rightly suspected that Maximilian wanted to exercise old claims on its hinterland. The math was daunting. Liechtenstein calculated Maximilian needed

30,000 soldiers. Even if the electors offered some troops, he would still need mercenaries at a cost of 120,000 florins. Liechtenstein told Maximilian to forget about a coronation. He couldn't afford it. Maximilian was undeterred and ordered Liechtenstein to get the money. "Work it out with Fugger," he said.

Liechtenstein met Fugger in Innsbruck and offered to sell him the two up-and-coming textile cities of Kirchberg and Weissenhorn that the emperor had snatched in the Landshut War. Liechtenstein threw in the surrounding countryside, including any castles in the area, to sweeten the deal. The sale offered Fugger tax revenue; he could collect whatever he could ring out of the citizenry. It also offered him a chance to join the landed gentry and slingshot his family into a higher social orbit.

Anyone with the means could buy a city. But there was a catch: The buyer had to be of noble birth. Fugger was, of course, a commoner. Despite his wealth, his coat of arms and his old-money wife, he was nothing more than a glorified peasant in the caste system. He and Maximilian had a way around that. Just as old Frederick could turn Charles the Bold into a king with a turn of his orb and a wave of his scepter, Maximilian could turn Fugger into a count. Political hurdles stood in the way because the lesser nobles—the knights—would resist being leapfrogged. They would have to be won over. But Liechtenstein promised to manage it. Fugger considered the offer. Kirchberg and Weissenhorn were close enough to Augsburg for Fugger to to keep an eye on. But the tax revenues were meager. Fugger could earn more on other investments.

While Liechtenstein worked Fugger, Maximilian worked the electors. Once more, this heir of Charlemagne who called himself Caesar came to an imperial diet to beg for money. Constance, a lakefront city near the Swiss border, hosted the diet. Maximilian argued that he needed the crown to legitimize his rule. The electors voted Maximilian 9,000 foot soldiers and 3,000 men on horse. This was helpful but only a token. The emperor would need more help to hack his way to the Eternal City.

Querini, the Venetian ambassador to the diet, wrote the doge and told him to relax. No need to prepare for an imperial invasion because the diet had given Maximilian almost nothing. But Querini had spoken too soon. The situation changed when Fugger agreed to the emperor's offer and bought Kirchberg and Weissenhorn for 50,000 florins. Fugger made a show of it. Rather than shipping cash into the battlefield to pay the mercenaries, Fugger sent wagons stuffed with gold coins and protected by a small army to the Constance diet. He parked the wagons in the public square to create the idea that the emperor had bottomless resources. It was an illusion, but it just might scare Venice into letting the emperor through unimpeded.

The theatrics caused a sensation. Querini alerted the doge and word spread that Maximilian had a banker who could produce impossibly large sums in an instant. Machiavelli was traveling through Switzerland at the time and ran into two Genovese businessmen. They told him that Maximilian visited Fugger in Augsburg and left with 100,000 florins. The story was not quite accurate, but it was close.

Maximilian signed papers proclaiming Fugger as lord over several cities and thousands of people. On New Year's Day, 1508, the people of Weissenhorn, the largest of the cities, gathered under the winter sky to pledge loyalty to a new master. The details are lost. But records of a ceremony in the Austrian city of Karnberg, not far from Fugger's factory in Arnoldstein, give the flavor of such events. There, a peasant sat on a round stone carved with the crest of the territory. The new lord, dressed as a peasant, approached the stone. After being introduced, the real peasant turned to the crowd of onlookers, pointed to the lord and asked, "Is he a righteous judge? Will he promote the well-being of our land and its freedom? Is he a protector of the Christian faith and its widows and orphans?" The people shouted, "This he is and will ever be so." The peasant gave the lord a symbolic rap on the ears and pledged his fidelity. We don't know if Fugger ever joined in a ceremony like this. But we know the citizens of Weissenhorn gave Fugger the keys to the city—keys that actually opened the city's gates—and read an oath: "I praise and swear that I will give Fugger my obedience, loyalty and support." The people of Schmiechen, which Fugger added to his collection a year later, did the same.

⚜

Shortly after buying Weissenhorn, Fugger wrote a letter that offered a defense of capitalism and revealed his worldview as never before. To modern ears, his arguments sound as unimaginative as those at a Chamber of Commerce mixer. But capitalism was still feeling its way and, although merchants had been around for centuries, big business was new. Fugger's arguments provoked his listeners because they were hearing them for the first time.

Fugger made his argument in a complaint to Maximilian about his latest fund-raising scheme. The emperor worried Fugger's contributions weren't enough to get him to Rome, so he tried to raise more with a financial tool created in Venice. Since 1171, Venice had been selling tradable financial certificates that offered a fixed rate of interest. This was the start of the bond market, now worth $80 trillion. That part of the story is well known. The forgotten part is that investors bought the bonds at the point of a sword. Venetian bankers and merchants had riches that the government wanted for conquest. Rather than raise taxes, it ordered investors to buy the bonds.

Maximilian drew up papers to make Fugger and the other bankers of Augsburg, Nuremberg and the other imperial cities buy his bonds. To the bankers, it was bad enough that Maximilian wanted to force this on them. Even worse was that the bonds came with no collateral, only Maximilian's promise to pay. Where he would get the money to repay was anybody's guess. Maximilian justified the move with a fairness argument that sounds familiar to modern ears. Fugger and the others might think they made their own breaks, but the truth was they benefited from being citizens of an imperial city. The empire provided security. Imperial protection let the merchants lead lives of peace and run their businesses without the distraction of invaders.

Fugger was furious. "His majesty wants to take it out of my pocket," Fugger huffed. To him, it smacked of a tax. He already paid property taxes. He and other Augsburg property owners had to pay 1 percent on the value of their real estate every year. Wasn't that enough?

In his letter, Fugger started with what he said was obvious: Companies like his benefited every level of society, producing jobs and wealth for all. Business could only work its magic if the government left it alone. If politicians threw up roadblocks and killed the profit motive, business had no chance. Merchants and bankers were good citizens, he argued. They treated each other and their customers fairly. Sure, self interest propelled them. But they knew better than to cheat customers. Reputation was everything and the need for credibility checked the urge to lie, gouge and steal. Hinting at the allure of tax havens (the Swiss border was only sixty miles away), he declared that other countries showed businessmen more respect. He then blasted those who condemned commerce and enterprise. They failed to understand that "it is for the common good that honorable, brave and honest companies are in the realm. For it is not disreputable but rather it is a wonderful jewel that such companies are in the kingdom." He ended the letter with a vague threat: "Reasonable people know this and would be wise to consider."

Who knows what he meant by the last line. But maybe the fact that it could mean anything was the point. Fugger wanted the emperor's imagination to fill the blanks. Maybe Fugger would refuse Maximilian future loans. Maybe Fugger would move to Switzerland. Maybe Fugger would fund the emperor's enemies. The last line is also noteworthy because of the implied insult. It suggested that the emperor was something other than reasonable. The implication would have shocked his contemporaries for its impudence.

Maximilian won the day; the bankers gave him a loan. But they gave him less than he wanted and Fugger's share was minimal. Fugger's jawboning paid off in another respect. Maximilian pledged to never again use force to get a loan.

⚜

Smart business people are politically neutral. Knowing that today's loyal opposition could be tomorrow's leaders, they play both sides of the fence and make friends with everybody. The fence for Fugger in 1508 was the Italian-Austrian border. Maximilian's desire to see Rome put Fugger in a bind. Venice and the Vatican were two of his best customers, and neither wanted Maximilian and an army of ravenous, booty-hungry mercenaries storming their way through Italy. Venice feared for its mainland holdings. The Vatican, whose secular inclinations never ran higher, feared losing territory of its own. Fugger could probably risk irritating Venice. Since Portugal had won the spice war, Venice's share of the pepper trade shriveled to almost nothing. Fugger had lost so much regard for Venice that he opened an office in Genoa, the republic's archrival. And Venice would still want to trade Fugger's copper even if Fugger did business with an enemy.

Fugger had to be more careful with the Vatican. Over the years, Fugger had come to dominate the business of transferring collection plate donations from Germany to Rome. Rome lived on the transfers. Italian bankers had the business before Fugger. But Fugger could move money more safely and efficiently than the others because of the size of his branch network. He had so many offices and handled so much money that he could create a closed loop where he could debit an account in one branch and credit an account in another. Actual coins never changed hands. This made him different from other bankers and endeared him to the Vatican because the pope could get his money without the risk of highway robbers seizing it en route. Like a credit card company taking a cut on every swipe, Fugger collected 3 percent on each transfer.

Fugger was more than just the Vatican's transfer agent in Germany. He was by now "God's Banker," the top financier to Rome. He had expanded the transfer business to eastern Europe, Sweden and parts of France. He took it upon himself to pay Swiss mercenaries to protect the pope, starting the tradition of the Swiss papal guards. He contributed 4,000 ducats (5,600 florins) to the papal campaign of Julius II and greased the cardinals' palms to get him elected. On the day Julius took the tiara, the coronation parade passed in front of Fugger's Vatican branch. The bank managers hung banners with the blue-and-white lilies of their employer. They wanted to remind Julius of Fugger's reach. Julius showed his gratitude by awarding Fugger the contract to mint the papal currency, the *zecca*. Minting had been the exclusive domain of the Florentines. Julius broke a five-year contract with the incumbent and awarded a fifteen-year deal to Fugger. Fugger served seven popes and minted coins for four of them, marking them with an *F* or the family symbol of a trident.

Fugger didn't need to be reminded not to help Maximilian march on Rome. But the Vatican reminded him anyway. Julius sent Bernardino Caravajal, his top man in Germany, to Augsburg to warn him to tread carefully. Caravajal's visit created all sorts of problems for Fugger. Augsburg was by now the financial capital of Europe. In addition to Fugger, the Welsers, Hochstetter and others played at high levels. The others would be angling to get the cardinal's attention while he was in town and steal Fugger's Vatican business for themselves. Determined to prove he was the richest of them all and the most valuable to Rome, Fugger hosted a party on the cardinal's first night with a twelve-course meal followed by music and dancing. Augsburg's rich and powerful came as well as the prettiest girls in town.

Caravajal enjoyed himself but remembered his mission. He told Fugger that Julius wanted Maximilian to stay home and that Fugger should not bankroll him or else. Fugger knew his best course was to stay neutral and sit the whole thing out. But that became impossible after the diet again refused to step up for Maximilian. To keep Maximilian happy, Fugger had to give him something. He gave him just enough to get him started, but no more.

Maximilian crossed the Alps with 10,000 men—only a third of what Liechtenstein said he needed. He got as far as Trent, north of Verona, when he ran out of cash. Maximilian refused to yield. He declared he would press ahead with a smaller contingent even if it meant getting killed. Better to die than to abandon the imperial crown. The emperor's attitude exasperated his advisors. "The wall of difficulties which opposes us is as hard as the head of the emperor," wrote a counselor, "and yet he will run against it without a helmet." His team devised a plan to keep the emperor breathing and their livelihoods intact. What about a coronation ceremony right away, on the spot, without the pope? Maximilian could get his friend Matthaus Lang, the bishop of Salzburg, to officiate. There was enough money in the till to hold a procession down the main street and scrounge up a proxy for the actual crown. Lang could, with full solemnity, put it on Maximilian's head and the pope could sanction the coronation from afar. The scheme was without precedent. Popes had always crowned the emperor. But the aides knew that Venice would fight if Maximilian entered its territory. Their boss might end up like his father-in-law Charles the Bold, who shortly after losing his jewels lost his life in battle and was barely recognizable after dogs dug into his remains.

Reason won the day. Lang crowned Maximilian in Trent Cathedral. Celebrants held a parade. Fireworks lit the sky. The imperial mint in Hall—the one run formerly run by Fugger's grandfather Franz—stamped coins with Maximilian's image and the word "Caesar." They put the coins in circulation to proclaim his greatness to the world.

Maximilian should have been happy but something nagged him: How could he be great if he settled for a coronation among the small, half-timbered houses of Trent rather than the temples of Rome? How could he be Caesar if a friend dressed in bishop's purple instead of papal white handed him the crown? Maximilian immediately regretted his ceremony and declared it a farce. If anything, it made him look weak. As soon as Lang gave him a crown, Maximilian took his forces farther south and into battle. He was more determined than ever to see the pope. Fugger, who must have been jarred by the emperor's insistence, risked the emperor's wrath and contributed nothing to the venture.

Venice met Maximilian and his soldiers at the frontier. Like his uncle Sigmund in his first battle with Venice, Maximilian surprised everyone by winning. He demanded money from Fugger to press on. This put Fugger back in the same spot as before the phony coronation. Once more, he had to choose between customers. Once more he gave the emperor just enough to do his part but not so much as to alienate the doge and, more importantly, Pope Julius. His 4,000-florin contribution was too little to make a difference and, as the Venetian forces grew in number, Maximilian's luck ran out. The Venetians killed his best commander, forcing Maximilian to retreat. The Venetians followed him into Austria. It became personal for Fugger when Venice attacked Fuggerau because the compound supplied the emperor with guns. Fuggerau had the strength to resist robber barons, Turkish looters and maybe even the Venetian army. But Fugger saw no value in trading bullets with the Republic. Fuggerau surrendered. As Fugger considered how to get his smelter back, Liechtenstein pleaded for more money. "God must help," he wrote Fugger. "I know of no other way."

God failed to intervene, but Fugger did. To save Maximilian, Fugger made him his fourth and largest loan of the Venetian war. He attached two conditions to his 20,000 florins. The first: Under no circumstances could Maximilian turn to the Welsers or any other Fugger rival for more money; he had to give Fugger exclusivity. The second: Maximilian had to immediately sign a peace treaty. All this crossbowing, cannon blasting and marching back and forth over the Alps was bad for business. If Maximilian wanted more cash, he had to make nice with Venice and stop scaring the pope. This time, Fugger gave Maximilian enough to force the Venetians back to Italy. Peace returned, the combatants signed a treaty and Fugger recovered Fuggerau.

4

❧

BANK RUN

If Fugger wanted to unwind, he could always find a seat at the Gentlemen's Drinking Room, the members-only tavern for Augsburg's elite. The average German in Fugger's time drank eight glasses a day of beer. Brewed under purity laws still in force, the beer was tough on the liver but safer than water from the sewage-filled streams. Inside the tavern, the men sat at long tables and swapped stories about servant girls, adventures at the Frankfurt fair and, if they were rich enough, their private zoos and golden saltcellars.

Others may have been better storytellers than Fugger, but it's hard to imagine anyone had better material. Only Fugger could describe the emperor as a friend or complain about the burden of yet another dinner with the papal legate. The men in the room most wanted to know the secrets of his success. But his secrets weren't all that mysterious, only hard to duplicate.

Fugger had a remarkable talent for investing. He knew better than the rest how to size up an opportunity and where to park his money for the best return at the least risk. He knew how to run a business and make it grow and how to get the most out of his people. He knew how to exploit weakness and negotiate for favorable terms. But perhaps his greatest talent was an ability to borrow the money he needed to invest. With what must have been enviable charm, he convinced cardinals, bishops, dukes and counts to loan him oceans of money. Without their support, Fugger would have been rich but no richer than the others at the club. The fund-raising—and with it the courage to risk debtor's prison if he couldn't repay—explains why he went down in history by the name Jacob the Rich. Financial leverage catapulted him to the top.

He borrowed in the most mundane way imaginable: He offered savings accounts. Banks litter every street corner these days. They cheerfully open accounts for anyone who walks in. But savings accounts were new in Fugger's time. Before they arrived, bankers funded loans and other investments with their own money and took in partners if they needed more cash. That diluted ownership, but they had no other choice. The easy way to raise money—borrowing—was off limits because of the church's ban on charging interest on loaned money. The church considered anything involving interest—even interest on lowly savings accounts—as usurious.

Venetians lived by the motto of "First Venetians, then Christians." They preferred making money to pleasing God. They ignored the ban and invented bank deposits. Venetian investors could leave their money with a bank, return a year later and get more back than they put in. Deposits gave banks a new way to grow and gave their customers an easy way to put their money to work. Everyone was happy except the church. The rest of Italy recognized the brilliance of savings accounts and offered their own. Germans respected canon law more than the Italians and observed the usury ban more faithfully but they, too, eventually came around.

Fugger's contemporary, the Augsburg banker Ambrose Hochstetter, took the retail route to deposit gathering. He accepted money from farm workers, maids and anyone else with something to spare. It took work to reach all these people, yet he still raised a million florins. Fugger followed a quicker but riskier path of taking money from big depositors. If a peasant withdrew money from the Bank of Hochstetter, Hochstetter himself would not notice. If a duke left the Bank of Fugger, Fugger could be ruined unless he had ready cash to cover the withdrawal. Both men would have found our modern banking system curious. They would be struck that a banker could run his institution into the ground and still keep his house, not to mention his freedom. They would scratch their heads over deposit insurance, although they would have liked the idea of someone else paying the bill for reckless behavior. They would be even more curious about our currency system where nothing but faith in the government, rather than gold and silver, backstops legal tender. Fugger and Hochstetter had enough trouble trusting that their coins weren't clipped. But currency backed by nothing but a promise? They may have said faith was for church, not for money. For them, banking was like any other business. A banker put his own money on the line and depositors put up theirs. Both sides accepted the possibility of catastrophic loss. Fugger promised to pay his investors 5 percent interest a year. The return was compelling, certainly more attractive than buying land or silver plate to store in a cupboard. Fugger targeted about a 20 percent return for himself. His fortune came from the 15 percentage-point spread between what he earned on investments and what he paid his lenders.

Savings accounts funded the biggest loan Fugger ever made to Maximilian. After the farce of the Trent coronation and the Fugger-decreed peace treaty with Venice, Maximilian took advantage of a spat between Venice and Rome (Venice claimed some papal territory, Julius excommunicated Venice) to renounce the treaty. He wanted to try again for Rome. In his desperation, he considered the unthinkable: an alliance with France.

Before the quest for a papal coronation consumed him, France had been Maximilian's obsession. His late wife, Mary of Burgundy, had died in a riding accident in 1482. She was the only woman he ever loved and their romance was one of the greatest and the most tragic in history. He wrote touching letters describing her beauty. He let her keep hunting falcons in their bedroom and let the birds go with them to church. Before they married, he wooed her with the gift of a diamond ring, an offering now described on the De Beers website as the world's first engagement ring. After she died, he hired a magician to summon her and, after France grabbed Burgundy, he went to war and tried to win it back for her memory. But now he wanted the imperial crown more than Burgundy and, to get it, he needed to go through Venice. He could only succeed if France and its large army joined him. Against the advice of his clear-eyed daughter Margaret, who warned of French betrayal, he struck a deal with his longtime enemy. They agreed to carve up the Venetian hinterland. France would get Brescia and Cremona up north and Maximilian would get Verona, Padua and what he wanted most: unobstructed access to Rome. The pope and

King Ferdinand of Aragon, eager to take Venetian territory in southern Italy, joined them.

Fugger liked the plan because victory looked assured. How could a combined force like that lose? He chipped in with his biggest loan yet; he agreed to give the emperor 300,000 florins, a sum large enough to pay 25,000 common laborers for a year. In return, Fugger received several more years of Tyrolean metal production. All of Fugger's deals were risky, but this one was a whopper and would leave him with dangerously little cash. Ill-liquidity was perilous, especially for a banker. If a large depositor asked to withdraw his money, Fugger might have to sell his fiefdoms, the Burgundian jewels and even his home to satisfy the claim. If things got really ugly, he could end up like his bankrupt cousin Lucas and have to flee to his grandfather's village. He'd be living in a hut, disgraced and surviving on gruel. But Fugger didn't dwell on the possibility of ruin. He had a war to finance.

Through his offices in Antwerp and Lyon, Fugger handled the money transfers from France with such speed that it enhanced his reputation as a financial miracle worker. Everything was in place to carve up Venice. The republic realized it could not fight four opponents at once and immediately surrendered territory to the pope and Ferdinand in order to concentrate on Maximilian and the French. The French routed the Venetians near Milan and took the city. Maximilian, too, won every territory he targeted. Venice only saved itself by invoking the sixteenth-century version of the nuclear option: It threatened to invite the Turks to Italy to let them sort it out. No one wanted that. Once peace returned, the French, as Margaret predicted, lost interest in Maximilian and did nothing to help him reach Rome. Without French support, he lost Padua and every other conquest to the Venetians except Verona. His debts to Fugger remained.

❖

Just as the war with Venice wound down, Fugger received alarming news: Cardinal Melchior von Meckau had died. The news could not have been worse. Meckau was Fugger's biggest depositor. He had given Fugger 200,000 florins and, with interest, Fugger now owed Meckau's estate 300,000 florins. The only trouble was that most of his cash had gone into the hands of Maximilian's mercenaries. He had enough to stay afloat for a while but not for long.

Meckau, a dodgy opportunist, came from a noble family in the Saxon city of Meissen. After completing his studies in Leipzig and Bologna, he became a priest and paid the required fee to become bishop of Brixen in what is now the Italian part of Tyrol. He moon-lighted in the secular world. Maximilian was too busy to administer Tyrol himself, so he assigned the job to Meckau.

Like Schwaz, Brixen had silver mines. Their output paled beside Schwaz, but they still had a lot of ore. The deposits belonged to the diocese. They might as well have belonged to Meckau personally. As bishop, he could sell the ore and, if he chose to cheat parishioners, deposit the money into his own accounts. That's what he did. He kept two personal accounts, one in Venice and one in Nuremberg. He moved his accounts to Fugger after he met him and learned how much interest he paid and how efficiently he moved money.

Meckau and Fugger helped each other. Shortly before Pope Al-exander VI—two popes before Julius II—died in 1503, Alexander promoted a number of bishops to cardinal. Meckau was the only

German. His installation came after Fugger's agent in Rome, Johannes Zink, of whom we will hear more shortly, bribed the pope with 20,000 florins. For his part, Meckau sang the praises of Fugger in Rome and attracted a number of high church officials to follow his lead by becoming depositors. Meckau also got him out of jams. During the incident years earlier when Maximilian got angry at Fugger and threatened to seize Fuggerau, Meckau was instrumental in getting the emperor to relent. Fugger became dependent on Meckau. He borrowed from him whenever he needed cash in a hurry. The Meckau relationship was among the factors that differentiated Fugger from his banking competitors. Their backers weren't as rich as Meckau.

Meckau's death sparked a treasure hunt. His assistants knew that the mines generated piles of money that vanished before they saw it. The money had to be somewhere. Two days after Meckau died, some monks rummaging through his belongings at the Brixen palace found a receipt. It disclosed that, with interest, Meckau had 300,000 florins on deposit with Fugger. The sum was unfathomable for the monks.

They also found a will. In it, Meckau gave his possessions to the Hospice of St. Anima, a clerical order in Rome to which he belonged. The will made no mention of amounts but the receipt was all the monks needed. The hospice demanded that Fugger pay the 300,000 florins at once. Nearby at the Vatican, Pope Julius heard about the money, too, and had another idea: Fugger should give him the money instead. As Julius saw it, the will counted for nothing under clerical law. Anything belonging to a cardinal belonged to the church, and Julius, as pope, was the church.

Fugger had few options. He could try to raise the money to pay off the pope by going back to his other investors. But that would put him even more dangerously in debt. He could also sell assets. But that would take more time than he had. And if he started dumping assets, rumors would spread that he was in trouble. That was suicide. The rumors would panic his other depositors and they would demand repayment, too. He'd be finished. Even if he could find a way to pay Julius, he could not pay all his creditors at once. Fugger was staring at a bank run. Grandpa's hut might not be so bad, at least compared to debtor's prison.

Fugger claimed that stress never bothered him. "When I go to bed," he once said, "I face no obstacles to sleep. I remove with my shirt all the cares and battles of business." During the Meckau crisis, he kept his cool. Of course, he said nothing about his plight. But he worried about rumors, so he kept up appearances by making loans to competitors and making his gift-giving visit to Schmiechen. He had money to burn or at least that's what he wanted everyone to think.

But he could stall for only so long. Out of time and out of options, he turned to his man in Rome, Johannes Zink, who he knew could get things done. Like Fugger, Zink was from Augsburg. He was shuffling papers for a living at a monastery when Fugger hired him to run his operation in Rome in 1501. Zink performed spectacularly, but the way he achieved success left a permanent stain on Fugger's reputation and made Fugger an easy target for reformers, including Martin Luther. Fugger had been trying to bust up the Italian monopoly on Vatican banking for years, but he only succeeded after Zink arrived. Zink took a different approach to winning business than his predecessors. He stopped talking about cost advantages and superior service. Instead, he endeared himself to Vatican officials with bribes and gifts. He went right to the top by contributing to papal election campaigns and doing odd jobs like being Meckau's bagman. Fugger became the lead banker to the Vatican within only a few years of Zink's arrival in Rome. The timing wasn't coincidental. Zink made it happen.

In the process of doing well for Fugger, Zink did well for himself. Among the many corrupt practices of the Renaissance church was the buying and selling of church offices. The jobs were for life and came with comfortable, tax-free incomes. High demand turned the sales into auctions where cash trumped qualifications. The Vatican got hooked on the cash, and outraged observers called the sales "simony," after Simon Magnus, an early Christian who tried to buy blessings. Zink bought more offices than anyone. He weighed the income stream against the up-front cost, liked the returns and bought as many as he could. All told, he bought fifty-six positions. They stretched from Cologne in the west to Bamberg in the east. He was a scribe in one city, a notary in another and a papal knight in a third. He delegated the work to underlings and he was rarely—if ever—in these places. He had five jobs in Augsburg alone.

Fugger never bought an office for himself but, through Zink, he bought for others. When an opening arose in the city of Speyer, a priest named Eberhard von Neuenhausen offered Fugger, who supervised the auctions in Germany, forty-eight florins. Neuenhausen was a senior priest at Augsburg Cathedral. He came from a noble family and had influential friends. He had a right to expect the job and looked forward to the money and respect that came with it. To his surprise, Fugger gave it to a thirteen-year-old seminarian instead. This was scandalous. Not only was the winner shockingly young, but he was technically ineligible because he lacked a degree.

Neuenhausen understood why he lost when he heard the

winner's name. The seminarian was Markus Fugger, Fugger's nephew. When Neuenhausen complained, Fugger told him the going rate in Rome for the post was 780 florins. The forty-eight florins Neuenhausen offered wasn't even close. Fugger didn't just turn Neuenhausen down when he offered to pay more. He compelled Rome to issue the equivalent of a restraining order. Neuenhausen fought back by accusing Fugger of simony before Maximilian and the Augsburg town council. They ignored him.

Of his many jobs, the only one Zink took seriously was the one with Fugger. He was in Rome for Fugger when Meckau died and it became his responsibility to save Fugger from a bank run. The pope was powerful, but even he had to follow procedure and clear up the matter of the will before he could grab the money. Stalling for time, Zink deliberately confused matters by spreading rumors about multiple wills. Then he and Fugger produced another claimant in the form of Maximilian. Meckau's territory in Brixen, like all church territory, fell under church law. But it also fell within the geographic boundaries of the empire. Why shouldn't the emperor get a cut? Maximilian filed a claim and ordered that no money change hands until the claim was settled. By this point, an exasperated Julius realized it would take forever before he got anything. Zink offered Julius 36,680 florins to drop his claim. He promised to deposit the money in the pope's personal account rather than a church account. Julius accepted. Fugger was saved. As Fugger knew, every pope had his price.

5

❧

THE NORTHERN SEAS

In November 1510, a Dutch ship set off from Danzig with 200 tons of Hungarian copper belonging to Fugger. The ship was sailing in the waters near the Hel Peninsula when a crew from another boat boarded and grabbed the cargo. The attack was the work of the Hanseatic League, the most powerful commercial organization on earth. It controlled the Baltic and North Seas and challenged anyone who dared sail its waters. The league's attack on Fugger sparked a long struggle that revealed Fugger at his strategic best and his willingness to take on all comers. To fight the Hansa, he employed tactical feints, high-level diplomacy and an abundance of tenacity. He was relentless. By the time the dust settled, the Age of the Hansa, when merchant adventurers ruled the seas and negotiated business deals with their fists, had given way to what historian

Richard Ehrenberg calls the Age of Fugger, when men behind desks conquered the world. Several factors conspired against the Hansa, but it was Fugger, undeterred by the enormity of the task, who gave the league the final push toward destruction.

The German cities of Lübeck, Hamburg, Bremen and Cologne created the league for profits and protection. They were small compared to Venice. None could afford to secure an entire coastline on their own. They pooled resources and gave each other trading privileges. Danzig and Bruges joined the group, as did every port city in northern Germany. London, far away on the Thames, let the Hansa set up a walled compound near London Bridge complete with warehouses, barracks and a beer garden that competed with local taverns with its Hamburg ale and Rhenish wine. Hansa law influenced English maritime law. The coinage of the Hansa towns, the Easterling, inspired the English word "sterling" and the word *hansa* inspired the name of the German airline Lufthansa.

At its peak, ninety cities belonged to the league. It was so powerful that even kings could not control it. With its unofficial capital in Lübeck, at the confluence of the North and Baltic Seas, the Hansa protected its monopoly by force. When the king of Sweden imprisoned German merchants for getting too uppity, the Hansa captured the Swedish fleet. When Norway became too cozy with English traders, the Hansa sent pirates to sack Bergen, took over the city's port and built a compound like the one in London. Discipline was paramount. The Bergen Hansa organized itself in small groups with "husbonds"—householders—to keep order and make sure Hanseatics observed the celibacy requirement. When the Hansa set its sights on the fishing grounds off Scania, it defeated Denmark and won a monopoly on herring. This mattered because herring formed a staple of European diets. "Days of fish" covered the church calendar. Without herring from the Danish Sound, Europe would have starved. The Hansa celebrated the victory over Denmark by adopting three dried fish as a symbol.

Hansa merchants had to be tough. To weed out weak recruits and build team spirit, Hansa captains dragged job applicants through smoking chimneys or tossed them into the sea and beat them when they surfaced. They stretched others on altars and whipped them to near death with wooden rods. This was Hansa boot camp and it highlighted the military nature of the organization. The Hansa was harsher on outsiders. Foreign merchants, including merchants from southern Germany, could save money by shipping on non-Hansa ships. But they risked having their cargo sunk or hijacked. In 1399, the Hansa sent Nuremberg a warning when it hauled copper to Flanders without the league: "If this practice should continue, you and yours would thereby suffer loss for which we would be very sorry." Others never got a warning. They just saw their ships destroyed.

Fugger kept his activities in Hansa country secret. He had to because the league was sure to retaliate if it knew what he was doing. He was too big a threat to ignore. The Hansa could dictate prices to fur trappers and fishermen. They had nowhere to sell but the nearest port. It was different with Fugger. Demand for silver and copper made him such an attractive business partner that he could try to play the Hansa towns off each other. Some towns might even prefer to leave the league if that was what it took to buy his metal. But the time wasn't right to go to war. The Hansa was still too powerful, so Fugger worked through front men. The ruse worked for years. As far as the Hansa knew, Fugger's only activity up north involved the church and money transfers. Little did it know that in one year alone, 1503, forty-one transports with Hungarian copper—Fugger copper—traveled from Danzig to Antwerp. The Hansa attacked him once it woke to his activities.

The fact that Fugger even considered challenging the Hansa spoke to his gall and the organization's waning power. The decline began in 1425, when the herring mysteriously left the Danish Sound for another spawning ground off the coast of Holland, where the Hansa had less influence. Then the Zwin River in Flanders silted up, spelling doom for the Hansa stronghold of Bruges and enabling the rise of independently minded Antwerp. In Russia, Ivan III, the father of Ivan the Terrible, had grown weary of the Hansa. On the same day in 1494 that the Fugger brothers accepted Jacob as a partner, Ivan expelled the league from Novgorod where the Hansa had been supreme. Novgorod continued selling to Hansa merchants, but it was now free to sell its furs and wax to others, including Fugger.

After the Hansa confiscated his copper, Fugger responded with a furious diplomatic assault that indicated his high regard for the northern trade route and his inflated belief, at least for now, in his own ability to dictate European economic policy from an office in Augsburg. Through Zink, he urged Pope Julius to retaliate, arguing that the Hansa's war mongering had disrupted Fugger's ability to collect and send money to Rome. Julius had excommunicated Venice in a recent dispute. Maybe he could do the same to Lübeck? Fugger then told Maximilian that the Hansa restricted his ability to lend. Unless Fugger could sell his metal up north, he would have no money to bankroll the emperor. How about an empirewide boycott of Hansa products?

The Hansa hadn't reached the top by bowing to authority and it had powerful friends just like Fugger. Sure enough, the pope took no action against the league and Maximilian gave only a halfhearted effort. He ordered the confiscation of Hansa goods but never enforced the order. Even in Augsburg, merchants continued to buy and sell from the Hansa. As far as they were concerned, this was Fugger's problem, not theirs.

The Hansa fought back with everything it had. Northern Germany was as much a part of the empire as southern Germany and Lübeck itself was an imperial city. It had access to the imperial legal system and representation at imperial diets. In a note to the imperial prosecutor in Nuremberg, it argued that Fugger was a dangerous monopolist and cited a rise in pepper prices and his control of Tyrolean silver as evidence. Maximilian led Fugger's defense. He shot off a letter to Nuremberg and argued that Fugger's activities were "valid, reasonable, honest and not monopolistic." Without directly answering the monopoly charge, he noted that Fugger risked his own money and that he deserved his profits because a bad bet could ruin him. Maximilian further argued that the critics had their facts wrong. They were confusing Jacob Fugger with all the other Fuggers who were out there doing business. Fugger had several uncles, cousins and nephews. Jacob Fugger himself only did a portion of the business attributed to him. Maximilian's final defense addressed Fugger's control of Tyrolean mining. Perhaps assuming that no one would dare challenge him, he denied that Fugger sold any Tyrolean ore and falsely claimed the crown used all the ore itself: "From these mines there is no trade with anyone on earth."

The Hansa kept up the attack. There was an imperial diet coming up in Cologne, and the Hansa worked with the prosecutor's office to demand the diet investigate Fugger and draft laws to cut down big business. This was becoming too hot for Fugger. Even if Maximilian vetoed the legislation, an investigation could damage him with inflammatory accusations and unwanted publicity. He needed to wrap this up. He settled the issue like he ultimately settled all issues—that is, with money. To quiet the Hansa, he paid Lübeck to repurchase the stolen copper. Nobody called it a bribe, but that was what it was. Lübeck dropped the charges.

Fugger let the Hansa win the day, but he continued the war by exploiting tensions within the group. His contemporary Machiavelli advised one to fight strong opponents by splitting them: "A captain ought to endeavor with every art to divide the forces of the enemy." Fugger never met Machiavelli, but he instinctively knew the concept. Danzig was the biggest city in the league and all the grain from the rich Polish heartland shipped through the city. With the help of Polish princes who hated the Hansa, Fugger struck a deal with Danzig to move goods freely through its port. The Estonian cities of Riga and Dorpat quickly followed. Russia was their most important trading partner. Without Fugger metal to sell to Russia, Danzig would run away with their business. Even Hamburg, a founding member of the league, gave Fugger privileges. The Hansa still existed in name after that but only Lübeck kept up the fight. It rejoiced in 1513 when pirates seized a pair of Fugger ships with three hundred tons of copper. But it no longer mattered. Herring, silt and Ivan III had enfeebled the Hansa. Fugger broke its back. Years later, Fugger invested in a Spanish trade voyage to the Indonesian Spice Islands and sent ships from Danzig to Spain to start the journey. Maximilian's successor, the emperor Charles V, warned Lübeck not to interfere with their passage. Leave the ships alone or else.

❧

Among the many services Fugger performed for Maximilian was saving Maximilian from himself. Self-interest, not loyalty, motivated him. He wanted to kept his client in the game and create new possibilities to soak him for more money and favors. One such episode came in 1511 when fever struck Pope Julius. The pope was almost seventy. As the illness dragged on, death seemed near. This gave Maximilian an idea. He would elegantly solve the imperial coronation question by getting himself elected pope. By being both pope and emperor, he could lift the emperor's crown to his own head and, with it, the power, he believed, to command all Christendom.

In a letter to his daughter Margaret, now regent of the Netherlands, Maximilian outlined the scheme. He would persuade the sick pope to name him heir apparent "so that on his death we may be assured of having the papacy and of becoming celibate and afterward a saint so that, after my death, you will be constrained to adore me, whence I shall gain much glory." He mourned he would never "see a naked woman again" but rejoiced that he would die as a holy man. He signed the letter, "Your good father, the future pope."

It was a crackpot idea. France, Venice and the other powers would never let Maximilian be both emperor and pope. To be sure, the emperor had limited power and the secular authority of the papacy stopped at Rome and the papal states. But if nothing else, the emperor-pope might try to grab all of Italy. Then there was the spiritual authority of the papacy. Who knows what mischief Maximilian could stir up with that?

Maximilian ignored the challenges. Rehearsing his campaign

themes with Margaret, he promised to set a better example than the lascivious Alexander, who hosted prostitutes in the Vatican and famously held a massive orgy, and the bellicose Julius, who wore armor and led troops in battle. They deserved the whip for their unchristian behavior, Maximilian said. He assumed if he raised enough money, he could bribe the cardinals and the job would be his. Wasn't money the way bishops got their jobs? Hadn't Julius himself, partly with Fugger money, paid off the cardinals to secure his own election? Maximilian estimated a cost of 300,000 ducats. He sent Liechtenstein to Fugger, telling him to do whatever it took. "Though the Fugger deny thee more than once, still shalt thou try yet again," he told him.

Liechtenstein might have been getting tired of this. It was always the same with Maximilian. The emperor dreamed up an adventure and Liechtenstein had to find a way to pay for it. Maximilian had already promised the next several years of mining output as well as revenues from a salt mine and other stray assets to Fugger. And he had already sold Fugger enough cities to make Fugger one of the biggest landlords in southern Germany. With almost nothing left to pledge, Liechtenstein offered the untouchables: the tax receipts of several Habsburg territories and the family's crown jewels. Short of offering Fugger the cities of Vienna and Innsbruck, Liechtenstein had nothing left in his bag. The jewels may have been worth more than the tax receipts. Over the years, the Habsburgs had acquired the jeweled crown of Hungary, a diamond-studded robe of Charles the Bold and other valuables that it kept in a collection of locked chests. Liechtenstein told Fugger they could be his.

Liechtenstein threw in a bonus. If Maximilian became pope, he would make Fugger papal treasurer. Fugger was already the Vatican's lead banker. But treasurer was a plum assignment because it came with a considerable fringe benefit: A monopoly on the alum mines outside Rome. The textile industry needed alum to make pigments. Rome had almost all the alum in Europe. Agostino Chigi, the papal treasurer under Julius, built Rome's largest fortune on alum. Taken together—the tax receipts, the crown jewels and the alum contract—Liechtenstein was making Fugger a fantastic offer. Fugger must have been tempted. But he understood the politics and refused to commit. As he hesitated, Julius recovered. Maximilian had moved on to other projects by the time Julius died the next year.

⚜

When Fugger reached his fifties, he started thinking about his living arrangements. He had been born into a wealthy family. Even as a young man living in his mother's house on Jew Hill, he looked like a person of means. He wore the gold beret and fur collars that tested the sumptuary laws. He traveled in a coach. He entered the Gentlemen's Drinking Room without a guard stopping him at the door. The distance between him and the rest of society became more apparent as he grew richer. He traveled with an entourage and held celebrations that awed with their extravagance. But he and his wife had no place of their own. They lived in the handsome, half-timbered house on the Wine Market that belonged to his mother-in-law. He stayed there because he liked it. If nothing else, it saved him from property taxes. Fugger may also have been thinking about appearances. Fugger was the pulse of the firm Ulrich Fugger & Brothers. He was the one with pull in Innsbruck and Rome, but it was Ulrich's name that was still on the door. It wouldn't look right to live in a bigger house than his older brother.

But after Ulrich died, Fugger had nothing holding him back. Fugger bought the house where he was living, along with two neighboring buildings, and demolished them. In their place, he erected a massive four-story building with arches along the ground floor, iron bars over the windows and Burgkmair murals to enliven the exterior. The Fugger Palace, as it came to be called, was the biggest house in the city and occupied a footprint that rivaled the Augsburg Cathedral. It served as a residence, a warehouse and the headquarters of Europe's largest business.

The palace had its own chapel, a stable for horses and a convenience that stunned visitors: running water. "There are fountains, even inside the rooms, with water conveyed by a device," wrote a visitor. While neighboring buildings had drab roofs made of slate, Fugger had expensive copper from his own mines. While others covered their windows with oiled parchment, he had glass from his trading partners in Venice. And in an age when keeping warm in the winter was almost impossible, he had heat—glorious heat from fireplaces and ovens—in almost every room. A fleet of servants kept them burning. The highlight was the Damenhof, a courtyard with a fountain in the middle and columns on the sides. It was the first Renaissance structure north of the Alps. With its tiles, arches and frescoes, it could have been in Florence. Clemens Sender, the Augsburg chronicler, claimed Fugger opened a portion of the house to beggars. There was no doubt a need. Poverty was everywhere. But there was no mistaking that the purpose of the building was commercial. Wagons full of merchandise shuttled through carriage doors nearly as wide as the city gates.

A half century later, two guests of Fugger's grandnephew

Markus gave detailed accounts. "At the Fuggers, the meal took place in a hall in which one saw more gold than color," wrote the butler of a visiting duke. "The marble floor was slippery like glass. A table filling the hall was laid with Venetian glass altogether worth more than a ton of gold. Mr. Fugger showed my master over the house which is so large that the Roman Emperor would have found room therein for his whole court." The French humanist Michel de Montaigne was even more enthused. "We were permitted to see two rooms in their palace," he wrote, "one of them large, high, and with marble floors, the other one filled with old and modern medallions, with a small cabinet in the back. These are the most magnificent rooms I have ever seen."

As Fugger stood inside and looked out the windows, he may have felt a twinge of satisfaction. He lived in the grandest house in a city that had become the financial capital of Europe thanks to him. He could see market stalls where the people of Augsburg, nestled far away from anything in the Swabian countryside, could find brocade from France, pepper from India and silks from China, all of which he had a hand in importing. He could peer down at those less fortunate; the drunken soldiers who taunted with swords; and the craftsmen, monks and beggars who shared the street with pigs, goats and chickens. Parades marched under him on festival days. To his right, Fugger could consider the spires of St. Ulrich and Afra, a Gothic masterpiece where three centuries later Mozart performed. To his left, he could see an even taller structure, the Perlach Tower, the clock tower whose height declared that businessmen, not the church, controlled the city.

And the people on the streets could look back at him and question why Fugger had so much and they had so little.

❧

As the year 1512 drew to a close, Fugger gathered his family around him. Christmas was a happy time in Augsburg where people celebrated with feasts, music and mystery plays based on the lives of saints. But Fugger wasn't interested in holiday cheer. He had business on his mind. His brother Ulrich had died three years earlier and his brother George had already been dead for six years. Fugger himself had no children, but his brothers had large families. As the relatives came together just after Christmas Day, Fugger informed them he wanted to bring his nephews into the family enterprise. The way he did it reveals Fugger as a bully. Like the many plutocrats who followed in his footsteps, he put aside considerations of fairness in pursuit of gain.

He started down the road ten years earlier when he rewrote the original partnership agreement he had with his brothers. That agreement, from 1494, allowed heirs to take the place of any brother who died. The heirs would have the right to cash out or, if they stayed, have a role in decision making. Fugger forced a change in 1502. He prohibited the heirs from liquidating. He also stripped them of any say in the business. All the power stayed with whichever brother died last. Fugger was the youngest, so he was the one most likely to be the last one standing. Sure enough, he outlasted George and Ulrich. With Ulrich's death, he took complete control. But by 1512, his brothers' sons were growing up and Fugger saw a need to bring them in and plan for succession.

Fugger informed the gathering that the firm would henceforth be called "Jacob Fugger & Nephews." But they shouldn't be fooled.

Fugger would keep power solely in his own hands. He showed them the new partnership agreement. It was filled with references to "I" and "my trade." The nephews were powerless. "They shall do nothing but what I command and give them permission to do," the document said. "If I direct one of them to do something, and afterward recall it to myself, they shall not dispute it." It ordered the nephews to always be honest with him, disclose to him every expense and conduct Fugger's business "in complete secrecy and to tell no one." It prohibited them from engaging in any business on their own and from signing anything without his consent. It gave Fugger the right to dismiss any of them, for any reason, at any time. The nephews and the others still had a claim on the money—Fugger didn't steal it from them—but it had to stay invested.

The most extraordinary part of the agreement allowed Fugger to arbitrarily change the terms without having to consult anyone: "In case I alter one or more of the above points or articles, and do it differently, or add anything which concerns this business . . . it shall be strictly adhered to by my nephews and their heirs." Fugger closed the proceedings by presenting a Bible. He made everyone lay their hands on the Bible and swear to honor the new contract.

6

⚜

USURY

Fugger spent the first half of his career making money. He spent the second fighting to keep it.

In the first phase, he had his greatest commercial victories. He won the silver contracts for Tyrol, created a mining giant in Hungary and put together a distribution network to sell his output to a diverse group of customers across the continent. He invested the profits from Tyrol and Hungary in new opportunities. In doing so, he created a formidable cash-generation machine that, year in and year out, added to his net worth. This was all he ever wanted. He never aspired to stitch his fiefdoms together and become duke of Swabia. He didn't even want to be the mayor of Augsburg. The Medici desire to turn wealth into political power was not in Fugger's makeup. Nor did he want to slow down. By all indications, he was happiest when striking deals or scrutinizing his ledgers. Nothing gave him greater joy than the chores required to make him richer.

Fugger would have liked the rest of his life to proceed in the same, linear way. In general terms, it did. He added to his fortune every year and he went from being merely rich to becoming the richest man on earth. But he also spent much of this period warding off attacks from a resentful general public and those who claimed to be its champions. He fought these opponents with the same vigor as he used against his commercial rivals. There was no hesitation and no ambivalence even when blood was spilled. He had a remarkable conviction in the justness of his actions. That's just how it was with Fugger. The way he saw it, God put him on earth to make money. He let nothing block what he perceived as God's will.

Fugger was now a different person from the dare-devil entre- preneur in his thirties who risked everything on a loan to Duke Sigmund, became perilously ill-liquid to sew up a long-term mining contract and traveled on horseback to supervise operations and make sure his contrarian bet on Hungary paid off. Now in his fifties, he was locking in at least some gains by diversifying into low-yielding real estate investments. But that was only a change in style. There was nothing—getting older, being married for twenty-five years, the loss of his brothers—that bumped him off the course of making money. The biggest change was, whether he liked it or not, that he had become a statesman as much as a businessman. The scale of his business and sweep of his activities inevitably entangled him in the big events of the day and made him a player in political affairs. As much as he may have enjoyed playing the game at the highest level, and though he claimed to sleep well at night, the requirements of managing the largest commercial enterprise in Europe must have been a terrible strain. Creditors, customers and suppliers demanded his attention. Kings and bishops from all over Europe sought his money. Only the emperor had more interests to juggle. The Augsburg artist Jörg Breu the Elder painted Fugger about this time. He looked frail and his gaze points to the heavens. It's easy to read this as Fugger feeling a sense of mortality, that this master of beating the odds knew he could not beat everything.

It was during this second phase of his career that he made his mark on history. When Thomas Carlyle put forth his great man theory, he created categories for kings, prophets and poets but none for businessmen. Why should he? They are enablers. Businessmen find the money for others to pursue greatness. They don't change the world. Fugger may not have passed Carlyle's test, but he changed the world enough to become the most influential businessman in history. No Rockefeller or Rothschild had more influence on the political events of his time.

His greatest contributions involved the Habsburgs. As we shall see, the first came in 1514, when he forced Maximilian to create the Austro-Hungarian Empire, a political entity that lasted four hundred years and played a prominent role in European history until its last breath in World War I. The second came in 1519 when Fugger bankrolled the teenage king Charles V and kept German-speaking Europe in the family's hands, putting the Habsburg empire—an empire that strode across much of the globe—on firm footing.

The frustrating thing about Fugger is that his achievements—both commercial and political—occurred so long ago that they seem to have little bearing on modern life. Fugger's destruction of the copper cartel and the kick he gave the Hanseatic League only matter today because of the lessons they teach. The importance of understanding the vulnerabilities of competitors and the motivations of customers; the benefits of being indispensable; the need to stay firm in the face of attack: These are lessons that apply in any age. As for the political achievements, they still mattered at the time of Napoleon and even Bismarck and Woodrow Wilson, but less so today. The European Union links Spain and Germany, not a royal family. Spain has lost its hold on Latin America and Austria has lost its hold on Hungary. The Habsburg influence on these places remains, most significantly in the fact that nearly 400 million Latin Americans speak Spanish, but the lines on a map that Fugger helped draw have been erased.

Another of Fugger's feats changed the world in a highly relevant way. This was his role in overturning the church's ban on usury—the charging of interest on loaned money. To the extent we can thank any single individual for our ability to borrow money to buy a house, lease a car or earn interest on our savings, we can thank Fugger.

⚜

The anti-Fugger movement that began with the Hansa protests expanded in proportion to Fugger's growing visibility. Fugger didn't hide his wealth. Just as the coat of arms gave him credibility, the wagons of gold he displayed in Constance attracted customers in an age when word of mouth defined public relations. But fame also brought scrutiny and vilification. In 1513, Fugger's success caught the attention of a group of Nuremberg intellectuals. Outraged by his wealth and methods, they seized on the church's usury ban to attack him with the larger agenda of ending what we now call capitalism. A cleric named Bernard Adelmann, who hated Fugger for blocking his bid to become bishop of Augsburg, led the group. The humanist scholar Willibald Pirckheimer joined him. Pirckheimer was a friend of Dürer's and a scholar of such distinction that Erasmus called him "the chief glory of Germany." It now seems inevitable that as trade and technology developed, feudalism with its lords, serfs and self-sufficient manor farms would give way to a market-based model—that is, an economy that divided resources based on what a person could pay rather than what he needed. Fugger argued this was best for all concerned. Free markets created jobs and growth lifted all boats. But the intellectuals in Fugger's time weren't buying it. They only saw clever men like Fugger grabbing all they could.

The only formal obstacle to Fugger was the church or, put more broadly, Christianity. Jesus had repeatedly condemned the rich. Fugger could dismiss a vague swipe like "You cannot serve both God and money." He could not dismiss "Lend and expect nothing in return" (Luke 6:35) because Rome had enshrined the comment with a ban on usury. Dictionaries define usury as the charging of unconscionably high interest rates. The church took the words of Jesus literally. It considered any demand for interest, regardless of the rate, as usurious. It condemned anyone who charged interest as a usurer. It threatened usurers with everything in its arsenal short of execution: excommunication, the withholding of absolution and the denial of Christian burial. Any one of these made the offender a social untouchable. The harshness of the punishments reminded Christians that the Lord would take action even if the church did not. God was all-knowing. He would spot usurers and send them to burn.

Fugger had no fear of excommunication. If the church excommunicated him, it would have to excommunicate all the other Christian moneylenders. This was inconceivable; there were too many of them. Nor did he fear damnation as a usurer. One of Fugger's strengths was an absolute conviction in everything he did. And nothing seemed fairer to him than receiving compensation for the risks he took. To him, Jesus did not literally mean "lend and expect nothing in return." The savior was simply issuing a blanket call for charity.

But Fugger couldn't ignore the usury ban. He had to take it seriously because his depositors took it seriously. Every time a depositor gave money to Fugger, they, like bankers, expected to earn interest. They took their 5 percent but felt dirty afterward. The Nurembergers circulated pamphlets about usury after the Diet of Cologne in hopes of putting a chill on bank deposits and destroying Fugger's fund-gathering machine. The attack hit Fugger where he lived. Unless he could raise money, he could not satisfy client demand for loans. And unless he could make loans, his business would shrink and his influence would vanish. As the attacks grew, Fugger decided it was no longer enough for the church to look the other way. He wanted the church to expressly legalize interest. He wanted Rome to say, Forget about what Jesus said. He didn't really mean it. He didn't mean interest was criminal in every case. If done right, charging interest conformed with Christian values. Fugger may have been the only one strong enough to join the fight. The battle he was about to lead held the transition from the feudal to the modern economy in the balance.

The usury debate went back centuries. Aristotle started it. He said it was fair to charge someone for a cow because a cow produced milk. But money was sterile. It produced nothing. Therefore it was unfair to charge someone for money. Aristotle's argument sounds more like a rationalization for an emotional reaction than a reasoned argument. He hated debt and the power it had to destroy. He called money lending a "sordid profession" and likened lenders to pimps.

No one cared about the usury debate in the Dark Ages when commercial activity was just a trickle in the stream. But as trade came to life in the eleventh century and lending began to power it, the victims of usurious practices multiplied. The church attacked the perpetrators for what it said was their own good. Their souls were on the line. The church had to save them. The Second Lateran Council, of 1139, condemned usury but stopped short of calling it a crime. Pope Urban III went further. He referenced Luke 6:35 and declared usury a mortal sin in 1187. Yet lending continued to grow, funding commerce while bankrupting more borrowers. In the *Divine Comedy*, an outraged Dante went further than Aristotle. Likening lenders to pimps wasn't strong enough. Dante likened them to sodomites. Thomas Aquinas, the great theologian, overlooked the commercial benefits. It made perfect sense to him to trade money for wheat or a horse. The buyer got something of fair value in return. But why should a person pay back more money than he borrowed? That was an unbalanced and therefore unjust transaction. Aquinas called for stricter enforcement of church law and was so incensed with the whole thing that he went further than Aristotle and Dante. He likened usurers to murderers. The people, or at least some of them, saw it the same way. In 1310, a council in Mainz forced cemeteries to exhume recently interred usurers. The decomposing bodies came up smelling foul and covered with leeches, worms, spiders and other supposedly demonic helpers. Their condition "proved" the deceased had sinned. The next year, Pope Clement V, spurred by Aquinas, reiterated the usury ban and overturned secular laws that legalized it. The church's enforcement arm got busy. Diocesan courts—there were hundreds of them—averaged about three prosecutions a year in the fourteenth century. Even more cases settled out of court.

The prosecutions only succeeded in shuffling the participants. Christians were sidelined and Jews filled the void. The church had a complicated relationship with Jews that expressed itself commercially by forbidding them from agriculture and the trades while letting them loan money. On the one hand, the church kept Jews from competing with Christians for "good" jobs. On the other, it let them monopolize a profession that could be even more lucrative. As long as people other than Christians made loans, the church said nothing. Nor did it take action against the flip side of the transaction; Christians were still free to borrow all they wanted. The approach was contradictory, but it let Rome fulfill its mandate of saving souls. Besides, who cared if a Jewish peddler came to a village and loaned a few pennies to a farmer? What was the harm in that?

But by the fifteenth century, lending was no longer about pennies and farmers. The economy was booming and lending had become big business. Envious of the Jewish monopoly, Christians snuck back in and became the biggest lenders of all. Rich Venetians and Florentines paid lip service to the usury rules—and eased their guilt—by calling interest by other names: penalties, processing fees, gifts, loss charges. It didn't matter what they called it as long as they didn't call it interest. Another ruse was to disguise interest with complicated currency transactions. But the results were the same: They gave out money expecting to get more money back. They could call it what they liked, but the "more back" was interest. The most famous bankers were the Medici. Other Italians were just as active. The Italians loaned to each other, loaned to their sovereigns and crossed the channel to loan to the English kings. They loaned to popes, cardinals and bishops. They loaned as if the usury ban didn't exist.

Change came in Germany a century later. Anxious to catch the Italians and lured by interest rates as high as 43 percent, German cities cleared the field of incumbents. Augsburg expelled its Jews in 1438 and used the gravestones from the Jewish cemetery to build a new city hall. A textile trader named Hans Meuthing became the first Augsburger to try finance on a major scale. He made a large loan to Archduke Sigmund of Tyrol, which was backed, just like Fugger's later loan to the duke, by the output of the Schwaz silver mine. Others jumped in, replacing Jewish lenders on transactions, large and small. The German satirist Sebastian Brant noted the development in his best-selling *Ship of Fools* (1494): "You borrow ten, eleven's due. They're more usurious than the Jew. Their business now the Jews may lose, for it is done by Christian Jews." Fugger took lending further than anyone, but even he, like the Italians, used dodges to mask interest. He took silver instead of cash for the Tyrolean activities, making the loan repayments look more like purchases than loans.

The Nuremberg circle smartly targeted moneylending as a way to contain Fugger and the new economy he was helping to create. They knew there was no quicker way to stop him than by turning off the cash spigot. Nuremberg is ninety miles northeast of Augsburg. Like Augsburg, it was a commercial city that reported to no one but the emperor. Nuremberg had Dürer and produced pocket-watch inventor Peter Henlein and globe inventor Martin Behaim. But Augsburg had Fugger, as well as Welser and Hochstetter, and was trouncing Nuremberg at the capitalist game. Nuremberg eyed it with envy. Civic rivalry might partly explain why Nuremberg school principal Anton Kress, shortly after Fugger paid the Hansa to leave him alone, wrote an essay condemning usury. Using words Fugger had heard before, Kress called moneylending unbrotherly and unchristian. Adelmann joined in and claimed that he had personally heard Fugger brag that "he had the pope and the emperor in his pocket." At Adelmann's urging, Pirckheimer fired a shot at Fugger by translating Plutarch's condemnation of usury from Greek into Latin. "Wretched usurers," Plutarch wrote, "preying on some poor and gnawing them . . . to the very bones." In case anyone missed the point, he cited Homer, comparing borrowers to vulnerable Greek gods and usurers to vultures "piercing into their entrails with sharp beaks."

Pirckheimer's translation, only a few pages long, might seem like more of a slap than an upper cut. He was merely translating an obscure text from a language no one spoke into one that only a few spoke. But in the sixteenth century his translation was a blast from a blow horn. Intellectuals and other opinion makers worshiped everything ancient and welcomed any form of mental stimulation in a world with too little to read. They were soon buzzing about it. Fugger had to respond. With his support, Augsburg schoolmaster Sebastian Illsung wrote a defense of lending by focusing on the narrow subject of the Augsburg Contract—the legal agreement Fugger signed with depositors that promised them 5 percent. Illsung argued the contract was valid if the lender, like the borrower, risked bankruptcy. Then a young theologian named Johannes Eck caught Fugger's eye by echoing Illsung's arguments in a university lecture. Fugger asked Eck to write a dissertation on the Augsburg Contract and enter a debate—a public showdown with scholars as judges—to validate it.

Fugger was taking a risk. The Augsburg Contract may or may not have been legal under church law. But it was in wide use and Fugger needed it to raise money. If Eck lost the debate and the judges declared the contract usurious, Fugger's depositors would refuse to give him money. This would be lethal. It was one thing to operate in a gray area. It was another to engage in a practice specifically ruled heretical. Fugger must have felt extremely confident because he sought nothing short of a Scopes trial, a winner-take-all smackdown pitting dogma against modernity, but with money instead of monkeys at the center. He had at least one precedent on his side. After theologians squared off over the subject of annuities—the interest-earning pension schemes that cities sold to raise money—the pope had sanctioned them. Maybe Pope Leo, who had replaced the "Warrior Pope" Julius II earlier that year, would do the same with the Augsburg Contract. There was also the fact that Leo was a member of the Medici banking family. Legalization would serve his personal interests. Even better was that Leo himself was a borrower of Fugger's. It goes without saying that Leo would be favorably inclined towards someone who gave him money.

Eck taught at the University of Ingolstadt. He later became notorious for reporting Luther's heresies to Rome and prompting his excommunication. He could advance his career if he won but faced ridicule if he lost. When Eck finished his paper, he submitted it to the university and asked it to host the contest. Universities usually approved such requests automatically, particularly when they came from one of their own. But the Nurembergers feared Eck would win. They pressured the school to refuse. After Adelmann accused Eck of being a Fugger stooge, the bishop with jurisdiction over Ingolstadt killed the contest. Other German universities refused, too.

The topic was too hot. None wanted to be part of a discussion of potentially heretical views.

Fugger refused to quit and when Eck drafted a letter asking Leo to force Ingolstadt to hold the debate, Fugger signed it. After getting no word, Fugger and Eck turned to Italy where, thanks to Venice and Florence, the universities were open-minded about lending. They found a willing participant in the University of Bologna, Europe's oldest university and among its most prestigious. Thomas Becket, Erasmus, Copernicus and Mirandola had studied there. On his way to Bologna, Eck passed through Augsburg. Fugger assigned him a translator and other assistants. Another Augsburger, the Dominican priest Johannes Fabri, made his own way to Bologna to argue the other side. For all we know, Fugger may have picked Fabri. It was a way of fixing the outcome. But Fabri appears to have been his own man.

On July 12, 1515, Eck and Fabri met at St. Petronius, the city's mammoth fourteenth-century basilica. The doors opened at four in the afternoon. Eager for a good show, students and professors came to watch and walked past an enormous painting of a hideous, two-mouthed Lucifer—a reminder of what awaited heretics—as they took their seats in the pews. Organizers engineered these things to entertain. They allowed heckling and encouraged cheering. Eck and Fabri went at it for five hours. Eck avoided scriptural references and focused on intent. Only evil intentions could make a transaction usurious, he declared. A lender committed usury if he aimed to harm the borrower. But he acted legally if he had a legitimate business interest. When his turn came, Fabri rehashed the old arguments; Aristotle, Aquinas and the rest. Eck thought he crushed Fabri. Three professors in the audience agreed with him. But the judges saw merits on both sides. They refused to call a winner and the contest ended in an unsatisfying draw.

Fugger might have been disappointed, but he could take comfort. The judges had refused to call the Augsburg Contract heretical. Eck and Fabri had presented a cut-and-dried case of charging interest on loaned money, and had given the judges a perfect chance to confirm Luke 6:35. But the judges refused to make a call, a call that could have put Fugger out of business. That was tacit approval. What's more, Fugger's letter to Pope Leo had gotten through and made an impact. Leo ignored the question about debate venues but, in a decree issued that same year, Leo went to the heart of the matter and signed a papal bull that, in direct contradiction of Aristotle and other ancient commentators, acknowledged the legitimacy of charging interest. "Usury means nothing else than gain or profit drawn from such a thing that is by its nature sterile, a profit that is acquired without labor, cost or risk." It didn't matter that money wasn't like a cow and provided no milk. Labor, cost and risk were enough to make it unsterile and make interest charges lawful. This was a thunderclap. Usury was a sin. But what defined usury? According to the new doctrine of the church, usury was no longer strictly about what Jesus said about charging interest. It was about charging interest without labor, cost or risk. And what loan didn't involve one of the three? As long as a loan passed that easy test, the lender was off the hook. Fugger's lobbying had paid off in spectacular fashion. He and others were now free to charge borrowers and pay depositors interest with the full blessing of the church. Leo's decree, issued in conjunction with the Fifth Lateran Council, was a breakthrough for capitalism. Debt financing accelerated. The modern economy was under way.

Fugger and Eck stayed in touch after the debate, and, as we will see, Fugger later tried to bring him to Augsburg as a preacher. Eck also earned a spot in history by going to Rome and successfully persuading the pope to excommunicate Luther and issue the warrant for his arrest—an arrest that, had it been carried out, would have resulted in Luther recanting or burning at the stake. Contemporaries whispered that Eck went to Rome under orders from Fugger. Hard evidence is lacking, but the record shows that Fugger was an early opponent of Luther and wanted to protect the papacy and his business in Rome. He often dispatched Eck to do his dirty work.

❧

After the usury debate, Fugger found himself under assault again, only this time in Hungary. Fugger had succeeded in Hungary because he had it to himself. Other German merchants thought Fugger a fool when he bought his first Hungarian copper mine. They said if the Hungarian nationalists didn't get him, the Turks would. For them, Hungary—where the Transylvanian count Dracula impaled Turks a generation earlier and displayed their heads on pikes—was too savage and unpredictable for investment. But the skeptics had been wrong for twenty years, and Fugger made a fortune mining Hungarian copper and exporting it around the world. What he didn't export in raw form, he turned into weapons for sale to princes and popes.

Fugger owned several mines in Hungarian territory. His biggest was in Neusohl in Slovakia, 130 miles northeast of Bratislava. None of the Hungarian mines was individually as productive as Schwaz. But together they produced 1.5 million florins' worth of profits over the years Fugger owned them. And that was just from copper. Fugger might have made just as much from silver but those figures are lost. More profits came from the guns cast in his Hungarian foundries. The money gave him a critical source of funds to loan Maximilian and others. Over his career, Fugger made more money in Hungary than on any other investment.

The outlook darkened in Hungary in 1514, when the Turks stepped up their attacks. They were looting more towns than ever and capturing girls to sell as slaves. To stop the Turks, Hungary appointed a Romanian warrior, Gyorgy Dozsa, to raise a peasant army and fight back. The Turks terrified the peasants and Dozsa easily found recruits. Once he had an army, he forgot the Turks and turned his forces on the Hungarian nobility and aimed to make himself king. The peasants hated the nobles even more than they hated the Turks. They jumped at the opportunity to attack the rich. In an early victory, Dozsa captured the fortress of Cenad and gave Dracula a nod by impaling the bishop. It looked as if Dozsa would overrun the country.

From Augsburg, Fugger tried to protect his Hungarian assets. He ordered Zink to bribe Hungarian priests to calm the peasants. He sent gifts to the Hungarian elite to win their favor. But he could only do so much. Help finally arrived when John Zapolya, Hungary's largest landowner, raised a force. He captured Dozsa and used him as a grisly example of what happened to rebels. Reflecting the sadistic practices of the age, he staged a torturous enthronement ceremony where he forced Dozsa to sit on a red-hot iron, wear a smoldering crown and hold a molten scepter. Then he burned Dozsa at the stake and gave his supporters a choice between death or eating alive their leader, then writhing in the flames. "Dogs," screamed Dozsa as they ripped off his charred flesh and consumed him.

Zapolya had won, but Hungary remained volatile. With the Turks on the loose and the peasants looking for a fight, Fugger's investments remained at risk. Division among the Hungarian nobility complicated matters and a war between rival noble factions loomed along with everything else. Fugger needed a permanent peace. The Hungarian royal family agreed. For years, it had been talking to Maximilian about a marriage alliance that would make the Habsburgs their protectors. But Maximilian was too busy in Italy to give it his focus. Now, with his treasure threatened, Fugger did something new. He gave Maximilian an ultimatum: Either strike a deal with Hungary or forget about more loans. Fugger had never before tried to manipulate Maximilian so overtly. In the past, if Fugger liked one of Maximilian's schemes, such as the phony imperial coronation, he was generous. If he objected to a project, such as Maximilian's papal venture, he delayed until the request went away. But he never initiated anything. He did this time. There was too much on the line to sit it out.

The threat worked. To appease Fugger, Maximilian sent an ambassador to Hungary to negotiate a marriage alliance—an alliance that promised the eventual handover of Hungary to the Habsburgs. No matter that the Hungarian people might object to Habsburg rule. No matter that it meant redrawing the map of Europe by creating the giant political tinderbox known as the Austro-Hungarian Empire. Fugger needed a Habsburg seizure of Hungary to protect his holdings.

To discuss details, Maximilian agreed to see King Ladislaus of Hungary and his older brother Sigismund, the king of Poland. The monarchs originally planned to meet in Lübeck because Lübeck was near Poland and Poland played a key role. Like kids trading baseball cards, Maximilian planned to give Sigismund the imperial possession of Prussia, home of the Germanic religious order of the Teutonic-Knights, in exchange for Hungary.

Fugger hated the idea of a Lübeck meeting because the Hansa were there. Concerned the Hansa would slander him while the kings were in town, he encouraged Vienna as an alternative. Besides, he wanted to attend and Vienna was an easy boat ride down the Danube. They accommodated him. In 1815, exactly three hundred years later, the great European powers met in the same city to engineer a peace treaty that won decades of European tranquility and made famous the term "balance of powers." The meeting was called the Congress of Vienna. It was more like the second Congress of Vienna. The first occurred when the three kings—Maximilian, Ladislaus and Sigismund—met in the city to consider the future of Hungary and, as a consequence, Fugger's copper mines.

The outcome hinged on personal chemistry and, to Fugger's delight, Maximilian and Sigismund liked each other. Maximilian called Sigismund a great prince and Sigismund invited him to hunt in Poland. They struck a deal that gave Fugger as much as he could hope. Hungary would immediately become an Austrian puppet and the Habsburgs would formally take over Hungary after Ladislaus's line died out. Poland would get Prussia and, as a sweetener, Maximilian promised not to ally with Russia, which was then at war with Poland. The kings sealed the accord with plans for not one but two marriages. Maximilian's grandson Ferdinand would marry Anne, the daughter of Ladislaus, and Maximilian's granddaughter Mary would marry Louis, Ladislaus's son.

Weddings are expensive—especially double weddings between royal families. Fugger gave Maximilian what he needed to pay for it.

In a letter written in Augsburg to the Tyrolean council, Maximilian explained in achingly honest terms why he had to put himself—and thus the state—further in debt:

> We cannot do this [the Hungarian takeover] unless the loan from the Fuggers is carried through. For without this we cannot go on, but will have to drop all the above dealings with both kings and abandon the plan for our children and theirs, and cancel all arrangements, and it will probably bring about the disadvantages and injuries suggested above if we finally abandon our meeting with them. If we knew any other method of finance, we would have been only too glad to spare you this, but we know of no other way.

After settling the financing, Fugger and 10,000 other wedding guests descended on Vienna. Fugger, like Charles the Bold when he went to Switzerland, brought his jewelry. The Habsburgs wanted to dress like Burgundians and needed Fugger's stones to create the illusion of family riches. Maximilian had nowhere near the means of his dapper father-in-law Charles, but he could look like him for a day thanks to Fugger. With Fugger in the pews at St. Stephen's, Maximilian's organist played a thundering *Te Deum* and Hungarian musicians played battle marches. Maximilian's secretary took offense with the military posturing of the Hungarians and dismissed them as "horse eaters."

The fine print of the marriage contract highlighted the complexity—if not the grotesque absurdity—of sixteenth-century royal weddings. Prince Ferdinand was too young to marry Anne, but their marriage was vital to the deal. To keep it on track, Maximilian, a widower, married her by proxy and agreed to take her as his wife if Ferdinand died before coming of age. Maximilian was fifty-five—exactly five times her age—and looked older because of the ravages of a puzzling disease new to Europe: syphilis. Cortez brought it back from the New World in 1504 and soon Maximilian, Erasmus and others had what they called the "French disease." The disease so ravaged Cesare Borgia that he took to wearing a mask in public. Luther complained about outbreaks at monasteries. Fearing death at any moment, Maximilian traveled with his casket just in case. "Ask God for my health," Maximilian told Anne at the altar. He put a crown on her head and declared her a queen of the empire. Louis and Mary wed in the undercard. Fugger saw the value of his Hungarian investment grow more secure with every vow.

While in Vienna, Fugger fished for business. Instead of awarding new depositors with toasters, he gave out diamonds, rubies and sapphires. He gave necklaces to the ladies and gold rings to the men. The gifts were a cost of doing business. His records show that he spent 9,496 florins, 18 shillings and 5 Rhenish hellers on the Vienna trip, including travel expenses. The effort paid off when George Szathmary, the archbishop of Gran, one of the richest men in Hungary, moved his accounts to Fugger.

From the standpoint of *Hausmachtpolitik*, the congress was a victory for all. For King Ladislaus, too weak to keep his family on the Hungarian throne without help, the agreement kept him in power and won a friend in the fight against the Turks. King Sigismund of Poland saved himself from a two-front war with the empire and Russia. Maximilian, by keeping Anne in Vienna until she married his grandson, attached Hungary as a satellite of Austria.

The Roman poet Ovid described the Trojan War hero Protesilaos as more deserving of love than war. Matthias Corvinus, the Hungarian king who had taken Vienna from Emperor Frederick, reworked Ovid's words and applied them to the Habsburgs. *Bella gerant alii, tu felix Austria nube* (Others wage war but you happy Austria wed). The words became a family motto. Fugger had now played a role in four Habsburg weddings. He and his brothers had dressed Frederick for the meeting with Charles the Bold that led to the marriage of Maximilian and Mary of Burgundy, and gave the Habsburgs the Low Countries. Later, Fugger's loans puffed up Maximilian and made his son Philip a more attractive suitor for Joanna of Castile— the wedding that gave Spain to the Habsburgs. Now Fugger's prodding brought about a double wedding and Habsburg control of Hungary.

The Habsburg triumph in Vienna was equally Fugger's triumph. Hungary might never completely embrace Fugger, but at least he had won more support from on high. He must have felt like a hero as he hobnobbed with the rich and powerful in Vienna. His efforts had united two kingdoms and stiffened the front lines of Christendom against the Turks. With his jewels glittering on Habsburg necks, he may have spotted guests admiring his diamonds and overheard them talking about what he and his money could accomplish.

⚜

After the wedding, Fugger struck a deal with Maximilian that points to a factor behind Fugger's rise: Capitalism was moving faster than society's ability to contain it. While commerce was barreling ahead, democratic institutions that could have curbed the excesses were evolving more slowly, allowing well-connected men like Fugger to have their way regardless of other considerations. After returning from Vienna, Fugger gave the emperor 100,000 florins for a lease on a smelting operation. It was a straightforward transaction except for one thing: Maximilian had already awarded the smelter to Hochstetter, Germany's pioneer of retail banking.

The Tyrolean council, the group of nobles who advised Maximilian in Innsbruck, was outraged when it heard about the deal. It complained that the cancellation of the Hochstetter contract would bring "disadvantage, expletives and ridicule." With Maximilian already dangerously stretched, the council wanted him to stay on good terms with Hochstetter, save face with other lenders and reduce his dependency on Fugger. Maximilian, when asking permission to borrow for the double wedding, pleaded with the council to let him have his way. "Do not leave us in such need," he wrote. "Our well-being is at stake." His request was nothing but a polite way of giving an order. In that instance, the council did as told.

The council had always played the role of rubber stamp in the belief that a strong ruler was better than a weak one. Sigmund's debt-financed pursuit of sex and luxury had left the duchy vulnerable whereas Maximilian's aggressive foreign policy had made it a powerhouse. The nobles only had one card to play if they objected. They could take up arms and try to oust Maximilian. But they still believed in him. And Hochstetter's smelter was hardly worth a rebellion. They gave up the fight and gave the smelter to Fugger.

⚜

Fugger was back in the Fugger Palace when a group of Maximilian's advisors showed up at the door. A fresh crisis had compelled the emperor to ask for more money. While Fugger and Maximilian were dancing in Vienna, Louis XII of France had died and his cousin Francis I, now king, had taken an army into Italy and reclaimed Milan from the Swiss. Francis chased women, drank hard and had a reckless streak that once nearly killed him during an aggressive game of tag. Machiavelli had called the Swiss the best fighters on earth. By defeating them, Francis made his reputation while destroying that of the Swiss. Invincible no more, Switzerland adopted a position of political neutrality maintained to the present day. The loss of Milan also set the stage for Fugger's final loan to Maximilian. The discussions over the deal offer a window into Fugger's negotiating tactics.

After the seizure of Milan, Maximilian wanted to race to the city and oust Francis. He sent the men to Augsburg to find the money to pay for the campaign. Fugger told the visitors that he had no interest, but that he would see them as a courtesy. As they got down to business, Fugger offered one excuse after another: Maximilian was already too deeply in debt, his collateral was thin and, in an objection that might have raised eyebrows among the negotiators, Fugger called the very idea of lending offensive because it was usurious. Even when Maximilian offered additional copper contracts, Fugger waved them off. He said he already had more copper than he needed. He added that he felt old and tired. He told the negotiators that he could die at any time and might not outlive the war. Besides, he told them, he had no children. He was thinking about selling his assets and unwinding the enterprise.

Liechtenstein, after years of faithful service to the emperor and his banker, had died before the Congress of Vienna. In his place came a new crop of advisors unfamiliar with Fugger and his negotiating tactics. They had never heard Fugger's vow to make money "as long as he could." They failed to appreciate that they were watching a rerun from the time of the Common Penny when Fugger, after complaining that lending was too much trouble, turned around and pursued lending with more vigor than before. Liechtenstein would have recognized the signs. The complaint about fatigue was code for wanting more collateral. The threat of liquidation was a demand for a higher interest rate. Maybe Fugger really was tired. But too tired to make money? Never.

Fugger also had doubts about the Milan campaign. Fugger thought it foolish to take on the French after what they had accomplished in Milan against the fearsome Swiss. He questioned whether Maximilian and his mercenaries were up to the task. Maximilian's men recorded Fugger's words. Fugger, they wrote, called the emperor's plan for a direct attack "strange and difficult to accept." When Maximilian offered a revised plan, Fugger called it "even worse."

Fugger's ears perked up only after Henry VIII of England took an interest. The French victory had stung Henry. It rankled him that foreign ambassadors hailed Francis as a military genius. Henry longed for a great victory of his own but he had yet to do anything significant in his six years on the throne. Anxious to prove himself and reverse French gains, Henry sent aides to the continent with an offer to fund a Habsburg attack. They made two stops. One was Innsbruck, to inform Maximilian. The other was Augsburg, to see Fugger. Henry feared the emperor would attack Venice instead of Francis if he gave him money directly so he handed it to Fugger instead. Fugger handled such matters professionally and Henry could trust Fugger to dole out the money as instructed. Henry transferred 100,000 crowns to Fugger's Antwerp branch and Fugger paid the bills for war from there.

Fugger also put up his own money. Maximilian paid him back with a favor. He let Fugger and the abused Hochstetter create a variation of the old copper syndicate. Fugger sabotaged the first syndicate twenty years earlier because he wanted to crush his competitors. This time Fugger was committed to the arrangement because he could control it. By joining with his only competitor in the copper trade, he could inflate prices.

When spring arrived, Maximilian marched into Italy at the head of 30,000 troops under the banner of the Habsburg eagle. It was the largest army he ever commanded and the one he had always wanted to command. He hoped it prefigured the one he wanted, one day, to march on Jerusalem. The French and Venetians were then laying siege to Brescia. Maximilian chased them back to their camps. With his superior manpower, he seemed poised for victory. The English looked forward to defeating the French and earning a return on its 100,000-crown investment. Then Maximilian, a man normally eager to fight, inexplicably gave up. The English were infuriated and suspected French bribes. Maximilian blamed an inability to feed his army, the coming of winter and inferior cavalry. The reasons made no difference to Fugger. He collected his commission from Henry and moved on.

✦

THE PENNY IN
THE COFFER

In 1514, Fugger made a loan to Albrecht of Hohenzollern, scion of the family that ruled the area around Berlin. The scheme to repay the loan triggered one of the most important events in history, the Protestant Reformation. The Reformation had many causes— Vatican corruption, lustful priests and church meddling in secular affairs all fed the rebellion against the Catholic Church. But Fugger lit the fuse. He midwifed the famous St. Peter's indulgence, the church fund-raiser that promised salvation for cash and prompted Martin Luther to write his Ninety-five Theses.

Fugger loaned to Albrecht to finance the sale of yet another clerical office. This time the job in question wasn't parish priest or church deacon. It was one of the most powerful positions in Germany, archbishop of Mainz. Among the seven electors of the Holy

Roman Empire, the Mainz bishop was the most powerful because he ran the imperial diets. He had one vote—the same as the others—but set the agenda. This gave him more authority than anyone in Germany except the emperor. His English equivalent was the Lord Chancellor. But King Henry could remove Cardinal Wolsey on a whim. The emperor could not touch the elector of Mainz. Mainz was the only city besides Rome allowed to call itself a Holy See. In 1514, Uriel von Gemmingen became the third Mainz elector to die in the space of ten years. The city had borrowed a huge sum to buy Gemmingen the job. The debt load exhausted its credit. Whoever took over for Gemmingen needed to find another way to pay.

Three candidates came forward to become bishop. The elector of the Palatinate suggested his little brother. Maximilian suggested his own nephew. Albrecht of Hohenzollern suggested himself. Despite being underage (he was twenty-four) and underqualified (no university degree) and technically ineligible (he already had two bishop seats—Magdeburg and Halberstadt—when the limit was one per customer) Albrecht had the best chances. Why? Fugger stood in his corner. Albrecht could pay whatever it took.

Pope Leo X, the pope who sanctioned charging interest for loans, would decide the contest. He was a corrupt pope in a corrupt age. Born Giovanni de' Medici, Leo was the second son of Lorenzo the Magnificent. Lorenzo had three boys. He said one of them was good, one foolish and the third shrewd. Giovanni was the shrewd one. Lorenzo raised Giovanni to become pope. He paid to make him a priest at age seven and a cardinal at fourteen. Offering some fatherly advice, Lorenzo instructed Giovanni to save his money and tend to his health. Giovanni observed the latter, devoting himself to hunting for the benefits of fresh air. But he loved to spend money and, upon becoming

Leo X, squandered the papal treasury on the most extravagant coronation Rome had ever seen. He gave money to strangers on a whim and hosted parties where prostitutes looked after the cardinals and servants brought food on gold plates. He wrote to his brother: "God has given us the papacy. Now let us enjoy it." For him, Albrecht's pursuit of Mainz offered an irresistible payday.

Albrecht borrowed 20,000 florins from Fugger to cover the fees. After stopping in Augsburg to get the loan documents, Albrecht's men went to Rome to collect the money from the Fugger Vatican office and win Leo's approval for the appointment. Dr. Johannes Blankenfeld headed Albrecht's delegation. In addition to representing Albrecht while in Rome, he and the others spent their time wandering the halls of the Vatican buying clerical offices for themselves.

The mission went smoothly until Matthaus Lang, the bishop of Salzburg, objected to Albrecht's accumulation of posts. Lang was one of Maximilian's top advisors and the bishop who crowned him in Trent. Lang's protest gave Leo an excuse to raise the price. Here the story took a strange twist. Blankenfeld later recounted how an unidentified figure approached him in the Vatican halls and spelled out Leo's terms. The pope wanted 10,000 ducats (a ducat equaled 1.4 florins) for his blessing. And he wanted the money deposited into his own bank account, not the Vatican's.

The mysterious middleman was probably Fugger's man Zink because only Zink, among all the people in Rome, knew enough about German politics and papal administration to be a credible go-between. Zink may have asked Blankenfeld to keep his name out of the records because of the sordid nature of the matter. In any case, Blankenfeld confessed surprise at the size of the demand, but not at the request itself.

In a later meeting, the unknown figure raised the demand to 12,000 ducats because, he joked, there were twelve apostles. Thinking quickly, Blankenfeld offered 7,000, arguing there were only seven sacraments. They settled at the original 10,000. This brought the total to 34,000 florins, or exactly double what Mainz had paid to install Albrecht's predecessor Gemmingen. Fugger transferred the money to the pope's account. With that out of the way, Albrecht had to come up with a way to repay Fugger. His men had an idea. They suggested a church-financing device called an indulgence.

❧

The faithful regarded the pope as heir to St. Peter and God's representative on earth. As such, he could wash away sins. The pope could take the meanest sinner and, with a blessing, secure him a place in heaven and save him from purgatory. Faith in the pope's redemptive ability gave him his power. The eleventh-century pope Urban II exploited this faith as a recruiting tool in the First Crusade. He offered soldiers forgiveness in the form of letters written in Latin and marked with a papal seal. The letters were called indulgences because Rome used them to indulge wickedness. Pope Urban expanded the program to include donors to the crusade, not just the fighters. Anxious to escape damnation, the people gave generously. The idea caught on. Bishops sold indulgences to build cathedrals. Frederick the Wise, the elector of Saxony, joined with the church on an indulgence to rebuild a bridge across the Elbe.

Leo liked the idea of the Albrecht indulgence right away because he understood better than anyone the ability to fleece the faithful. He summed it up with another of his arresting statements: "How very profitable has been this fable of Christ." But he and Albrecht had to take care. While churchgoers could support a crusade or a construction project, even the most naive would question the bailout of a banker. The plotters needed a cover story. They found one in St. Peter's Basilica.

Pope Constantine had built the original St. Peter's in the fourth century, choosing the site then occupied by the Circus of Nero. Charlemagne kneeled on its floor in the year 800 for his crown. By the sixteenth century, the old wooden structure teetered near collapse. Julius II broke ground on a replacement made of marble, planned to be as grand a structure as anything on earth. He ran out of money before he could finish. Leo took up the project and recognized St. Peter's as perfect for indulgence financing. Peter was a martyr for Christ, one of the apostles and the founder of the church. Who could refuse him an appropriate resting place? Publicly, Leo would declare an indulgence for St. Peter's. But it was as much an indulgence for Fugger. Behind the walls of the Fugger Palace, the pope and Fugger would split the money. St. Peter's would get half. Fugger would get the other half.

❧

Once Fugger and Rome settled on a price and put the plan in gear, a pudgy Saxon priest dressed in black led a solemn parade into the mining town of Annaberg, near the Czech border. The priest's name was Johannes Tetzel, and he was the greatest of the indulgence peddlers. He and his crew carried Bibles, crosses and a large wooden box with locks on the side and a picture of Satan on top. A priest held aloft a velvet cushion with a gold braid. The cushion carried the pope's indulgence order. Fugger auditors trailed the priest. The city's notables met the parade with lit candles. As the group marched toward the city's church, solemnity gave way to excitement. Bells rang in the steeple. The townspeople, from the elderly to the school-children, dropped what they were doing. Not much happened in Annaberg and they would have been happy to see anyone. They found these visitors particularly thrilling because they knew they brought with them God's greatest gift: the gift of salvation. The excitement turned into a frenzy inside the church. The organ boomed and the people sang full-throated hymns. The visitors lifted a giant red cross affixed with the papal banner. "God himself could not have been given a more magnificent welcome," wrote a witness.

After silencing the crowd, Tetzel spoke. He started slowly, laying the groundwork for his pitch by explaining indulgences. He had come to raise money, he said. The pope—God's agent on earth—was building a magnificent church to honor St. Peter. He needed them, the good people of Annaberg, to help by buying his certificates. Tetzel said these magical letters cancelled every sin. Steal from a widow? Kill a baby? Deflower the Virgin Mary? Indulgences absolved them all. He helpfully offered a progressive fee schedule. Kings, queens and bishops should pay twenty-five florins. Counts, barons and cathedral directors should pay twenty florins, merchants three and workers one. Prayer sufficed for those with no means. He told the audience that a customer could buy an indulgence for himself, his wife and even dead relatives. He played off guilt as much as self-interest. "Open your ears," he said. "Hear the father saying to his son, the mother to her daughter, 'We bore you, nourished you, brought you up, left you our fortunes, and you are so cruel and hard that now you are not willing for so little to set us free. Will you let us die here in the flames?'" He summed it up in a jingle: "As the penny in the coffer rings, the soul from purgatory springs."

Tetzel said a lot that day. He went beyond the salvation offer and promised riches. The mines of Annaberg, he said, would fill with silver if the people gave their support. But one thing he didn't mention was Albrecht and Fugger. As far as the listeners knew, Tetzel worked for St. Peter's and St. Peter's alone. The Fugger agents setting up a table made from a wine barrel knew better. One of them unlocked the box with Satan on top and prepared to collect the cash. He kept the box near his feet to guard it.

Tetzel and the auditors traveled the countryside for months, taking the act to Berlin, Braunschweig, Görlitz, Jüterbog and other cities. No place was safe. Lauingen, a little town near Augsburg, received two visits. Tetzel met resistance in Saxony. When he tried to return to his home state, guards stopped him at the border. The Saxon duke, Frederick the Wise, considered the St. Peter's indulgence to be competition for his own fund-raising scheme. Frederick's business was relics. He kept the world's greatest collection in a palace in Wittenberg. The 19,000 items included what was purportedly a tooth from St. Jerome, a branch from the burning bush and a crust of bread from the Last Supper. The church promised forgiveness to those who saw the items. Pilgrims traveled to Wittenberg and paid to have a look. Relics were valuable and counterfeits were everywhere. Fugger sometimes trafficked in fakes made in Italian workshops. Whether Frederick had fakes didn't matter. The church certified his thorns, teeth and bones as real. That was enough for the pilgrims who came to see them.

In Saxony, there lived a thirty-three-year-old scholar from a mining family who had once studied to be a lawyer. Some later remarked on his debating skills and called him The Philosopher. Others remarked on the clarity of his speaking style and called him the Wittenberg Nightingale. In the nineteenth century, Carlyle put him alongside Napoleon and Shakespeare and declared him a "Great Man." But for now he was just a humble academic known around Wittenberg as Martin Luther.

Luther had heard about Tetzel from Saxons who had gone out of their way to buy indulgences. Barred from the duchy, Tetzel put them up for sale just over the border in Jüterborg in the state of Thuringia. Reports of the sale reached Luther. The campaign outraged Luther and the consequences of his outrage shook Europe to its foundation. Luther recognized indulgences for what they were— a scam Rome invented to cash in on popular fears of damnation. Luther found the St. Peter's indulgence all the more offensive because it targeted Germans. The indulgence peddlers left France, Spain and other countries alone because these places had rulers strong enough to stand up to Rome. They refused to let people like Tetzel into their kingdoms, particularly if they were shipping indulgence proceeds out of the country. Germany was too fragmented to resist and let Rome have free rein. Germany had long been the venue for some of Rome's worst abuses, and Luther could take it no longer. Enraged by what he heard about Tetzel, he composed ninety-five arguments against indulgences, his famous Ninety-five Theses. Item 67 told it straight: "The indulgences, which merchants extol as the greatest of favors, are in fact a favorite means for money-getting."

Luther timed publication to coincide with All Saints' Day, the one day of the year when Frederick opened his relic collection to the public. Wittenberg would be full of pilgrims eager to see the holy teeth, bones and thorns. Wanting to make a splash, Luther nailed a copy of his list to the door of Wittenberg Cathedral on Halloween, the night before the holy day. All the pilgrims would see it. He also sent it to highly placed individuals, including none other than Archbishop Albrecht of Mainz. Luther was ignorant of Albrecht's role in the scheme and hoped to persuade him to stop Tetzel. The letter speaks to Luther's naiveté. His remarkably sycophantic language speaks to his low social standing and the prevailing etiquette.

"Father in Christ and Most Illustrious Prince," he began, "forgive me that I, scum of the earth, should dare to approach Your Sublimity. The Lord Jesus is my witness that I am aware of my insignificance and my unworthiness. May your highness look upon this speck of dust and hear my plea." After referring to the "racket of indulgences," he found his nerve. He told Albrecht, "It is high time you looked into this matter," and asked him to "utterly suppress" the indulgence campaign. Albrecht never responded. But he did send a copy to the pope.

8

✤

THE ELECTION

When Fugger sat in his front row pew at St. Moritz, the church of Augsburg's elite, he seethed. It offended him when the priests mumbled Scripture and delivered ill-prepared sermons. In letters to friends, he complained that the priests read too few masses and lit too few candles. He fumed that some saints' days went unobserved.

For Fugger, the job of priest was too important to leave to amateurs. He and his contemporaries considered priests to be agents of redemption, capable of converting life on earth into life after death. They believed that priests, by saying masses, taking confessions and reciting prayers, could deliver them to heaven. But priests were human and many fell down on the job. They ate and drank too much, kept mistresses, and, in what offended parishioners the most, neglected their duties as divine middlemen.

It was one thing for a priest to disappoint a blacksmith or peasant. It was another to disappoint Fugger. He had the wherewithal to fight back. Aiming to upgrade the quality of local preaching, he launched a mini-Reformation at his church that put him at odds with his bishop, dragged in the pope and, if one believes the theory of one of his servants, nearly got him murdered.

The battle for St. Moritz wasn't just about a rich man stamping his feet until he got his way. More than anything, it was about someone trying to save his soul. Yes, Fugger is a recognizable figure to modern observers. He manufactured products, loaned money, signed contracts and fought competitors. Apart from the primitive technology, Fugger could have been a Russian oligarch, a Latin American telecoms boss or an American railroad baron from the nineteeth century. But this impression of Fugger overlooks the fact that he lived at a time when people built their lives around the church and man's mission was to serve the Lord and strive for heaven. Fugger and his contemporaries not only believed that God created man, that Christ is the risen Lord and that sinners burned in hell. They also believed in a formulaic approach to salvation. If they said their prayers, confessed their sins and, yes, earned extra credit by paying indulgences, they would sidestep the flames. Hence, Fugger's interest in St. Moritz. He wanted to save himself.

Fugger first became involved in local church affairs under different circumstances. While his brothers still lived, the head priest of St. Anne, another Augsburg church, complained of cramped quarters. Wouldn't it be great to add a chapel beautiful enough to credit the Savior and big enough to accommodate a crowd? The idea

captivated the Fugger brothers, and Fugger made it happen after Ulrich and George died when he built a funeral chapel to honor their
memory.

The chapel gave him a chance to publicly declare his greatness
in a socially acceptable manner. With thoughts of immortality, he
hired a famous organ maker, a noted ironmonger and, for the most
important feature—the design of the crypts—he turned to Maximilian's favorite—Dürer. For the Fugger Chapel, Dürer contributed
three designs: one of the resurrection of Christ and two of Samson.
Fugger wanted to protect Dürer's creations and insisted on an iron
gate that opened during mass but otherwise stayed closed. Only he
and the priests had keys.

The St. Moritz dispute began in 1511 over a storage place
for holy objects. Fugger and other community leaders built one
behind the church. For whatever reason, the foundation that ran
St. Moritz—a group comprised entirely of priests—objected. Fugger and the others felt insulted and diverted donations to other
churches. Tensions escalated when the priest who ran the foundation
retired and created a chance to upgrade the staff and the worship
service. Fugger wanted a theologian instead of a hack and campaigned for Johannes Eck, his champion in the usury debate. The
foundation hated the idea. Eck was a brilliant but arrogant hothead.
They also bristled at Fugger telling them what to do. Not wanting
the job that much anyway, Eck bowed out and Fugger asked another
theologian, Johannes Speiser, to apply. Speiser refused at first and
only agreed after Fugger said he would match Speiser's church pay
with his own money.

Finding a candidate was the easy part. Now Fugger had to con-
vince the foundation. This was a challenge because the foundation

didn't need his money and, unlike the emperor, could survive without him, thanks to large landholdings that gave it financial independence. Rather than let Fugger take over, it preferred to go without a new sacristy, a new chapel or whatever else he might offer. The foundation compromised by letting Speiser preach but only in the afternoon. This was an insult; few people, if any, went to church in the afternoon. Fugger was furious and he doubled his efforts to make Speiser the lead priest.

In the middle of the controversy, Fugger took a seat in a coach and travelled thirty-two miles west to Dillingen on the north bank of the Danube. He was going to dinner with Christoph von Stadion, the bishop of Augsburg. Stadion lived in a ten-story castle with a round dome built in the eleventh century. After dinner, Fugger became violently ill—so ill that the aides traveling with him thought he would die. They got sick, too, but one was strong enough to pack Fugger into the coach and race him back to Augsburg. Doctors tended to Fugger through the night and he recovered the next day. Years later, one of the servants who had accompanied Fugger on the visit wrote down the story and attributed the illness to poison. Fugger should have had an ally in Stadion because Fugger had supported him when he sought his seat. But Stadion sided with the priests, prompting Fugger to condemn his "ungratefulness and treachery."

Whether this was an assassination attempt or not matters less than what the episode symbolizes. Fugger had enemies and some of those enemies might have hated him enough to try to kill him. All we know for certain is that Fugger never again had a kind word for Stadion. He kept fighting for Speiser. He ordered Zink to take the matter to the pope.

Leo was having a hectic year. He was campaigning for a crusade, selecting a record thirty-one new cardinals, and keeping an eye on the trial of some plotters who had tried to kill him. But like the politician doing a favor for a contributor, he wanted to keep Fugger happy. He ordered the foundation to let Fugger have his way. The foundation appealed to a clerical court, but here, too, Fugger prevailed. Speiser became the lead priest at St. Moritz. Back in his front-row pew, Fugger could now sit back and listen as a true theologian delivered erudite sermons and recited all the prayers. He may have smiled. By getting what he wanted, he could feel more confident about his own salvation and less concerned about purgatory's fire.

❧

About this time, Fugger hired a nineteen-year-old Augsburger named Matthaus Schwarz as a bookkeeper. Schwarz stayed with Fugger and his successors his entire career. Although he became a critical part of the organization, he is less interesting for his own accomplishments than for the glimpses he left of Fugger. We know a lot about Schwarz because he commissioned a series of portraits that capture him through all the phases of his life. One shows him naked, another wearing armor and another with him in Fugger's Golden Counting Room, quill in hand. He is sitting at his worktable as Fugger looms over him giving instructions. File drawers with the names of Fugger's branch offices occupy the background. Schwarz, who loved fashion, wears a green doublet with slashes cut in the sleeves. He offers a lively contrast to Fugger in his black tunic and black hose. The only bit of color on Fugger is his gold beret. The picture is crudely done and has a cartoonish effect that would have horrified

Dürer. But the Schwarz picture is important because it is the only one of Fugger practicing his craft.

Schwarz's literary efforts spanned two genres—fashion and management. In addition to his portrait book, he wrote a textbook on accounting that shows the emphasis Fugger put on accurate records. Schwarz, like Fugger, apprenticed in Venice. He studied bookkeeping there but wrote that he understood "little more than nothing" about accounts before joining the firm. After spending time with Fugger, he recognized the folly of Fugger's competitors who believed they could live without detailed figures: "These little men write down their dealings in poorly kept scrapbooks or on slips of paper, stick them on a wall and make their reckonings on the window sill." Fugger, in contrast, had clerks in each of his offices. They monitored every transaction and let nothing sneak through. The offices had to update the figures every week and close the books at year-end, no exceptions. Once they did, managers sent copies to Augsburg where Fugger's staff translated the figures into Rhenish florins and, in another first, combined statements from all the branches into a single statement. The Italian banks had statements for each branch but never bothered with consolidation. Fugger could see the big picture like no one else. By knowing exactly where he stood at every moment, he always knew how much he had to lend or whether he needed to cut back. He knew if he was carrying too much inventory or too little cash. He knew how much he might be able to fetch for his jewels or factories. And he knew exactly, down to the last kreuzer, how much he was worth. Schwarz noted with disdain how others lost track of the numbers and how they expressed shock when they went bankrupt. They deserved their fate, Schwarz seemed to say. They were idiots.

Schwarz described Fugger's pioneering use of auditors—something the Italians later copied—and his insistence on involving three people in statement preparation as a tool to deter fraud. "Rarely will three people share the same views when it comes to bad intentions," Schwarz wrote. "This way, the master will not be cheated and the servants will remain honest against their will." Fugger was the chief auditor. While reviewing the ledgers for Neusohl, his big Slovakian mine, he fumed when he spotted that a general manager spent too much on food and lodging. "I don't know what is going on here," Fugger scribbled in the margin.

Schwarz intended his work as a textbook for young Germans interested in business, and he gave his readers investment advice that probably came from Fugger himself. A business person, he said, should keep a third of his assets in cash, a third in investments and a third in merchandise, and brace himself for steep losses at any moment. It went without saying that he should personally own real estate. Investments fail and cash diminishes with inflation but land endures.

⚜

In *The Wealth of Nations*, Adam Smith argued that capitalism provides for all or at least does as much as can be hoped. It succeeds because of what Smith called "the invisible hand." An individual looking out for No. 1 is "led by an invisible hand to promote an end which was no part his intention," he wrote. "By pursuing his own interest he frequently promotes that of the society more effectually than when he really intends to promote it." In other words, individuals out for gain did more for the common good than deliberate state efforts to do the same. That's the theory. The reality is that the pursuit of self-interest, if left unchecked, leads to crony capitalism, where those in power conspire with a handful of rich businessmen to look out for themselves and undermine others. Private individuals, not the state, still own the property. But wealth is concentrated in the hands of the few. And the lack of competition stills the invisible hand and its beneficial effects.

Fugger didn't see himself as an opponent of the common good. He pointed to the thousands of workers he employed in his mines, warehouses and factories. He could also point to his payments to suppliers that allowed them to employ thousands more. Without those jobs, many, if not most, of the workers would be landless peasants or even beggars. That's why Fugger referred to business as a "wonderful jewel." It took care of people. Besides, Fugger certainly had no objection to prosperity for all. He was simply doing what businessmen do. Like anyone else in his situation, he used every advantage he had to make money. Fugger would have been a fool not to exploit his special relationship with the emperor, particularly when there was no other path to extraordinary riches than through royal connections. He wasn't being crooked as much as he was being practical.

But the Tyrolean council, after the emperor's latest costly adventure in Italy, saw it otherwise. It was convinced that Fugger's cozy relationship with the emperor held back economic development and, more importantly, threatened the duchy with bankruptcy and made it vulnerable to a foreign takeover. Looking to calculate the damage, they totted up numbers on Fugger's latest contract with the emperor and came to a damning conclusion: The deal was outrageously lopsided. Fugger had loaned the emperor 130,000 florins and, in return, would earn a profit of 466,000. As with previous deals, the emperor would repay by giving Fugger silver and copper from his mines. But the value of what Maximilian gave on this deal was far less than what he got. Once Fugger sold the metal in the open market, he would earn a profit several times what he loaned. A rubber stamp no more, it demanded a diet to investigate the findings and overturn the agreement.

The council had inspected the books because the state's finances were exhausted. The output of the Schwaz silver mine, the largest silver mine on earth, should have eased Tyrol's financial burdens. But it instead allowed Maximilian to mortgage future income and run up massive obligations. Maximilian had taken office with a promise of fiscal discipline. Now it was clear that Maximilian was just as bad as Sigmund. The only difference was that Sigmund spent his money on love and Maximilian spent his on war. Sigmund had several mistresses and dozens of illegitimate children to support. Maximilian borrowed to pay troops and buy guns to fight Venice. The difference in how they spent it didn't matter. The state was broke in any case and, like in the days of Sigmund, it had no money to drain swamps or build bridges, let alone provide for the courts of Maximilian's daughter Mary, the future queen of Hungary, or of Anne of Hungary, the wife of his grandson Ferdinand.

Fugger and Maximilian didn't invent sovereign debt but they stretched it to a new extreme. Through their partnership, Tyrol had become an experiment in the limits of public borrowing. These days, governments routinely borrow for as many as 30 years. Investors assume taxpayers will be there to pay as the bills come due. But loans were almost always short term in Fugger's time. Fugger went farther than his predecessors by making loans that went out as far as eight years. He trusted Schwaz and its silver would be there for him well into the future. His wager paid off but later investors, including Fugger's heirs, got a tough lesson in royal finance at the end of the century when Maximilian's great-great-grandson, Philip II of Spain, defaulted on the loans used to fund the Armada and his wars with England.

In combating the council, Fugger could argue that he deserved a high return because the emperor was an unsafe credit. As a sovereign, Maximilian was above the law. Nothing other than the threat of revolution and the desire to preserve his good name compelled him to repay. A contemporary of Fugger's nailed it when he said, "Leaders act as they please." Another risk was the price of silver. A lot could happen in eight years. If silver prices crashed, Fugger could be stuck with losses instead of profits. But there are fair profits and ridiculous profits, and the council charged that Fugger's profits were ridiculous. The auditors had made inquiries and found that other bankers would have loaned to the emperor at 10 percent interest. Fugger's interest exceeded 50 percent. Maximilian may have had no head for figures, but the terrible terms suggested something other than faulty arithmetic. It suggested fraud. The council could not believe anyone, let alone the emperor and his experts, could have entered into such horrible agreements if they had known the details. Fugger must have lied to them.

The report contained other bombshells. It found that Fugger sometimes paid the emperor less for copper than the emperor paid to have it produced. In other words, Maximilian was losing money with every shovel of ore. Another finding noted that Fugger and other merchants often loaned to the emperor with diluted currency or in wool or silk that Maximilian's people didn't know how to value. Maximilian may have thought he was getting 40,000 florins worth of coins or goods. The truth was he got far less.

Not everything in the report was true. It was full of errors and exaggerated claims. But it nevertheless put Fugger in a dangerous spot. If Maximilian agreed with the council and turned on him, he could be finished. No one mentioned Jacques Coeur, once the lead banker to Charles V of France. But Coeur might have been on Fugger's mind. Coeur had been the richest man in France. His palace in Bourges rivaled that of the king and made him a target for the envious nobility. The king liked Coeur—Coeur funded his wars and enabled his victories—but he needed the nobles more than the banker. Caving to the pressure, Charles tossed Coeur in jail and snatched his holdings. Coeur escaped by bribing his jailers but never regained the king's favor. Coeur died in exile in Italy. Some members of the Tyrolean council wanted the same for Fugger.

The council argued Fugger's contracts with the emperor were invalid because Fugger had abused the emperor's trust. Moreover, Fugger had corrupted Tyrolean officials and manipulated copper prices by flooding the market with copper from his smelter in Fuggerau. The officials offered Maximilian 400,000 florins of their own money—an amount equal to several years of Schwaz's output—to break with the banker.

Unfortunately for them, Fugger was worth more to the emperor than that. The council could keep its money, Maximilian told them. Maximilian closed the diet and went back to his business. He was willing to risk a rebellion because he was about to embark on the most important project of his life. The project would cement Habsburg hegemony in Europe if successful. To make sure it did, he needed Fugger.

❧

If the story of the imperial election held a universal truth it was this: Left to their own devices, many politicians will milk a financial opportunity for all it's worth. Why shouldn't they? After all, once in power, the point is to stay in power. The more money a politician has, the more he can spend on private armies, television commercials, ballot-box stuffing or whatever else he has to do.

The election campaign began in 1517, when Maximilian dragged his casket and weary body to the Netherlands to beg his grandson Charles to succeed him. Maximilian considered emperor to be the best job on earth. He believed that the possessor of Charlemagne's crown could rule all of Europe. But his time was ending. He was now fifty-eight, and syphilis was eating him alive and a riding accident had badly damaged one of his legs and left him in horrible pain. He needed to set the stage for the future before it was too late. Charles, seventeen, was a confused teenager still learning how to be a king. But as monarch of Spain and the Netherlands, he already knew the burdens of the crown. The prospect of adding Germany to his duties intimidated him. Charles shared none of his grandfather's romantic ideas about the job. Charles hesitated and Maximilian had to appeal to family honor to get him to come around.

The Golden Bull, the constitution of the Holy Roman Empire, mandated an election but inertia had made the events meaningless. Just as Frederick had passed the crown to Maximilian, Maximilian believed he would pass it to Charles. Besides, before Maximilian revitalized the office with his determination, cunning and Fugger's money, no one even wanted it. A generation earlier, the electors had to beg Maximilian's father, Frederick, to take the imperial crown. Frederick dithered for months before agreeing because the job had few powers and could be more burden than benefit.

This election was going to be different because for the first time in memory, it was going to be contested. The French king, Francis, the dashing adventurer who had stunned Europe by defeating the mighty Swiss, feared Charles. He knew that if Charles became emperor, he'd have Francis surrounded. Charles would use his influence in Germany to attack him in Italy, then come looking for him in France. Francis could stop him by becoming emperor himself. With self-preservation in mind, he announced his candidacy. "The reason that moves me to seek the empire," he said, "is to prevent the Spanish king from doing so."

Francis was the better qualified of the candidates. Several years older than his rival, he was considered by Machiavelli and others to be the strongest and most capable king in Europe and, should the day come, they wanted him to lead the fight against the Turks. The fact that he was French and the empire was German posed no hurdle. The rules said nothing about nationality and, besides, Charles was no more German than he was. Charles may have spoken German to his horse, as the wags noted, but at court he spoke French.

As the contestants knew, greed drove the electors and the race would be an auction. And why not? An election between the rich king of Spain and the rich king of France offered the electors a spectacular opportunity for gain and a once-in-a-lifetime pay day. Maximilian warned Charles against frugality. "If you wish to gain mankind, you must play at a high stake," he said. "It would be lamentable if, after so much pain and labor to aggrandize our house and our posterity, we should lose all through some pitiful omission or penurious neglect." Francis spoke the same way. When an advisor suggested persuasion as a low cost alternative, Francis dismissed his naiveté: "If I only had to deal with the virtuous, your advice would be expedient. But in times like the present, when a man sets his heart on the papacy, the empire or anything else, he has no means of obtaining his object except by force or corruption."

To pay the bills, the candidates needed financing. Fugger was the most obvious banker for Charles. He had long served the Habsburgs and had unsurpassed resources. But he made no assumptions. Charles had never been to Germany, had never met Fugger, had presumably seen the scathing report of the Tyrolean Council and already had his own set of bankers in Spain. These bankers included several Italians as well as Fugger's Augsburg rivals, the Welsers, who had operations in Spain because of their work in the Portuguese spice trade. Charles could go to any of them. But Fugger had no intention of letting anyone except himself, least of all the Welsers, win the deal.

Just as the election got underway, Fugger prepared a marketing campaign. Louis of Aragon, an Italian cardinal, was coming to Augsburg as part of an exhausting sightseeing tour that, over nine months, would take him to forty-eight cities in eight countries and would include a visit with Leonardo da Vinci. Louis planned to cap it off by meeting Charles in the Netherlands. Confident that Louis would report everything he heard to the young Habsburg, Fugger treated him like royalty. After the cardinal arrived, he gave him a tour of the Fugger Palace. He showed him the Fugger chapel at St. Anne and threw him a party. The cardinal enjoyed himself. "These Fuggers entertained my master with dancing and the company of many beautiful ladies in their garden," wrote Antonio de Beatis, a writer Louis brought to take notes. Fugger boasted to the cardinal that the funeral chapel cost him 23,000 florins and that he had loaned money to every bishop in Germany.

Fugger's publicity assault worked and made Beatis gush over what he saw and heard: "These Fuggers are among the greatest merchants to be found in Christendom, for without any outside help, they can lay their hands on 300,000 ducats in ready money and still not touch a hair of their property, which is by no means small." He went on to praise the Welsers but added that "they are in no way to be compared with the Fuggers."

⚜

As it happened, the imperial diet was meeting in Augsburg that year. The Turks led the official agenda; Pope Leo wanted the electors to fund a crusade and sent the papal legate to Germany to press the case. He had been in a panic since the Turks captured Belgrade in 1521 and created a path into Hungary and, from there, the rest of Europe. He feared Rome would fall just like Constantinople and, if that happened, Christendom itself would perish. But the electors could care less about the Turks. The election and the inevitable payoffs consumed them. Three of the electors—Bohemia, Palatinate and Frederick of Saxony—leaned toward Charles. As long as Charles paid them fairly, he could have their votes. Three others—Trier, Cologne and Fugger's client Albrecht of Mainz—leaned toward Francis. If he greased them, they were his. Nothing was certain until the electors actually cast their votes. But as the Augsburg diet got under way, it looked like a dead heat with each candidate confident of at least three votes.

The seventh elector was Joachim of Brandenburg. He led the House of Hohenzollern, which produced Albrecht of Mainz and later produced Kaiser Wilhelm I, who with Bismarck unified Germany, and Kaiser Wilhelm II, who led Germany into World War I. Joachim joked that he only cared about falcons, but he had founded a university and reformed the justice and administrative systems of his territory. Clever with money, he worked with Fugger on the indulgence scheme for Albrecht. Now he employed his talents to extract all he could from Maximilian and Francis. The Habsburg negotiator in Augsburg, Max von Berges, called him "a devilish man regarding money matters." His French equivalent said Joachim was "blinded by greed."

Francis tried to preempt the bidding with a spectacular offer. In addition to cash, he offered his niece, the princess Renée. This tantalized Joachim because the Hohenzollerns—B-grade players in the game of *Hausmachtpolitik*—had historically made nothing better than local matches. A Hohenzollern might marry a duchess of Pomerania or a countess of Mecklenburg, but never someone from a powerful house like the Valois. But as the ascent of Albrecht showed, the Hohenzollerns were climbing the ladder. A Valois marriage would be another boost. Renée, however, dashed their dreams. She defied Francis and skipped off to marry a French duke.

Before Francis could deliver another princess, Charles offered one of his own—his sister, the Spanish princess Catherine. He threw in a dowry of 300,000 florins. Joachim liked the offer—the Habsburgs were now as prestigious as the Valois—and he accepted. But he insisted Charles pay a third of the money up front. As Fugger suspected, Charles lacked the cash. Only Fugger could deliver it quickly, so Charles turned to him. Fugger insisted the negotiators produce a marriage contract first.

The families held a provisional wedding at the diet with only the bridegroom in attendance. A wedding without the bride might seem a hollow event. But Augsburg celebrated for three days anyway. The city regarded the Habsburg-Hohenzollern union as good for business and security. Fugger, always willing to throw a party, hosted a costume ball.

After Joachim came over to Charles, support for Francis evaporated. The other electors saw what Joachim got and demanded their own payoffs in return for votes. As the papal legate fumed over the inability of the electors to care about the Turks, Maximilian corralled them in a room to negotiate the bribes. Maximilian invited a special guest to the meeting: Fugger. Since the diet of Constance, where Fugger produced the wagons of gold, the Fugger name was magical. No one doubted he could pay whatever Charles promised. There is no record of what Fugger told the electors. Maybe he said nothing and his mere presence was enough. In any case, all seven electors signed a pledge for Charles.

⚜

The Golden Bull decreed the election occur in Frankfurt. By voting in the city of the Franks, the empire honored the memory of Charlemagne, who was king of the Franks before becoming emperor. The electors wanted cash and Fugger got busy on the logistics. He needed horses, wagons and armed guards to transport sacks of gold to Frankfurt. He needed gifts to bribe every lord whose borders he crossed. And he needed one more essential item. Despite his boast about being able to whip up 300,000 ducats in an instant, he didn't actually have the money. He had to raise it. But this is where he excelled. As evident already in his dealings with Duke Sigmund, when he persuaded friends and family to loan him all he needed without the benefit of a track record, he knew how to woo investors. Now, thirty years later, he had the best track record of any banker in Europe. If there had been telephones, he could have raised all he needed with a few calls. As it was, he raised the money with face-to-face conversations at the diet. The largest deposit came from Duke George of Brandenburg. George was forty-six and related to Frederick the Wise. He met Fugger for the first time at the diet. He owned ore deposits near the border with Bohemia and shared Fugger's interest in mining. After George invested, Fugger wrote to him for the rest of his life. These letters, resembling the letters CEOs write every year to shareholders, are among the few Fugger letters that survive. Fugger keeps a formal tone, but he nonetheless reveals his thoughts about religion, social unrest and late-paying Habsburgs. The letters are among the most important documents in the historic record about Fugger.

Fugger had everything in place to pay the bribes when he received shocking news from Spain: Charles wanted to use other bankers and cut him out. Fugger had pushed too hard for favorable terms and made Charles opt for a cheaper course. The details are missing, but it may have been that Fugger demanded more valuable collateral than the others. None of the bankers, at least not as individuals, could loan the required sums, but they could collectively. The group was all Italian except for one, Fugger's rivals—the Welsers. The aides to Maximilian were aghast because only Fugger had credibility with the electors. The electors might jump if Charles went with the Welsers. One of the aides condemned the Welsers as worthless: "We could never find a way to get a loan or a penny from the Welsers, so we always had to go to the Fuggers." Fugger himself must have been furious. The electors didn't sign on for Charles because a Welser was in the room. They signed because Fugger was in the room. Charles tried to appease Fugger by throwing him a bone. He assigned him to handle the money transfers and hold the necessary documents in his safe. This was easy money for Fugger. But it was the loan Fugger wanted. The profits on the loan would dwarf those from transfer fees. He had to get back in.

❧

As the electors groveled for cash, Albrecht Dürer grabbed his easel, brushes and sketch pads and headed to Augsburg. He was the greatest German artist of the age and an excellent businessman. Sensing an opportunity for commissions, he counted on wealthy dignitaries at the diet lining up for their portraits. Dürer specialized in woodcuts because woodcuts could be mass-produced and sold several times over. He stamped a logo on every one to deter counterfeiters. But he knew the dignitaries didn't want woodcuts. They wanted luminous oil paintings on canvas. That's certainly what Fugger wanted. When his time came, Dürer had him turn slightly to capture a bit of his profile. Dürer, his golden locks tucked under a cap, began with a quick charcoal sketch. That way, Fugger could be on his way quickly. Dürer would fill in the colors later.

Fugger sat for several portraits in his life but the one Dürer painted in Augsburg is the best. It shows Fugger wearing his gold cap and a cape with a fur collar, and offers a sharp contrast to the portrait of Maximilian painted at the same time. The emperor looks tired. His brilliant jewels are unable to hide the fact that death looms. Maximilian's daughter, to whom Dürer tried to sell the painting, hated it and refused to buy it. Fugger was the same age as the emperor but looks wide-awake in his portrait. The gaze is calm, intelligent and dignified—a look of confidence. The painting now hangs in the Augsburg city museum.

❧

Just as the diet concluded, Martin Luther appeared at the gates of Augsburg. The pope wanted him to recant and had ordered him to Augsburg to give a statement. The pope promised not to arrest him if he showed up, but Luther thought about Jan Hus, the Czech reformer burned at the stake for heresy in 1415. Hus, too, had been promised safe conduct. Luther prepared for the worst. "Now I must die," he said.

In his Ninety-five Theses, Luther denied the pope's ability to absolve sins, thereby attacking the bedrock of papal authority and power. Cardinal Cajetan, a papal emissary in town for the diet, intended to bully him into retracting his statements. Cajetan was a Dominican who made a name for himself when he debated Pico della Mirandola before the priest's arrest. Although Cajetan defended papal authority to the last, he was himself a voice of reform who argued against Vatican extravagance. He got a strong dose of extravagance in Augsburg, where he stayed as a guest of Fugger's at the Fugger Palace. Luther met Cajetan at the palace and surprised him by holding his ground. Instead of apologizing, Luther argued scripture and, threats notwithstanding, refused to renounce anything in the theses. The third and final meeting between the two ended with a sputtering Cajetan ordering Luther out of his sight. Luther was staying with the monks around the corner at St. Anne. The monks liked Luther and his message. They feared authorities might arrest and even kill him if he left through a main gate. They showed him a secret passage in the city wall. A horse waited for him on the other side. As much as he disliked horses, he needed to make a quick getaway. Luther escaped Augsburg undetected.

Although Luther had been in his home, Fugger might not have seen him during the visit. Luther was still an obscure figure and Fugger had the electors on his mind, not a Saxon monk. For his part, Luther didn't need to meet Fugger to form an impression. He could create one from seeing the Fugger Palace and hearing about Fugger's exploits from the St. Anne brothers. However he formed his opinions, this much is clear: He left Augsburg with a new target. Over the next few years, Luther wouldn't leave Fugger alone.

The encounter with Luther closed a difficult trip for Cardinal Cajetan. When the legate finally got the diet to consider the Turks, the debate became a one-sided harangue against Rome. The electors were not Lutherans, at least not yet. But even before Luther became popular, Germans were turning against Rome. The indulgence campaign, the sale of church offices and the lazy and lecherous priests: Many Germans, including some of the electors, had lost patience with all of it. Popular anger with Rome would soon have dangerous consequences for Fugger.

❧

Maximilian had taken his family to the top, but he had nothing to show for it financially. Fugger had made all the money and Maximilian only had debts. He complained at the Augsburg diet about not having a penny to his name and that he had to borrow from Fugger just to eat. He had felt miserable at the diet and, once it broke, he took the few pennies he had and set off for Innsbruck, the city where he wanted to be when he died. When he was young and full of dreams, he built the city's most famous landmark, the Golden Roof. The roof was a gilded balcony covered with gleaming copper that looked over the town square. It was a skybox for watching tournaments and a monument to himself. It featured the coats of arms from his territories and two giant reliefs. One showed him laughing with his court jester and his chancellor. Another showed him with his beloved Anne of Burgundy. When he reached Innsbruck, he found his self-promotion counted for nothing. Innkeepers refused him lodging because of unpaid bills. Unable to find a bed, he limped to Wels, halfway between Innsbruck and Vienna. Maximilian loved songbirds and attendants brought some to his room. Maybe they reminded him of Mary and her falcons. He died listening to them sing.

Maximilian's death voided the pledges the electors made to Charles and gave them a chance to soak the contestants for more money. It also liberated Fugger. With his longtime client and protector in the ground, Fugger became a free agent. Europe's richest banker could now pursue what worked best for him even if it did not include the Habsburgs. If Charles didn't want him, it was fine with him. He would find another way in.

9

❧

VICTORY

When a banker thinks he might lose a deal, he sometimes invokes a tactic known as "bid 'em up." He gets his client to pay a price so high that no other bidder can afford to stay in the game. The bid might be so large that it puts the client at risk of bankruptcy. That doesn't matter. What matters is that the banker wins the deal and gets his fee. Fugger didn't invent the phrase "bid 'em up." But the death of Maximilian offered him the opportunity to use it for what may have been the first time.

The moment Maximilian died, Fugger ordered a courier to race to Paris with the news. He wanted to ingratiate himself with King Francis by being the first to tell him about the death. It was Fugger's way of signaling that he was open for business and ready to help the French king win the election. Of course, Fugger preferred Charles.

Fugger had become the richest man in Europe by financing the Habsburgs in little Austria. The prospects of financing them in Spain and the New World dazzled him. But he had put too much faith in Maximilian and too little effort into wooing Charles directly. He had pushed too hard for good terms and stirred up too much mistrust among the Austrian nobility. And now with the election coming back up for grabs, he faced the real possibility of being shut out. No matter that the electors wanted Fugger in the deal because he was the only banker they trusted. The teenage king of Spain wanted to leave him on the sidelines.

Fugger couldn't let that happen. He was the preeminent financier in Europe. A loss would not only embarrass him but, infinitely worse, endanger his empire. The Habsburgs might cancel his agreements if he backed France. Charles might rip up his silver contracts and give them to the Welsers or one of the others. That could trigger the nightmare scenario of anxious depositors demanding withdrawals. Like in the terrifying days after Meckau's death, Fugger could not pay everyone at once. Debtor's prison loomed again.

With everything on the line, Fugger fell back on his greatest advantage: scale. He could offer a candidate more money than anyone. By reminding the electors of his resources—a promotional campaign he began with Louis of Aragon's garden party and continued until election day—he could push the price of victory so high that no one else could compete. His competitors would drop out and he would be the only banker left. He made a bet on the ambition of the rival kings, counting on them to keep bidding and send the price high enough to shove his banking competitors off the field.

To pull it off, he had to demonstrate to Charles that he held the cards. This is where Francis came in. Fugger wanted Charles to know one thing: that if Charles didn't choose Fugger, Fugger would snub him right back and put his resources—the largest pool of uncommitted capital in Europe—behind France. It was that simple. He wanted Charles to understand that he, not the electors, would decide who became emperor, and that if he backed Francis, the Habsburgs would lose the Holy Roman Empire—the largest political jurisdiction in Europe—and their hopes of global domination. Fugger support of Francis would create its own problems. Fugger would still have to deal with the Habsburgs. But whether or not Fugger ever intended to actually back Francis didn't matter. What mattered was whether the Habsburgs believed that he could, that they believed he might actually betray them for the French king. That's why Fugger sent the courier to Paris. That's why he continued to apprise Francis of the latest news in the following weeks. That's why he directed his nephew Anton, who had replaced the aging Zink at the Vatican, to stay in touch with Francis's people in Rome. Fugger couldn't go so far as to give Francis a direct sales pitch without infuriating the Habsburgs. But there was nothing to prevent Francis from coming to him. With his innocent overtures, Fugger was trying to engineer an approach from Francis.

A situation now arose that gave Fugger another chance to prove his value to the Habsburgs. Württemburg was a German duchy near the French border. A number of cities within the duchy belonged not to the local ruler, Duke Ulrich, but to the empire and its Habsburg stewards. This infuriated Ulrich because the cities paid taxes to the empire and not to him. When Maximilian died, Ulrich seized the moment. He sent soldiers to the cities and claimed them. But he had misjudged the situation. Although Maximilian was dead, the Habsburg power structure remained in place. It would fight the duke if it could raise money to pay an army. Fugger used the opportunity to showboat. He gave the Habsburgs 113,000 florins to hire mercenaries.

Dürer sketched a scene in the war. It shows the overwhelming disparity between the Fugger-backed forces and those of the enemy. In the foreground, a line of cannons with impossibly long barrels aims at a castle. The Habsburg soldiers manning the cannons look confident about finishing the job in time for dinner. One pities the defenders. They have nowhere to go. The image leaves no doubt that the Habsburgs would triumph, which they did. This was a great victory for the Habsburgs because it gave them Stuttgart, a strategic holding given its proximity to France.

The episode proved again that Fugger was a friend worth having. In the aftermath, an exasperated Margaret, Charles's aunt and campaign manager, asked Charles to quit fooling around and borrow from Fugger before it was too late. Leaving aside that Fugger had more resources than the other bankers, she cited an ethical obligation: "He accomplishes so many favors and services for us that you are duty-bound to acknowledge him."

Time was running out for Charles. Realizing before Charles that whoever had Fugger would win, Francis reached out to Augsburg just as Fugger expected. The way Francis saw it, Charles and he were even in the battle for funds. Charles had the Welsers and the Italians. Francis had the bankers of Lyon and some Italians of his own, as well as money raised by selling royal lands and seizing, in the name of the state, the inheritance of his budget director. But Francis knew he had to do better than just match Charles's offer. He needed to make the choice easy for the electors by not only outbidding Charles but by vastly outbidding him. With that as his aim, he asked Fugger for 300,000 ecus, the equivalent of 369,000 florins. Francis made the offer as enticing to Fugger as possible. He promised speedy repayment out of French tax revenues plus a 30,000-ecu commission. If Fugger agreed, Francis could double what Charles had offered. Francis couldn't lose with that kind of money. No matter how many other bankers Charles added to his consortium, Charles could not match Francis and Fugger. Fugger's strategy of bid 'em up had seen to that. With any luck, Francis would get all seven votes, not just a simple majority. He would have a mandate to unite France and Germany under the House of Valois.

Fugger leaked word of Francis's offer to the Habsburg camp. Von Berghes, the Habsburg man in Augsburg, pleaded with Margaret to reason with Charles. He declared that Charles absolutely had to borrow from Fugger or all would be lost. "Regarding Fugger, Madam, the king will have to work more with him, whether he wants it or not," Von Berghes wrote. "The electors want to have Fugger's word and nobody else's." He added that Charles should have used Fugger from the start: "If we had done that from the beginning, it would have greatly been to the king's profit and progress to his business." Pressure came on Charles from all sides. The commissioners running the election wrote Charles to say the electors "have neither faith, letters nor seals from any merchants other than the Fuggers."

Meanwhile, the electors became greedier. A year earlier in Augsburg, Joachim of Brandenberg had won a Habsburg bride and a 300,000 florins dowry for his pledge to Charles. Now, with the bidding war in full swing, he broke his promise. He told Fugger, whom he said "he particularly trusted," that he would back whomever Fugger backed, and he specifically asked whether Fugger's personal guarantee only applied to Charles or whether it applied to Francis, too.

⚜

Across the channel in England, Henry VIII was in his tenth year as king and, at age twenty-nine, still athletic and handsome. He divorced Catherine of Aragon fourteen years later and split with Rome. For now he was still friends with the Holy See. Pope Leo came to him with an idea. Henry should enter the race and try his luck at becoming the first Englishman since the earl of Cornwall in 1256 to win an imperial election.

Leo feared Charles and Francis as threats to the Vatican. Francis already occupied Milan. If he became emperor and no longer had to contend with the Habsburgs, he could easily sweep down the peninsula and snatch Rome. Charles was a bigger threat. With much of southern Italy already in his control, Charles could muster imperial troops in Naples and attack Rome from the south.

Leo needed a spoiler. It had to be someone strong and someone with sufficient credibility and cash to compete financially. Leo considered backing Frederick the Wise, the Saxon elector. The other electors liked Frederick and he had already been considering a run. But when ultimately forced to declare, he demurred. He said he "preferred to be a powerful duke rather than a weak king." That left Henry. Leo could count on Henry, if elected, as a buffer between Rome and any continental power that tried to attack. But first he had to get him to run.

This was not the first time someone approached Henry with the idea of becoming emperor. Six years earlier, when Maximilian was still alive, Maximilian feared he himself might not live long enough to see Charles come of age and become emperor. He surprised Henry by offering to adopt him as his son and persuade the electors to name him emperor. Henry laughed it off, but he took the pope's request seriously. From his island off the coast, he envied Charles and Francis. He longed to have their power. He could get that by becoming emperor. He believed if the German princes backed him with money and guns, he could become the most powerful sovereign in Europe. He warmed to the idea and agreed to run. Leo gave him a letter outlining his support.

This was a stunning development and could cut either way for Fugger. If the electors liked Henry, Henry could win the race and leave Fugger out of the deal. Conversely, more candidates meant more bidders for electoral votes. More bidders meant higher bids— bids that only Fugger could finance. A third candidate could make Fugger even more valuable.

Henry sent his councilor Richard Pace to Germany to work the electors. Pace knew Germany. He had negotiated with Fugger when Henry subsidized Maximilian on his final Italian campaign. The election mission was more delicate. Henry wanted to stay on good terms with the other candidates and told Pace to offer Henry as a candidate only if, in the course of conversation with an elector, the elector himself suggested it. If that happened, Pace should mention that Henry was of "German tongue," even though he spoke no German. He should also promise bribes. Henry, without understanding the possible costs, assumed his Hansa friends in Lübeck would loan him all he needed.

Frankfurt suffered that year from an unusually hot summer and Pace became ill en route. Only his devotion to Henry drove him on.

In Cologne, he met his first elector, the city's bishop. He left the meeting encouraged and wrote Henry to say Cologne might come his way. In Mainz, he met Albrecht. Albrecht demanded secrecy but, in a cinema-worthy moment, he hid Francis's campaign manager behind a curtain to eavesdrop. Next, Pace met the shrewd and greedy Joachim. Joachim gave Pace additional encouragement. The bishop of Trier, a fourth elector, offered even more. Pace was thrilled. Everything seemed to be coming together. He sent Henry another update. Get ready to come to Germany, he wrote. He had the votes.

❧

As the electors descended on Frankfurt, the Habsburg camp became anxious and spread a rumor that Francis would invade Germany if he won. Although the rules allowed foreign emperors, the public, conditioned to hate France by centuries of war, would not tolerate a Frenchman. Mobs took to the streets and looked for Frenchmen to kill. Worried about being mistaken for French, Pace fled Frankfurt for Mainz. By stoking the mob with invasion rumors, the Habsburgs engaged in a Renaissance case of voter intimidation. They wanted the electors to think the mob would hang them if they voted the wrong way.

The voting took place in Frankfurt Cathedral. Made of red sandstone and home to the skull of St. Bartholomew, it sits close to the Main River. The location let the electors come by barge and avoid the mayhem on the streets. Once inside, they had to walk forty paces toward the altar, turn right, and head through an antechamber that led to a wooden door. The door was so small and hidden that the uninitiated would never find it. It opened to the election chapel.

Only the electors could go in, ducking their heads and maneuvering their fat, game-fed bodies through a narrow frame. Then it was down a step to a chapel with a vaulted ceiling, a stone floor and a small window above a cross. The electors had the most power, the biggest egos and the grandest lifestyles in Germany. They lived in palaces the size of shopping malls. For the election, they huddled in a room the size of a donut shop and had to stay until they reached a verdict even if it took weeks. They had to sleep on straw mats, relieve themselves in buckets and live on whatever food and wine their servants brought. The rules cut rations to bread and water if they failed to decide after thirteen days.

When the tocsin rang, the electors, dressed in scarlet robes, took their places in the chapel to cast their votes. They held a mass and Albrecht administered an oath. As the electors thought about how to vote, they swore to make their decisions free of influence and corruption. "My voice and vote, on the said election, I will give without any pact, payment, price or promise or whatever such things may be called," they said. "So help me God and all the saints." Outside, the crowds grew. Just in case Francis attacked, Charles's people hired an army led by the knight Franz von Sickingen for protection. Sickingen was the most powerful knight in Germany. He could raise an army as easily as Fugger could raise money. By putting him on the payroll before Francis did, the Habsburgs made sure he would cause no trouble.

The electors negotiated until the last. Although Albert had encouraged Pace, he followed his brother Joachim by refusing to accept promises from anyone but Fugger. Elector Louis of Palatinate asked Fugger to personally sign a pledge. With the electors insisting on Fugger, Charles was unable to resist any longer. He agreed to borrow from the Augsburg banker. This sealed the outcome. Anything could happen in the election chapel but if the electors wanted Fugger, they had to vote for the Spanish king. Two weeks after the electors came to Frankfurt, they emerged from the church, squinted in the daylight and announced the outcome. They gave the crown to Charles in a unanimous decision.

Charles's supporters greeted the news in different ways. The mob in Frankfurt got drunk and rioted. Antwerp held a joust. In Augsburg, Fugger offered to host a multiday celebration. City officials refused him the permit. They wanted to control the show and treated the town to a modest fireworks display instead. Henry rejoiced despite his loss—anything was better than a victory for the French! He held a mass in London and, after hearing how much Charles spent on bribes, told the Duke of Suffolk he celebrated his defeat:

> When the king's highness had well perceived and pondered the great charges and profusion of money expent by the said king of the Romans for the obtent of that dignity, his grace did wonder therat and said that he was right glad that he obtained not the same.

When Fugger completed the final reckoning, he, too, might have wished someone else picked up the tab. The "profusion of money expent" on bribes came to 852,000 florins, including, curiously, 600 florins for Lamparter, the university rector who had married Fugger's illegitimate daughter Mechtild. The Italians contributed a fifth of the total. The Welsers only a sixth. Fugger's share came to 544,000 florins, an amount considerably more than requested by Francis. He had just made the biggest loan the world had ever seen. And this time, there were no mining rights standing behind the loan, only a promise to pay from Charles. The loan was unsecured.

Fugger had always made loans backed by solid collateral—a silver mine here or a city and its tax rolls there. It is what kept him solvent. He lowered his standard for the imperial election because he had to win. But he recognized that Charles, unlike his poverty-stricken grandfather, was rich beyond imagination. Twenty-seven years had passed since Columbus landed in America. Gold and silver from the New World—a Habsburg-controlled world—was already coming back to Europe. Closer to home, the Habsburg possessions in Spain and the Netherlands were two of the richest parts of Europe. Still, it was one thing to be rich on paper and another thing to have cash on hand. Whatever the case, Fugger was now at the mercy of a nineteen-year-old creditor 1,200 miles away from Augsburg in Spain.

Even worse, the imperial diet immediately demanded that he betray Fugger. The lawmakers feared that Charles would put his own interests before those of Germany and drafted a thirty-four-article contract to keep him in check. It demanded that Charles defend the empire and the church; enter no foreign wars without its consent; use only German and Latin for official business; hire only German speakers for imperial offices. Article 19 had a commercial agenda. It demanded Charles investigate Fugger and other rich bankers. "We should consider," it read, "how to limit the big trading companies which have up to now governed with their money and acted in their own interest and caused damage, disadvantages and burden to the empire, its citizens and subjects through their rise in prices."

Habsburg ambassadors signed the document on behalf of Charles a week after the vote. With that, Charles launched an investigation into the man who just put him in office.

❧

Charles looked more like a footman than a king. He was slim, ungainly and cursed with an oversized lower jaw—the Habsburg jaw—that made it difficult to chew. Embarrassed to be seen when eating, he dined alone. He was quiet and sober. He cultivated carnations and took the imperial choir along when he traveled. He lacked the rakish flair of Francis and the robust energy of Henry. Maximilian thought his appearance repulsive but would have been impressed by his intellect if he had spent more time with him. "There is more at the back of his head than appears in the face," said a papal official. Like Maximilian, Charles made the rookie mistake of believing the election gave him dictatorial power: "It is our view, that the empire of old had not many masters but one, and it is our intention to be that one." After the election, he convened the Cortes, the Castilian parliament, and demanded tax increases to pay his election debts to Fugger. The Cortes resisted. It saw no reason to pay for Charles's empire building and his debts to a German banker. There was nothing in it for Spain, the lawmakers argued. Germany wasn't a promising new possession like Cuba or Mexico. It offered the people no riches, only entanglements in France and Italy. The body begrudgingly approved the tax hike but only after Charles made compromises. After the vote, Charles went to Germany for his coronation as king of the Germans and appointed his former tutor, the bookish Cardinal Adrian of Utrecht, to rule in his absence.

Wool workers in Segovia, incensed by the tax hike, seized the city hall ten days later and captured the town clerk. They cinched a rope around his neck, beat him with wooden bats and hung him by his feet to die. This was the first act in the Revolt of the Comuneros, a sixteenth-century Spanish civil war incited by Fugger's demand for repayment. Toledo, Tordesillas and Valladolid followed Segovia's lead. In Madrid, the militia joined the rebels. Most of Castile belonged to the insurgents after five months. Talk spread of overthrowing the king. Fugger agents in Spain sent updates to Augsburg. One was a monument of understatement. "Spain is not well," it read.

Charles stayed in Germany and let Adrian cope with the uprising. Thirteen Castilian cities belonged to rebels when Charles bowed before the electors in Aachen Cathedral and swore to protect the church, the weak and the innocent. Fugger, now sixty-two, stayed home. His nephew Ulrich watched in his stead as Charles received the crown, orb and sword. We can assume Ulrich spoke to Charles or his counselors. We can also assume he outlined the consequences of a Habsburg default and argued how it would ruin the emperor's reputation and make future borrowing impossible. We can assume this because Charles got busy for Fugger immediately after the diet. He wrote to Adrian from Germany, demanding that he find a way to collect the taxes and to forward the money to Augsburg.

The request floored Adrian. Had Charles forgotten Madrid and other cities belonged to the rebels? He told Charles to be realistic. "Your Highness is making a great error if you think that you will be able to collect and make use of this tax," he wrote. "There is no one in the Kingdom, not in Seville or Valladolid or any other city who will ever pay anything of it." Adrian questioned his former pupil for even asking: "All the grandees and members of the council are amazed that Your Highness has scheduled payments from these funds."

Fugger may have been asking himself how this could be happening. He had always been careful. Now he risked the same end as his cousins, the Fuggers of the Roe, who had lost it all when the taxpayers of Leuven refused to pay Maximilian's bills. Fugger now found himself in the same corner.

Brushing aside Adrian's rebuke, Charles ordered him to mobilize the army and arrest and execute the rebel commanders. Adrian, who later became pope, dutifully attacked. The Habsburgs won back the rebellious cities one by one and, after taking Toledo, ended the war. The loser was Fugger. To ensure peace, Charles signed a treaty that cancelled the tax hikes. With that, Fugger could no longer count on the Spanish people to pay the election debts. If he hadn't already, he might have now questioned himself for not demanding collateral. In what should have been his greatest moment, Fugger found himself in the most vulnerable position of his life.

❖

At some point in the middle of the imperial election, workers nailed a plaque onto a high brick wall on Augsburg's eastern edge. Latin words covered the plaque. They described what became Fugger's most enduring legacy—more memorable even than putting Charles on Charlemagne's throne. Fugger probably wrote the words himself. After acknowledging his brothers, he attempted modesty before lapsing into self-praise.

The brothers Ulrich, George and Jacob Fugger of Augsburg, who are convinced they were born to serve this city and feel obligated to return property received from the all mighty and just God, have out of piety and as a model of openhearted generosity, given, granted and dedicated 106 homes with all fixtures to the diligent and hardworking but poor fellow citizens.

The plaque described the Fuggerei, a housing project for Augsburg's working poor. The settlement remains in service 500 years later, housing the poor just like always. The only difference is the tour buses. It is Augsburg's top attraction. Visitors from as far away as Japan and Brazil come to see how people lived in the Age of Fugger. They peer inside the houses, stroll the neatly ordered grounds and take pictures to capture the achievement of Augsburg's great banker and philanthropist.

Fugger started the project by buying four small houses at the bottom of Jew Hill on a creek that ran into the Lech. The Welsers sold him the houses, but it's unlikely they ever spent much time in the area. The neighborhood was coarse, dirty and working class. If Augsburg had enemy territory for the bankers, this was it. Crews cleared the land for a set of two-story row houses with small gardens behind each. They built a hospital on the grounds to tend to the sick, a wall to keep out the riffraff and three gates to let in residents. The official papers called the development the Houses at Hood Point but no sooner did it open than it became known as the Fuggerei. Like Fugger's similarly named factory in Austria, it translates to the Place of Fugger.

There was nothing on its scale in Europe. Leiden had its St. Anne almshouse and Bruges had its *Godshuisen* (God's Houses) for the elderly. Augsburg had several homeless shelters. But none was more than twelve units. The Fuggerei smashed precedent with 106 units. At five people per unit, the Fuggerei could house more than 500 people or one in every 60 Augsburgers.

Thomas Krebs built the Fuggerei. It was his second job for Fugger. He had also built the sacristy at St. Moritz. At the Fuggerei, he gracefully combined form and function. The top floor of each house had a separate entrance so that a family living upstairs would not inconvenience the family below. Each unit had 450 square feet with four rooms—two bedrooms, a living room and a kitchen. The kitchen had a stove that doubled as a heater and a window to the living room that let a mother keep her eye on the kids. Tenants used chamber pots and emptied them into the creek that ran through the settlement. Recognizing the comforts of private life, Krebs, with Fugger's approval, purposely omitted a central square from the complex. He and Fugger wanted the settlement to be a refuge from the bustle of public life, not an imitation of it.

Late in life, Dürer wrote books on artistic theory and, after being dazzled by a schematic of Tenochtitlan in Mexico, pronounced his views on city planning. He rejected the quaint randomness of medieval cities, with their twisting alleyways and mix of styles, in favor of symmetry, unity and proportion. Krebs felt the same. He made the rooflines at the Fuggerei even with the surrounding walls and the streets between the houses straight. The sameness of the homes created a sense of order and kept the costs down by eliminating the need for multiple designs, but made the houses hard to tell apart. Krebs solved the problem by painting a number on each house, giving each one its own address. Written in Gothic script, these were the first house numbers in Augsburg. Along the same lines, he gave each house a uniquely shaped doorbell pull—some curled, some square, some shaped like anchors—that allowed residents to identify their entrances in the dark. He livened up the place with gables that matched those on the homes of Augsburg's rich. The simple elegance of the Fuggerei attracted imitators. Row houses with similar proportions popped up in Augsburg and other cities in the years following.

If Fugger had wanted a lasting monument to himself, there were flashier options than housing. He could have built another chapel or given a stipend to another priest like he gave Speiser at St. Moritz. If he wanted to help the poor, he could have given money to the church and its programs to feed the needy. These alternatives would have satisfied a common sixteenth century motive for charitable giving: guilt relief. In his last will and testament, the Cologne businessman Johann Rinck spoke for his class when he confessed, "Commerce is hard on the conscience and the soul." Public relations also motivated givers and it no doubt motivated Fugger. With enemies gunning for him, he sought to project a generous image. He wanted people to think, as they walked past the gates and looked into the neatly maintained houses and gardens and saw children playing by the fountain, that he had a heart and that, despite his wealth, he cared.

Fugger never said what attracted him to housing. The bylaws of the Fuggerei spoke only of his desire "to honor and love God, to help day laborers and hand workers." This was boilerplate. But the admission rules provide some clues and give an example of how rich people—then and now—believe themselves to know what's best for the poor. For starters, Fugger refused to let people live in his houses for free. A tenant had to pay one florin a year to stay at the Fuggerei. That was a bargain; the price came to only a quarter of the market rate. But it was a sufficient burden for tenants, given that a weaver at his loom had to work six weeks to earn the required amount. If someone wanted to live in Fugger's complex, he or she needed a job to afford the rent.

Another condition excluded beggars. Augsburg was full of them. Some Augsburgers liked having them around as an outlet for soul-saving largesse. But Fugger was suspicious. For him, the poor fell into two camps, the worthy and the unworthy. Day laborers working odd jobs might be poor, but they deserved sympathy and assistance. The beggars scurrying into Augsburg each morning when the gates opened were undeserving. By excluding them from the Fuggerei, he betrayed a core belief: Everyone had a duty to work. It was his way of saying, Get a job.

The town council felt the same. During Fugger's lifetime, the council passed increasingly harsh laws against begging. The first outlawed door-to-door panhandling and sleeping on church stairs. The second required them to carry a license in the form of a lead medallion. The third prohibited begging entirely. Beggars slipped in every morning despite the laws. Better vigilance would have kept them out, but the city couldn't screen everyone. The Fuggerei, a city within a city, could. Its guards kept beggars out.

Fugger insisted on a curfew. Like the gates of Augsburg itself, the gates of the Fuggerei were locked at night. Those who came late had to pay a penny. The penalty aimed at excluding drunks and prostitutes. A drunk, after a night at the tavern, couldn't afford the fine and a prostitute, who might only earn a penny or two for an evening's work, needed accommodations even more economical than the Fuggerei. Fugger led a temperate and disciplined life. He expected the same of his tenants.

One rule was particularly striking: Tenants had to say prayers for Fugger, his nephews and his late mother. Prayers, even those made by third parties, counted as points toward admission into heaven. Fugger wanted the points. But he asked for little compared to others. Residents of Augsburg's St. Anton hospice had to attend church for an hour a day and recite two prayers—the Lord's Prayer and the Hail Mary—fifteen times every morning and evening. They had to say three other prayers before and after meals. If a mass took place in the house chapel, they had to say fifty Lord's Prayers and fifty Hail Marys. Noncompliance meant expulsion. Fugger required only three prayers a day and, consistent with his appreciation of privacy, took it on faith that the residents prayed as asked. Maybe he thought that, with five hundred people praying for him, three prayers a day from each were enough.

Fugger created an endowment for the Fuggerei to last generations. In the letter that created the endowment, he commanded that it exist "as long as the name and male line of the Fuggers lives." Over the years, weavers, distillers, toy makers and artists called the Fuggerei home. There was at least one butcher. He kept a slaughtering table out front. The most famous resident was Mozart's great-grandfather Franz. He lived in the house at Mittelere Gasse 14, from 1681 to his death in 1694.

Eighteen generations later, the male line of Fuggers continues and so does the Fuggerei. It is now a residence for elderly Catholics. The Fugger family pays for the upkeep from timber sales on the land Maximilian sold to Jacob. It still charges the equivalent of one florin a year, or eighty-five euro cents. If the Fuggerei lifted Fugger's image while he was alive, the improvement may have been limited to Augsburg. But in terms of a lasting legacy, Fugger could not have done better.

10

✦

THE WIND OF FREEDOM

In 1891, the president of Stanford University needed a motto for his new school. He turned to the words of the sixteenth-century German writer Ulrich von Hutten. Hutten spent his life arguing for social justice and urging revolution. In Palo Alto, David Starr Jordan found parallels between Hutten's struggles and his own fight for academic freedom. There was one phrase of Hutten's that particularly resonated. *Die Luft der Freiheit weht* (The wind of freedom stirs). Since 1906, that obscure German phrase has encircled the Stanford Tree in the school emblem.

Before the imperial election, Fugger's enemies were commercial rivals, assorted lawmakers and some humanists upset by the rapacious character of big business. After the election, the general public joined in the condemnation. Fugger became a target for workers fed up with the changes sweeping Europe. Like Jordan at Stanford, the people took inspiration from Hutten. Hutten wrote a series of pamphlets that targeted Fugger. Hutten was to Fugger what Ida Tarbell was to John D. Rockefeller. He was the one who made Fugger a public enemy.

Hutten wrote with passion, power and courage. While another social critic, Erasmus, used his pen like a classical pianist, reserving his brilliance and perfect Latin for the elite, Hutten blasted a trumpet for all to hear. He was born in 1488, at a castle outside Frankfurt, into a family of knights. His father recognized that young Ulrich would never be a warrior and sent him to school to learn Latin and read the classics. Constantly on the run from creditors, he bounced around different universities before taking to the road as a roaming intellectual. He won notice with a poem that turned a petty rent dispute into a struggle between barbarism and modernity. Maximilian liked his work and made Hutten his poet laureate in 1517. He crowned Hutten at an Augsburg ceremony within earshot of Fugger's office. Hutten was a young man on the rise. Needing someone with a quick mind to send on a diplomatic mission, Albrecht of Mainz hired him as a counselor.

Hutten, like Maximilian, Erasmus and Cesare Borgia, suffered from syphilis and his illness sparked his first thrust against Fugger. It came in an essay, considered the first medical testimonial, in which Hutten described his boils as "acorns from whence issued filthy stinking matter." The standard cure—mercury—killed as many as it saved. In Augsburg, Hutten learned that West Indian natives used a safe remedy made from the bark of the guaiacum tree. He proclaimed it a miracle cure and, in a digression praising oatmeal and denouncing the German craze for spiced food, he blamed Fugger for the spiraling price of pepper. Hutten would have been furious to know that Fugger later won the monopoly for guaiacum imports and used Hutten's tract to boost sales. The pioneering physician Paracelsus, who had studied with Fuggerau alchemists, later debunked guaiacum. Fugger's nephews fought back with papers attacking Paracelsus.

Hutten earned a good living as an elector's counselor, but his sense of mission overwhelmed his desire for comfort. He joined Luther in attacking the papacy and pointed out Fugger's complicity: "The Fuggers have earned the right to be called the princes of the prostitutes. They have set up their table and buy from the pope what they later sell for more . . . There is no easier way to become a priest than to be friends with the Fuggers. They are the only ones who can achieve anything in Rome."

Hutten's most exhaustive attack on Fugger came in a dialogue called *The Robbers* (1519). In keeping with the ancient Greek practice of putting imagined words in the mouths of real people, he cast Franz von Sickingen, the knight the Habsburgs hired for security during the imperial election, as his hero. Sickingen had charisma, leadership skills and the ability, based on a series of successful campaigns, to attract volunteers for profitable, mercenary adventures. As the owner of several castles and estates, he lived in luxury and, owing to his intellectual curiosity, kept his homes full of poets, musicians and artists. Hutten was his favorite. Rome wanted to arrest Hutten for calling the pope the antichrist. Needing a place to hide, Hutten found shelter with Sickingen.

Sickingen and Hutten, as knights, belonged to a dying order. The word "knight" was as much a social class as it was a job description. Knights were the lowest order of the nobility, but they were

A portrait of Jacob Fugger that appeared on the cover of a sixteenth-century Fugger family chronicle, in which he looks characteristically shrewd and unyielding. *(Courtesy of the Fuggerei Museum, Augsburg, Germany/Bridgeman Images.)*

A roughly contemporary painting showing Fugger's hometown of Augsburg, Germany. *(Augsburger Monatsbuilder by Jorg Breu I [1480–1537], c. 1531; courtesy of Deutsches Historisches Museum, Berlin, Germany; Copyright © DHM/Bridgeman Images.)*

Imperator Cæſar Diuus Maximilianus
Pius Felix Auguſtus

Holy Roman Emperor Maximilian I (ABOVE) and his grandson
and successor Charles V (BELOW) both relied on Fugger's loans
throughout their lives to keep their family, the Habsburgs, on a
firm political footing. *(Portrait of Maximilian I: Early sixteenth-century
woodcut by Albrecht Dürer; courtesy of Private Collection/Bridgeman Images.*
Portrait of Charles V: *Painting by Christoph Amberger [c. 1505–1562/63];
courtesy of Musée des Beaux-Arts, Lille, France/Bridgeman Images.)*

These two woodcuts show some of the typical work that would have been done at the silver and copper mining operations Fugger owned at Schwaz and at Arnoldstein, through which he made much of his money. *(Workers hoisting leather buckets from mine shaft, 1556: Courtesy of Universal History Archive/UIG/Bridgeman Images. Blast furnace for smelting, 1556: Universal History Archive/UIG/Bridgeman Images.)*

The famous *Ermine Portrait* of Queen Elizabeth I of England, in which she is wearing the Three Brothers, one of the world's largest diamonds. Before it became a symbol of Elizabeth's wealth and power, it belonged to Jacob Fugger. *(The Ermine Portrait by Nicholas Hilliard [1547–1619], 1585; courtesy of Hatfield House, Hertfordshire, UK/Bridgeman Images.)*

At the center of this portrait is Pope Leo X, whom Fugger convinced to overturn the Church's ban on money lending. *(Portrait of Leo X, Cardinal Luigi de Rossi and Giulio de Medici, 1518: courtesy of Galleria degli Uffizi, Florence, Italy/Bridgeman Images.)*

Martin Luther was outraged by the Church's sales of indulgences, which were engineered as a scheme to pay back one of Fugger's loans. Luther didn't target Fugger as directly as did his supporter Ulrich von Hutten, who publicly demanded that Jacob Fugger & Nephews be shut down. *(Martin Luther by Lucas Cranach the Elder [1472–1553]; courtesy of Kurpfalzisches Museum, Heidelberg, Germany/ Bridgeman Images.)*

A sixteenth-century woodcut depicting a battle scene from the German Peasants' War, the first great clash between capitalism and communism. Fugger financed the army fighting for the nobility, saving his own fortune and saving free enterprise from an early grave. *(Copyright © SZ Photo/Bridgeman Images.)*

TOMAS MVNCER PREDIGER ZV ALSTET IN DVRINGEN.

A woodcut portrait of Thomas Müntzer, one of the main leaders of the German peasant revolt, who believed in the abolition of private ownership. He and Fugger are iconic opposites in German history; during the Cold War, West Germany put Fugger on a postage stamp and East Germany put Müntzer on a five-mark bill. *(Hand-colored woodcut, c. 1600; courtesy of Private Collection/ Bridgeman Images.)*

Fugger didn't entrust just anyone with the details of his business, but a few people did benefit from his money-making expertise. Here Fugger stands in his Golden Counting Room, teaching his apprentice Matthaus Schwarz about the art of bookkeeping. *(Jacob Fugger in his office, 1518; courtesy of Private Collection/Bridgeman Images.)*

A portrait of his nephew and protégé Anton Fugger, who inherited the business after Jacob died. *(Portrait of Anton Fugger by Hans or Johan Maler [fl. 1510–1523], c. 1500–29; courtesy of Louvre-Lens, France/Bridgeman Images.)*

Two pieces of Fugger's legacy today, both still standing: (ABOVE) a postcard depicting the Fugger Palace, now occupied by several Augsburg businesses, as it looked in the nineteenth century; (BELOW) a recent photo of the Fuggerei public housing project, which remains in operation. *(Fugger Palace: Courtesy of the Private Collection Archives, Charmet/Bridgeman Images. Fuggerei: Courtesy of De Agostini Picture Library/G. Dagli Orti/Bridgeman Images.)*

nobles nonetheless and had privileges that commoners lacked, such as the right to carry swords. Commoners had to step aside when a knight came through or risk being struck down for insolence. Although Sickingen was rich and powerful, the days of knights had passed. Guns were now widespread, reducing the importance of individual battlefield heroics. Monarchs increasingly valued infantry over talent with a horse and sword.

Out of work and needing to supplement meager feudal dues from their estates, knights took to highway robbery. They saw nothing immoral in it. They were noblemen and, as such, believed themselves entitled to grander lifestyles than commoners. If they had to cut throats to obtain the entitlements, so be it. The knights even tried to enshrine their often murderous activities in imperial law, although the attempt failed. Fugger hated the knights because highway robbery disrupted trade and made his staff afraid to travel. He had personally escaped their attacks, but his cousins, his son-in-law and other acquaintances had been victims.

In *The Robbers*, Hutten pits Sickingen in conversation with a Fugger manager. What has Fugger ever done for anybody, Sickingen asks. He never plowed a field nor built a wall. Nor, as a money-lender, did he even take risks. A trader could be stuck with unsalable merchandise and lose everything. But a banker, safe behind a desk, is always covered. If a borrower defaults, the banker takes the borrower's property and sells it at a profit.

The Fugger man is outraged. "We? Thieves?" Knights are the real crooks, he says. They're savage criminals. What else is a highway robber if not that? Sickingen responds with an argument that only a knight could accept. It's one thing to take money with physical strength. That's "honest theft." What Fugger does—earning money with trickery—is truly criminal. "You do not steal by force but by underhanded practices," Sickingen says. Sickingen's anger turns to disgust when he considers how Fugger bought his way into the nobility. Knights earned noble status by risking their lives for their lords. They are truly noble. All Fugger ever did was swindle the innocent. Hutten condensed his feelings in a blistering generalization: "The great robbers are not those whom they hang on the gibbet. They are the priests and the monks, the chancellors, the doctors and the great merchants, especially the Fuggers."

Hutten was relentless. He followed *The Robbers* with a tract that called on Emperor Charles to "abolish the mercantile monopolies" and "stop the drain of money to Rome by the Fuggers." In another, he claimed Fugger once tried to still his pen with bribes: "Fugger money won't silence me, not when it concerns freedom for Germany." Hutten's attacks hit a nerve with the public and printers pumped out copies of his works. Owing to Hutten, Fugger became a symbol of oppression in the popular imagination.

Hutten's solution to Fugger and Germany's other ills came down to a single word: revolution. He campaigned to throw out the old order in favor of a centralized power structure with the emperor on top and knights replacing the bishops and dukes as regional administrators. He called for a German church built on Lutheran principles. He demanded the liquidation of Jacob Fugger & Nephews and the other giant banking houses. Unwilling to stop there, he called for the execution of their leaders. The bankers, he said, deserved "the gibbet." He vowed to make the revolution happen or die trying: "I'll play the game and all the same, even though they seek my life."

Luther wanted change as much as Hutten but disagreed with Hutten's call to violence. He tried to steer Hutten to peaceful measures. "You see what Hutten wants," wrote Luther to a friend, commenting on Hutten's call to arms. "I do not wish that we should fight for the gospel with fire and sword. I have written the man to this effect." In the same year as *The Robbers*, Luther offered his own attack on big business in his *Treaty on Usury*. While Hutten wanted to kill the rich merchants, Luther, a technocrat, suggested regulation in the form of price controls. Luther argued that a merchant should charge no more than his costs plus a trifle—the wages of a laborer—for his efforts. To enforce the rule, he advocated self-regulation because, as he sarcastically noted, government officials were useless. "We Germans have too many other things to do," he wrote. "We are too busy drinking and dancing." But Luther's pacifism only went so far. If the government found a flagrant violator, it should hang him.

Luther's prescriptions showed a hopeless misunderstanding of human motivation. No reasonable business person would build a factory or even buy a loom for no more than laborer wages. But Luther's list of sharp practices—price fixing, monopolies, padding the scales—betrayed real-world knowledge. Merchants used these "dangerous and wicked devices" to "skin" their customers, he wrote. He mentioned no names, but he might have had Fugger in mind throughout. A merchant who drives down prices to put rivals out of business? Fugger. A merchant who strives to corner the market? Fugger again. A man "who cares nothing about his neighbor"? Fugger would deny this, but his poor neighbors, despite the Fuggerei, might have appreciated more charity from the man. Later that year, in his *Open Letter to the German Nobility* (1520), Luther pleads with the princes to crack down on big business. This time, he dispenses with the generalities and attacks Fugger directly: "We must put a bit in the mouths of the Fugger."

❧

Even without the direct assaults, Luther would have had Fugger's attention by now because of his enthusiastic use of a fairly new technological device: the printing press. Gutenberg made his first press in 1450. Its use only took off in the 1520s. This was in large part due to Luther himself. His popularity, the sheer volume of his output, and the fact he wrote in German kept the printers busy. The presses in Germany produced just thirty-five works in the German language in 1513. In 1520, they printed 208, of which 133 were written by Luther. As Luther's sermons, rants and musing found their way to the presses, he developed a huge following. All of Germany seemed to support him. As the papal envoy to Germany reported to Rome, "Nine of ten support Luther and the tenth hates the Pope." Fugger almost had another chance to meet Luther in 1521. The diet that year was scheduled for Augsburg. But because of logistics, the electors moved it to the Rhineland city of Worms. A more experienced politician might have better gauged the public mood and made peace with the monk. But Emperor Charles, living in Spain and untroubled by indulgences and the sale of clerical offices, was naturally inclined to see him as a heretic. Besides, the pope wanted Luther's head and Charles wanted the pope. He needed him as an ally against France. So Charles ordered Luther to appear before him and the electors. He would give Luther one more chance to recant.

Hutten was under a papal arrest warrant when he snuck into Worms to see Luther the night before the first hearing. He begged Luther to lead a revolution and promised to follow him until the end. Now was the time to attack. The people liked the emperor,

Hutten told Luther. But they hated the princes. They hated Rome. And they hated the rich merchants. If the peasants joined with the knights—an unlikely coalition given the class barriers and snobbery of the knights—they could take over Germany and purge it of wickedness. Luther refused. He didn't want to fight the princes. He wanted them to join him against Rome.

Luther's appearance at the Diet of Worms defined the Reformation. Despite the risk of being arrested and burned as a heretic, he appeared before Charles, his prosecutors and a packed meeting hall. Just as in the Fugger Palace four years earlier when he sparred with the cardinal, he refused to recant. His conscience forbid him from doing otherwise. In declaring such, he uttered the phrase that made him immortal. "Here I stand," he told the emperor. "I can do no other."

A riotous crowd was gathered outside to support him. When he emerged from the hall, the crowd mobbed him. Frederick the Wise pushed his way through and greeted Luther with beer in a silver mug. Frederick enjoyed the moment. His boy had done well. The other princes and Fugger, however, had reason to fear. Rebels had scrawled a picture of a leather boot on the walls of Worms. This was the symbol of the *Bundschuh,* a peasant revolutionary movement. The graffiti was a blood-chilling warning to the elite. Luther endorsed nonviolence, but by facing down the establishment and winning, he showed that anything was possible. Luther had ignored Hutten when Hutten wanted Luther to lead an armed revolt. But to the followers of the *Bundschuh,* "Here I stand. I can do no other" wasn't about a negotiated settlement. It was permission to attack.

Fugger's nephew Ulrich represented Fugger at Worms. Compared to the drama of Luther, Ulrich's activities at the diet seemed trivial. But they mattered greatly to Fugger. With little hope of Spanish tax revenue, Fugger had ordered Ulrich to find other forms of repayment. Ulrich struck a deal with the Habsburgs, but it offered less than Fugger hoped. Charles acknowledged his 600,000 florins of election and other debts; he didn't deny that he owed the money. But rather than pay at once, he assigned 400,000 florins, or two-thirds of the obligation, to his nineteen-year-old brother Archduke Ferdinand. Ferdinand governed Austria and agreed to satisfy the obligation by extending the mining concessions a few more years. Charles said nothing about how he intended to pay the other 200,000 florins, only that he would somehow make good. The agreement left Fugger unsatisfied but solvent, and let him sidestep the disastrous end of his cousins.

Charles gave Fugger a job as part of the deal. Private individuals owned Augsburg's printing presses. Recognizing the danger of free speech, Charles took them over and assigned Fugger to run them. The emperor hoped to censor Luther, Hutten and anyone else opposed to him or the pope by putting Fugger at the controls. But as he and Fugger discovered, control of the presses could not still the opposition.

❧

Inspired by Worms, Hutten wanted to do more than criticize. He wanted action and after Luther turned him down, he concentrated his zealous energy on recruiting Sickingen, the powerful knight, to lead the revolution. Sickingen had a limited education but he enjoyed ideas. In the evenings, he and Hutten dined by candlelight and Hutten read to him from Luther or his own works. Sickingen initially laughed at Hutten's rebellious chatter. But little by little, Hutten made him a revolutionary. Their evening conversations became not about whether to fight but how to fight. Sickingen invited other knights to the castle. Lacking Sickingen's money and property, they felt even more aggrieved than their host and signed a pledge committing them to war. Hutten, Fugger's enemy, finally had what he wanted. He had a chance to take the field.

Contemporaries called the coming conflict the Knights' War. The knights didn't fight for territory and the sake of *Hausmachtpolitik* but for ideas and systems. It was a class war that put the entire system at risk. An aide wrote to Duke George that it had been centuries since he and other German princes faced a greater threat. The Knights' War heralded a new phase for Fugger. He had previously financed military campaigns for his clients. This time, he funded soldiers for himself as much as anyone. Fugger embodied the system Hutten sought to capsize. If the system went down, so would Fugger. He had to defend it.

The knights selected Trier as the first target. Near Luxembourg, Trier belonged to the elector—Bishop Richard von Greiffenklau. Fugger knew Greiffenklau from the imperial election. Greiffenklau was in the room with Fugger and Maximilian when Fugger guaranteed Maximilian's lavish bribes for Charles. Fugger paid Greiffenklau 40,700 florins for his vote. By taking on a bishop who was also an elector, Sickingen could attack papal and secular oppression in one stroke. He considered Trier vulnerable. The other ecclesiastical electors—Albrecht of Mainz and Herman of Cologne—were Greiffenklau's natural allies, but they were not inclined to fight. Sickingen assumed Greiffenklau would be on his own.

Sickingen also expected help from within the walls. He believed the people of Trier, inspired by Luther and Hutten, would side with the knights and he only had to light the spark. Full of confidence, he looked ahead and planned to take the war along the length of the Rhine once he took Trier. He would take his revolution across Germany from there. He needed resources to fund his ambition and sent Hutten to raise money in Switzerland where anti-Vatican sentiment ran high.

The knights numbered 10,000 and easily seized the towns on the way to Trier. Trier itself posed a greater challenge. As the attacker, Sickingen could choose the timing of the fight but not the terms. Knights preferred to engage the enemy on horse in an open field. The feast of Michaelmas was approaching. Nothing would suit Sickingen more than to play the role of the archangel Michael, who defeated Satan with sword and shield. He would ideally confront Greiffenklau, one on one, in a dramatic fight to the death. Then the world would see who deserved to live and who should die. But Trier would be siege warfare, not a fight in an open field. The outcome would not depend on the thrusts and parries of Sickingen's sword but on the power of his guns and his stores of ammunition. Cannons had made knights obsolete. Now Sickingen depended on them.

When Sickingen reached the city, he shelled it like Almeida had shelled Mombasa, but with less success. Sickingen discovered he had underestimated Greiffenklau. Like Julius II, the warrior pope, Greiffenklau was more fighter than priest. In the days leading up to the siege, he inspected the towers, walls and weapons. He gave a rousing speech. He shed his bishop's robes for armor. When the battle came, he told the soldiers when to fire. Sickingen shot letters over the wall exhorting the people of Trier to rebel. They ignored him and rallied around the bishop. Sickingen soon ran out of gunpowder and limped back to Ebernburg to wait out the winter and gather strength for another assault.

Fugger and his allies worked on a faster schedule. Fugger gave money to the Swabian League, a military organization that kept the peace in southern Germany, to fight the knights. The league hunted down the rebels one by one in their homes. With his friends either killed or in custody, Sickingen fled Ebernburg to a more formidable castle in Landstuhl. Greiffenklau followed him and pummeled the sandstone walls with his cannons. One of the shells sent Sickingen crashing into a shattered roof support and ripped open his side. Sickingen, poetically felled by a cannon, finally got his dramatic confrontation with Greiffenklau, but only as he lay dying and Greiffenklau climbed over the rubble to accept his surrender. "What has impelled thee," the duke asked, "that thou hast so laid waste and harmed me and my poor people?" Sickingen was short of breath and struggled to talk. "Of that it were too long to speak," he said, "but I have not done nought without cause. I go now to stand before a greater lord."

He died the same day. His death enfeebled the knights as a political class and consigned to history this colorful vestige of the Middle Ages. The princes chased the knights from their castles and made sure they never returned. In Swabia and Bavaria alone, the lords seized twenty-six castles and destroyed the ones they didn't want for themselves. They torched the castle in Absberg. They set gunpowder into the eight-foot walls of Krugelstein castle and blew off the top. The Augsburg guard captain took his men into the forest to blow up the old castle in Waldstein. For Fugger, the triumph in the Knight's War removed an immediate threat by finishing Hutten's days as an agitator. Hutten was still in Switzerland three months later when

Fugger's tree bark let him down. He died from syphilis with a pen as his only possession. But his dream of violent struggle survived in the hearts of a larger, less predictable force. This group hated Fugger and his friends as much as he did. They were Hutten's would-be allies, the great mass at the lowest rung of society and the followers of the *Bundschuh*. They were the peasants. Their anger and resentment was coming to a boil.

❧

The Renaissance gave rise to a new breed of professionals that instantly won the scorn of the general public. The people hated their haughty manners and fancy robes. They hated their use of Latin and their bewildering arguments. Hutten called them "empty windbags." Another writer likened them to locusts: "They are increasing like grasshoppers year by year." Another remarked on their ability to sow chaos: "In my home there is but one and yet his wiles bring the whole country around here into confusion. What a misery this horde brings upon us."

Who were these windbags, locusts and misery bringers? They were, of course, lawyers. Arising from the swamps of canon law, they made their secular debut in Fugger's lifetime. They arose because the emergence of capitalism and the growth of trade necessitated a new, modern body of law and practitioners to make sense of it. The old legal system, known as customary law, used common sense to settle disputes and torture to extract confessions. It worked well enough on feudal estates where everyone knew each other, but failed to keep pace as society transitioned from the medieval to the modern. Rather than develop a new system, society adapted an existing system that was robust enough for commerce and dovetailed with the Renaissance love of everything ancient. This was Roman law, a set of laws Emperor Justinian I codified in 529 to govern the empire and apply common rules from Egypt to England.

Roman and customary law took contrary views of property rights. Customary law, based on Christian values, saw property as communal. To the extent anyone owned anything, it came with a duty to share. The peasants who plowed a lord's fields could hunt in those fields and fish in his streams. Everything belonged to everyone. Roman law, on the other hand, honored the individual over the communal and emphasized the privileges of property ownership instead of the duties. Under Roman rules, a lord paid the peasant for his work and, if the peasant wanted to hunt in his fields, the lord charged him a fee. The Roman system went hand in hand with capitalism because it acknowledged private ownership of property. The princes liked the Roman system because it put property in their hands and left them with more than they had before. The rich merchants liked it because they discovered that a good lawyer could use clever arguments to defeat common sense and win cases they should have lost. Ambitious parents liked it because a legal career could provide a path to riches for their sons. They dreamed their sons would one day work as imperial advisors, town councilors or as hired guns for rich men like Fugger. German universities filled with law students. But the common people hated the new system. The peasants, miners and the working people in the cities viewed Roman law as a system designed not for justice but for deprivation, and as a contrivance unsuitable for those who wanted to live free. They saw Roman law as a system made for slaves and masters.

❧

When the imperial diet came together in Nuremberg in 1522, Luther was back *in absentia* as the main event. Frederick the Wise had refused to hand him over for trial. He had hidden the monk in Wartburg Castle in Thuringia under the alias Junker George (Junker Jörg) and made him grow a beard as a disguise. One year earlier, Charles had a chance to arrest Luther but honored his pledge to leave him alone if he attended.

With the emperor worrying about Luther, a special committee of the diet gathered to fulfill the emperor's postelection pledge to investigate Fugger and other bankers. The committee went over the same ground as the Hansa-inspired effort from years earlier and planned legislation to straitjacket the plutocrats. Fugger was unsure of the emperor's protection. Maximilian had been in his pocket, but Charles was his own man. Fugger had never even met Charles. Unable to predict what Charles would do, he fought the committee on its own terms—that is, with lawyers.

Lawyers staffed the antitrust committee at the Nuremberg diet. They knew what Rome said about monopolies. With irritating pedantry, the staff opened the hearing on the bankers by citing the Greek origins of the word monopoly—*monos* for one, *pōlion* for trade. Legal arguments gave way to venom. The committee said financiers hurt the economy more than "all the highway robbers and thieves combined." It cited the example of Bartholomaus Rehm, an Augsburg banker who had hijacked a wagon train belonging to Fugger's rival Hochstetter a few months earlier. After authorities arrested Rehm, he bribed his jailers and escaped. The committee declared that a textbook example of how financiers did business. First they broke the law. Then they bought their way out. Never mind that Hochstetter, himself one of the biggest bankers in Germany, was the victim in the story, or that the law already had ways to deal with crooks like Rehm. The bankers still had to be stopped.

Fugger hired Conrad Peutinger, the best lawyer he could find. Peutinger had a law degree from Bologna and served as the city manager for Augsburg. He had previously done legal work for Gossembrot and other members of the ill-fated copper syndicate. He had also performed odd jobs for Maximilian. Years earlier, before Hutten became an agitator, Peutinger was the one who nominated Hutten for poet laureate. Peutinger's daughter had placed the laurels on Hutten's head. In his spare time, Peutinger pottered around Augsburg looking for ancient Roman inscriptions to translate. His collection of artifacts included the Peutinger Map, a one-of-a-kind fifth-century diagram that showed the Roman-created, trans-European road system.

Peutinger told the diet that high pepper prices were regrettable but it was unfair to blame the bankers. The fault rested with the king of Portugal and his restriction of supply. He reminded them that there would be no pepper at all if the merchants failed to pass on their costs. As for high metal prices, they benefited society because they allowed mine operators to pay high wages. He advised them to leave the bankers alone because the market was complex and hard to regulate. Who knew what unintended consequences might arise from legislation? The committee was unmoved. With the words *monos* and *pōlion* in the forefront, they declared the bankers violated statute.

Politics played a role. Delegates from Augsburg, Frankfurt,

Cologne and other beneficiaries of big business endorsed Peutinger's views and fought for the status quo. But they lacked the votes in the committee, where the interests of small business dominated. The group drafted legislation that limited a commercial enterprise to no more than 50,000 florins of equity and no more than three locations. If enacted, Fugger—whose equity exceeded 2 million and whose operation had hundreds of offices—would be back to selling textiles out of a back room.

Fugger had tried to fight fair by hiring Peutinger. When that failed, he went back to the tried-and-true methods and bribed influential members of the diet to drop the proceedings. He hoped to settle the matter once and for all. He partly succeeded; the diet broke up before taking action. But to his disappointment, the chief imperial prosecutor, Caspar Marth, took up the fight. Citing Roman law, Marth ordered the bankers to appear in court and face trial. Marth lived in Nuremberg and was influenced by the Nuremberg circle who stirred the usury controversy. Marth nailed a summons for Fugger to the door of Augsburg City Hall. He wanted to embarrass the banker. It was trial by press release.

Marth's attack so angered Fugger that it cracked his usual calm. He was in "very bad humor," said an imperial official. The fact that Charles still owed him money made it even worse. His temper may have explained what he did next. As he was fighting Marth in the spring of 1523, he hit Charles with a sharply worded collection notice. Fugger could not force Charles to pay and the courts were no help because Charles was chief justice. All Fugger could do was appeal to Charles's decency and need to maintain his reputation among creditors. Given the age and Charles's position as the most powerful man on earth, the letter shocks for its bluntness. Fugger follows protocol, but missing from the letter is the look-upon-this-speck-of-dust sycophancy found in Luther's letter to Archbishop Albrecht. Fugger's tone suggests his confidence that Charles would realize he needed to keep Fugger happy. But first Fugger had to slap him in the face.

Most Serene, All-Powerful Roman Emperor
and Most Gracious Lord!

Your Royal Majesty is undoubtedly well aware of the extent
to which I and my nephews have always been inclined to serve
the House of Austria, and in all submissiveness to promote
its welfare and its rise. For that reason, we co-operated with
the former Emperor Maximilian, Your Imperial Majesty's
forefather, and, in loyal subjection to His Majesty, to secure the
imperial crown for your Imperial Majesty, pledged ourselves to
several princes, who placed their confidence and trust in me as
perhaps in no one else.

We also, when Your Imperial Majesty's appointed delegates
were treating for the completion of the above-mentioned
undertaking, furnished a considerable sum of money which was
secured, not from me and my nephews alone, but from some
of my good friends at heavy cost, so that the excellent nobles
achieved success to the great honor and well-being of Your
Imperial Majesty.

It is also well known that Your Majesty without me might
not have acquired the Imperial Crown, as I can attest with
the written statement of all the delegates of Your Imperial
Majesty. And in all this I have looked not to my own profit. For

if I had withdrawn my support for the House of Austria, and transferred it to France, I should have won a large profit and much money, which were at that time offered to me. But what disadvantage would have risen thereby for the House of Austria, Your Majesty with your deep comprehension would understand.

Taking all this into consideration, my respectful request to Your Imperial Majesty is that you will graciously recognize my faithful, humble service, dedicated to the greater well-being of Your Imperial Majesty, and order that the money which I have paid out, together with the interest upon it, shall be reckoned up and paid, without further delay. I pledge myself to be faithful in all humility, and I hereby commend myself as faithful at all times to Your Imperial Majesty.

Your Imperial Majesty's most humble servant. Jacob Fugger

The letter had an immediate effect. Charles wrote Prosecutor Marth and ordered him to drop his case against Fugger and the other bankers. Charles was direct: "In no way will I allow the merchants to be prosecuted."

❧

The protection Charles offered Fugger showed one thing. If a businessperson becomes so hated that reformers call for his scalp, he better have the ruler in his corner. It's a fair bet that Marth and his supporters would have thrown Fugger in jail if Charles had not constrained them. Fugger's indispensability saved him. Maximilian had needed Fugger so desperately that it was sometimes unclear who was in charge. Charles, too, had come to realize that Fugger was a good man to have on his side. But imperial protection couldn't save Fugger from everything. He had to fight some battles on his own.

On August 6, 1524, less than a year after Charles called off the dogs in Nuremberg, the sun rose over Augsburg at five and the city came to life. At eight, Fugger was probably at the window watching a group of demonstrators outside city hall. They were workingmen who, in this city of splendor, struggled to feed themselves. Thirteen hundred came to the square that day—one of every twenty Augsburgers—and they were all angry at Fugger.

The protestors believed it unconscionable that Fugger had everything and they had nothing, that they lived on oats and he ate pheasant, that he wore furs and they wore rags. They agreed with Hutten and his accusation that Fugger became rich on the backs of the poor. But their immediate concern was something other than social equality. They were angry that Fugger sought to oust their priest, a populist reformer named Johannes Schilling. When word leaked of his attempt, they marched on city hall.

Schilling preached at the Church of the Barefoot Monks, the Franciscan church of the city's poor. Of the many Augsburg priests who sympathized with Luther, Schilling was the most strident. He told the congregation to ignore Rome and seek truth in the Bible. This made sense to his listeners because it offered them a more credible path to salvation than the one of indulgences, relics and Hail Marys. Egged on by Schilling, they wanted to break with Rome and, while they were at it, crush the establishment. Alarmed, Fugger wanted to run Schilling out of town.

Schilling had numbers on his side. Nearly 90 percent of Augsburgers were either poor or close to it. But the town administrators answered to Fugger and the city's other rich men. They stood firm and told the mob the priest had to go. The next day, the crowd returned with knives, swords and pitchforks. As tension built, Fugger faced a choice. He could stay in his palace and hope the demonstrators would leave him in peace, or he could flee to Biberbach Castle, the nearest of several fortresses that he owned in the countryside. Flight was risky because of highway robbers. Fugger could try to pay them off but, if the robbers were desperate, they might ambush Fugger's coach, strip it of valuables and slit the banker's throat. Another reason to stay home was the strain of the journey. By this time, Fugger, now sixty-five, was old and sick. He had outlived all six of his brothers and he was among the few in town old enough to remember a world before globes, pocket watches and syphilis. The journey might kill him. Still, the risk was worth it because, behind the thick walls of Biberbach, the protestors could not touch him. It would take cannons, which only the government had, to flush him out. As the noise in the streets grew, Fugger grabbed his cap, called for the horses and headed for his coach.

Peutinger, the city manager and Fugger's lawyer, negotiated with the protestors. Peutinger had been in this situation before. Three years earlier, he and the town council exiled another Franciscan priest, Urbanus Rhegius, for preaching Luther. Now Peutinger looked for compromise and offered to bring back Rhegius if the mob abandoned Schilling. The protestors held firm because they preferred Schilling. Rhegius was an intellectual. Schilling spoke from the heart. They could connect with him and his passion in a way they never could relate to the cerebral Rhegius. At Schilling's urging, they did things like throw salt on the holy water and tear apart sacred books. Peutinger could not sway them. He agreed to let Schilling stay.

Peutinger's surrender was a trick. He only wanted to scatter the crowd. Three days later, the mayor reported to work in armor and the city council renounced the promise to the protestors. Like a dictator seizing the television networks to control the flow of information, the council sent guards to occupy Perlach Tower and make sure protestors sent no signals to confederates beyond the gates. It reinforced the armories and arrested some of the protest leaders. After a quick trial, it pronounced two weavers involved in the protest guilty of treason and sentenced them to death.

The city's execution grounds were just outside the gates. Authorities usually invited the public to watch the hangings and beheadings. Public killings had a social function. They demonstrated the consequences of criminal behavior. Such events were well-attended. But in the case of the weavers, the council feared demonstrations and told no one. It quietly beheaded the men in front of city hall before dawn and cleaned up the blood before anyone knew what happened. Fugger returned home after things calmed down and wrote a letter to his client, George of Brandenburg, the duke he befriended at the Augsburg diet. He explained the events and how he and the council had defended the true teachings of Christ.

⚜

Historians love to study battles because they are turning points. Waterloo, Saratoga, Gettysburg, Stalingrad. Each changed the course of history. Fugger played a part in one such encounter. The Battle of Pavia in 1525 marked a shift in the Italian Wars that had been raging more than thirty years. The Habsburg victory at Pavia, financed by Fugger, cemented the family's dominance in Europe.

No city had changed hands more in Fugger's lifetime than Milan. At one time or another, the French, the Habsburgs, the Swiss and, at rare intervals, even the Milanese themselves controlled it. Milan was the largest city in northern Italy after Venice. It was the hub of the Italian textile trade and a gateway to the rest of the country. Its exposed location on the plains, spreading from the banks of the Po River, made it easy to attack. Maximilian had considered it of such strategic importance that he chose the daughter of a Milanese duke for his second wife.

Charles had taken Milan from France in 1521 and now, four years later, Francis personally took the field to win it back. He surprised the imperial mercenaries guarding the city and chased them to the walled city of Pavia. Winter was approaching and Francis thought that cold and hunger would flush them out. As supplies ran low and the mercenaries grew impatient about not receiving pay, they were about to give up when money—money from Fugger—arrived to pay and supply them. The cash kept the forces together just long enough for Charles's commander, the marquis of Pescara, to storm out of Pavia for an all-or-nothing attack on the French.

On February 24, the day Charles turned twenty-five, Francis led a cavalry charge only to find himself well ahead of his artillery. A century earlier, King Charles VI suffered the worst military defeat in French history when the British and their longbows killed three dukes, eight counts, a viscount and a bishop at the Battle of Agincourt. Pavia claimed fewer lives but in a significant way was more devastating because the imperial forces captured Francis. In the game of *Hausmachtpolitik*, this was checkmate. Pescara's daring, not Fugger cash, won the day. But there would have been no battle without Fugger to keep the troops in the field.

Fugger had given Charles the money after Charles brought him a new opportunity: He leased him the Almadén mercury mine in the Maestrazgo mountains of central Spain. Metallurgists used mercury to extract gold and silver from ore. The Maestrazgos, one of only two mercury sources in Europe and the largest source on earth, belonged to a religious order when Pope Leo died in 1521. The new pope happened to be Adrian of Utrecht, the former tutor of Charles V and his stand-in during the Revolt of the Comuneros. Adrian, now Hadrian VI, took the mines from the order after becoming pope and gave them to Charles. Charles, in turn, sold Fugger a three-year lease on the mines for the enormous sum of 560,000 florins. This was the deal that funded Pescara through the winter.

Once Fugger had the lease, he sent German mining engineers to Spain to increase output. The mine yielded only modest profits despite their efforts. Fugger would have made more money if not for competition. In addition to the Maestrazgos mines, Charles owned the continent's other mercury mine, in Idrija, Slovenia. After leasing Maestrazgos to Fugger, he leased Idria to Hochstetter. Fugger and Hochstetter colluded on silver, but they competed on mercury.

Still, Fugger was satisfied because the Maestrazgos lease made him whole on the election loan. That's because only half of the 560,000 florins loan total came out of Fugger's pocket. The rest cancelled the remainder of the election debt. The financing of the imperial election had been a wild ride for Fugger. But it played out as he had hoped. With sources of income that encircled the globe and a citizenry that included 40 percent of Europe's population, Charles, as Fugger had foreseen, turned out to be creditworthy.

The loan for the Milan campaign helped Fugger in another way. Charles was in his palace in Valladolid when he heard about the capture of Francis. On that same day, he signed a decree, probably drafted by Peutinger, that sanctioned the existence of monopolies in the metal industry. That wasn't all. He also killed the investigation into big business that he had promised after becoming emperor. He notified the imperial diet that his investigators found "no unseemly nor criminal enhancement of prices in Germany or elsewhere." He singled out Fugger and his family for leading "honest, upstanding, Christian and god-fearing lives" and praised Fugger for opposing the "Lutheran heretics." With that, Fugger had nothing more to fear from the diet or the prosecutors.

Fugger, in his collection notice to Charles, had asked the emperor to consider what "disadvantage would have risen thereby for the House of Austria" if he had backed Francis in the election. If Charles hadn't considered the disadvantages before Pavia, he might have considered them afterward. Francis, now a prisoner awaiting transport to Spain, may have been thinking the same thoughts.

In 1525, while King Francis languished in jail, Charles approached Fugger with a plan to break Portugal's lock on the spice trade. The idea was to get to Asia, not by sailing around Africa like da Gama, but by going around South America like Ferdinand Magellan had done three years earlier when his fleet became the first to circumnavigate the globe. By approaching from the east, Spain could sail to the Spice Islands in what is now Indonesia and avoid the Portuguese controlled waters off India.

Fugger agreed to take part and loaded five ships with copper in Lübeck. He sent them to Spain, where they joined a fleet captained by García Jofre de Loaísa. Loaísa planned to trade the copper for nutmeg, cloves and whatever else he could find. Unfortunately for Fugger, storms scattered the fleet and only one ship reached the islands. The Portuguese knew the ship was coming and captured it. Fugger lost his entire investment.

The most interesting aspect of the episode is that Fugger's involvement supports the idea that he funded Magellan's voyage. Officially, Emperor Charles and the Flemish businessman Christopher de Haro paid for Magellan. But according to a lawsuit Fugger's nephews later brought, Haro merely fronted for Fugger. The Fuggers claimed that Haro owed them 5,400 ducats, the exact amount Haro had invested in Magellan's journey. Haro denied owing anything and claimed the money came from his own pocket. There is no question that Fugger and Haro worked with each other; Fugger employed him as his agent on the Loaísa venture. But there is no other record of Fugger backing Magellan, so Fugger's participation is unclear. The lack of documents is easy to explain. Portugal, which hated Spain, was one of Fugger's best customers, and Fugger had no interest in alienating it. That also explains why we have only German records and no Spanish ones of Fugger's funding of Loaísa. Fugger wanted to keep his two-timing secret.

11

⚜

PEASANTS

In 1525, Germany exploded into the largest mass uprising Europe had ever seen. Called the German Peasants' War, it left behind a country of scorched fields, incinerated villages and ravaged monasteries. About 100,000 people lost their lives. So extensive was the barbarism and devastation that the war deterred future generations of would-be rebels. It took another three and a half centuries before the European working class, with the French Revolution, found the courage to try again. Frederick Engels, the collaborator of Karl Marx, wrote a book on the war and argued it prefigured the clash between capitalism and communism of his own day. "It is high time to remind the German people of the clumsy yet powerful and tenacious figures of the Great Peasants' War," he wrote in his preface. The opposing camps of modern times, he said, "are still essentially the same."

Fugger and Engels would have had little to talk about. Fugger, as events will show, defended private ownership to the last. Engels would have taken everything Fugger had and given it to the people. But both saw the rebellion in economic terms. Referring to the peasants as "common riffraff," Fugger argued with unintended irony that the peasants only thought about money. He dismissed their complaints about fishing rights, corrupt priests and inequitable justice. To him, the grievances were a smokescreen for what he considered their real objectives: debt forgiveness and wealth redistribution. Fugger's creation of the Fuggerei housing project showed that he respected anyone who put in a full day's work. But the rebellious peasants failed to qualify. To him, they were lazy parasites looking for handouts. "They want to be rich without working," Fugger wrote in a letter to his client Duke George of Brandenburg. Fugger was more than an observer of the Peasants' War. He was a catalyst. To peasant leaders, he was an oppressor. Many would have been happy to kill him. Forced to take a side to preserve order, Fugger became an agent in their annihilation.

The war began with a countess who lived in a castle in the Black Forest. The countess of Lupfen was an enthusiastic knitter. To wrap her yarn, she used snail shells as spools. They were just the thing—lightweight, the right size, and more attractive than sticks. In the fall of 1524, she ran low and ordered her peasants to suspend their chores. Fetch her some snails, she commanded. It was a trivial request, the sort of order only a pampered countess could get away with. But this day was different. The peasants were in the middle of the harvest and too busy for silly errands. Enraged, they threw down their tools and went on strike. One observer, shocked that the normally obedient peasants defied a countess, said it was as if the crops

demanded water or the cows asked for food. That was an overstate-
ment; there had been protests before. The significance of Lupfen
was that it spread. Before long, peasants across Germany followed
the example.

In Memmingen, sixty miles from Fugger's home in Augsburg,
some 10,000 peasants gathered in the fields outside town. A fur-
rier named Sebastian Lotzer was among the few in that large group
who could read and write. He wrote a petition to the Swabian
League, the regional army that Fugger funded in the Württemberg
and Knights' Wars. Lotzer's document became the manifesto of the
movement. Some of the demands in the Memmingen Articles—tax
relief, hunting privileges, fishing rights—were progressive. Others—
the end of private property and serfdom, and the right to choose
one's own priests—were revolutionary.

Archduke Ferdinand was the most powerful member of the
league. He took notice of the peasants after the exiled duke Ulrich
tried to enlist them in a scheme to regain his duchy. Ulrich wanted
their numbers and offered the peasants privileges if they helped him
chase the Habsburg occupiers out of Stuttgart. Ferdinand wanted
to attack. But the league depended on mercenaries and they were
still limping their way back from Pavia. Besides, Ferdinand had no
money for them. He told the league's commander, George von
Truchsess, to stall while he looked for funds. Hochstetter, the Augsburg banker who sometimes worked with Fugger, hemmed and
hawed. The city of Ulm expressed doubts about strategy. Others
politely declined. After much effort, Ferdinand found a backer. He
wrote Truchsess with the news: "We inform you that we have arranged to borrow from the Fuggers."

For Fugger, this was no time for hesitation, no time for tactical quips of being old and tired, and no time to argue about terms. He recognized the need for haste and became the league's most enthusiastic financier. He knew he and his business were in danger and unless Truchsess defeated the rebels, the peasants would overrun Augsburg and hunt him down. A secondary consideration was commercial. Fugger and other Augsburg merchants had spent hundreds of thousands of florins for goods at the Frankfurt spring fair. With peasants in control of the roads, wagons could not safely transport the items to Augsburg. Fugger wanted to disperse the peasants and liberate his inventory.

Truchsess was a member of the minor nobility. He was one of several remarkable figures who emerged during the war, but he had none of the clumsiness of the tenacious and powerful peasant leaders that Engels venerated. Truchsess cut a striking figure with his powerful frame, curly hair and neatly trimmed beard. Over the ensuing months, he was everywhere. He demonstrated a mix of daring, cunning and single-mindedness that no peasant leader could match. Fugger was lucky to have him on his side. Truchsess had experience with peasants. In 1514, he led troops against the Poor Conrad rebels that ended with the torture and imprisonment of nearly two thousand of their number. In Memmingen, confronted by Lotzer's manifesto, he masterfully strung the peasants along. When they presented demands, he asked for more information. When they gave him the information, he asked for clarifications. He went to meetings where he scheduled more meetings. This continued for weeks and the peasants grew frustrated. But Lotzer, who knew Scripture but nothing about the duplicity of the powerful, became more enthusiastic as Truchsess pumped him with reassurance. He wrote a constitution calling for a peasant-led Christian brotherhood to replace the

princes, bishops and bankers at the top of society. The talk of frater-
nity prompted Leonhard von Eck, the money-loving chancellor of
Bavaria, to make a joke. "I'm repulsed by the peasant offer of brotherly love . . . I'd rather the Fuggers share some of theirs."

❖

Fugger was in no mood for brotherly love. A splinter group from
Memmingen had parked itself outside the gates of Weissenhorn,
the largest of his fiefdoms. They had stolen a cannon and were now
shelling the city walls.

A priest from the little town of Leipheim named Jacob Wehe led
the group. He had grown weary of talk in Memmingen. He thought
all of Lotzer's negotiations and manifestos were getting the peasants
nowhere. Using parish funds, he stocked sixty wagons with provi-
sions, recruited 3,000 peasants and marched north. He targeted
Ulm, the headquarters of the Swabian League and a regional powerhouse. Its looms produced even more cloth than those of Augsburg
and the city was home to what is still the world's tallest church, the
spidery Ulm Minster. To take Ulm would be a tremendous victory for the peasants. Wehe first turned to smaller targets in search
of weapons. His path took him into the heart of Fugger country.
Biberbach, the castle where Fugger had fled during the Augsburg
uprising, surrendered without a fight. So did Pfaffenhoffen, another
Fugger fiefdom. Weissenhorn was the next stop.

Fugger was fond of Weissenhorn. He had poured money into
the city after Maximilian sold it to him in 1507. He renovated buildings, gave money to weavers to buy looms and created a trade fair.
The population stood at only a few thousand. But with Fugger's

help, Weissenhorn had emerged as a rival to Ulm and was gaining on it every day. Still, there was sympathy for the peasant cause behind the walls. The guilds supported the prevailing order, but the workers supported the peasants for the same reason that thousands of peasants had congregated in Memmingen. They felt exploited by their social betters and wanted revenge and a better life. In a scene now immortalized in a painting on the old city wall, the mayor met Wehe when the priest arrived at the gates. Wehe offered him a choice between obliteration and submission. The mayor refused to surrender. Wehe ordered his men to bring out the guns. He started firing and troops behind the walls fired back. Weissenhorn would not have normally had the forces to resist. But as the peasants massed in Memmingen, Fugger took advantage of the time wasted on negotiations to hire soldiers and ship them to Weissenhorn to defend the city. Weissenhorn was not going to let itself go down like Biberbach and Pfaffenhoffen. It was going to resist with all its might. The shooting went on all day and, by nightfall, the peasants had still gotten nowhere. Supporters threw food over the wall for the peasants. But the peasants needed stronger guns more than food. Not wanting to waste his ammunition on a futile cause, Wehe gave up.

He marched the next day on an easier target, the neighboring abbey of Roggenburg. What happened in Roggenburg revealed the disarray of the peasant movement. A rich bishop ran the abbey. The bishop had once tried to divert the streams to bypass Weissenhorn and throw a wrench into Fugger's development efforts. He fled before the peasants arrived and left the abbey unguarded. Wehe and his men destroyed the church and its organ. They grabbed the silver plate and emptied the wine cellar. A drunk peasant put on the bishop's hat and stood at the altar as his friends playfully bowed before him.

When peasants took over a settlement, the smart ones looked for weapons and treasure. The rest drained the wine cellars and pantries. When there was no more loot, they set fire to the buildings. Tapestries, paintings, libraries went up in flames in the name of social justice. At the height of the conflict, much of the country was burning and most of the peasants were drunk. "A more drunken, more full-bellied folk one had hardly ever seen," wrote a witness. If not for the bloodshed, it was debatable whether the rebellion was "a carnival's jest or a war . . . and whether a peasants war or a wine war."

Truchsess, flush with Fugger cash, selected Wehe and his mob as his first target. They had attacked Fugger. Now Fugger's captain, before confronting peasant bands elsewhere, would go after them. Informed that Wehe was back home in Leipheim, Truchsess took it over. His dogs found Wehe crouching in a secret passage in the rear of his parsonage. "Sir," Truchsess said upon confronting Wehe. "It had been well for thee and us had thou preached God's word instead of rebellion."

"You do me wrong," Wehe said. "I have not preached rebellion but God's word."

"I have been informed otherwise," Truchsess said. The sun was setting over Leipheim when Truchsess escorted Wehe to a meadow for his execution. Wehe said a prayer and put his head on the block.

Fugger might not have wanted executions. But he could justly claim self-defense. There were plenty of men like Wehe who would love to slit his throat. So, like it or not, as the head of Wehe, the assailant of his fiefdoms, rolled in the grass, Fugger had his first victim. Fugger blamed Luther for the war, writing to Duke George that the monk was "the initiator and primary cause of this uprising, rebellion and bloodshed in the German nation."

Blood was spilling everywhere. An early incident in the war involving the countess Margarethe von Helfenstein dramatized the stakes and gave legitimacy to Fugger's concern for his personal safety. The countess was the illegitimate daughter of Maximilian. When Ferdinand ordered her husband to defend Weinsberg Castle, she thought she would be safer with the count than at home so she went with him to Weinsberg. Count Helfenstein slew every peasant he met on the way. Peasants followed him to the castle and looked for revenge on the morning of Easter Sunday. Helfenstein lacked a Fugger-financed army. The peasants scaled the walls and captured him and his wife. When the countess begged for mercy, the peasant leader, a baker named Jacklein Rohrbach, pinned her to the ground. "Behold, brethren," he said. "Jacklein Rohrbach kneels on the emperor's daughter." Helfenstein offered Rohrbach his fortune—60,000 florins. Rohrbach laughed and forced Helfenstein to run a gauntlet. He made the countess watch as his men skewered her husband with spears. The Black Hoffman, a gypsy woman who traveled with the peasants, killed him with a final jab. Rohrbach made the countess wear the gray tunic of a peasant and put her on a manure wagon bound for the nearby city of Heilbronn. "In a golden chariot you came. In a dung cart you leave," he said. "Tell that to your emperor." She clutched her son to her breast and cried that she found consolation in Christ. "I have sinned much and deserve my lot," she said. Her son became a priest and she died in a convent. Archduke Ferdinand vowed revenge: "The crime must be chastised with an iron rod."

⚜

Peasants had taken Heilbronn early in the uprising and peasant leaders had made themselves comfortable in town hall. As the leaders plotted strategy, they found the Memmingen Articles hopelessly tame. For one thing, the manifesto said nothing about big business. The Heilbronn peasants considered big business just as responsible for their oppression as the church and the princes. They corrected the omission in a version of their own. "The trading companies, such as the Fuggers, the Hochstetters and the Welsers and the like should be dissolved," read one of the articles.

Not knowing when and if the rebels might come for him, Fugger stayed in Augsburg. With the countryside in flames and Biberbach in peasant hands, no place was safer than home. He joined the planning to defend the city. Like Weissenhorn, Augsburg made a call for soldiers. Precaution was no guarantee of safety. In Austria, the people of Salzburg rose up against Matthaus Lang, the bishop who crowned Maximilian in Trent and oversaw Fugger's mining contracts in Schwaz for the emperor. Lang came from a rich Augsburg family. He was greedy and cruel. After buying his job as bishop, he revoked ancient privileges and raised the taxes on city dwellers and peasants alike. The threat of Luther gave him an excuse to take by force what he failed to get through edict. "First I must undo the burghers," he said. "Those of the country must follow." Like Julius II and Greiffenklau in Trier, he was a cleric with the heart of a general. He left the city in search of troops and returned battle ready on a white charger with four companies of soldiers. After Lang executed a peasant who had liberated a condemned Lutheran priest, the peasants joined with the city dwellers looking for revenge. They surprised Lang's men with sickles and pitchforks, and chased Lang up the hill to Salzburg Castle. The castle had high double walls and was set against a cliff. Cannons could not bring it down. But Lang was trapped. The people of Salzburg, facing no opposition, pounded the gates as Lang cowered inside. He spent four months inside before Truchsess finally sprang him. The four months of bombardment took its toll on Lang. He lost his mind to insanity.

❧

Of all the peasant leaders, Thomas Müntzer was the most dangerous to Fugger. It was not because he had the most guns but because his populist agenda held enormous appeal. A priest from Thuringia, Müntzer was a self-proclaimed mystic who believed in communal property and that only the abolition of private ownership could clear the path for grace. His followers cheered when he promised God would come to kill the rich. "If someone wants to properly reform Christendom, one must throw away the profiteering evildoers," he declared. "The lords themselves are responsible for making the poor people their enemy." The contrast between Fugger and Müntzer could not have been greater. One was the archcapitalist and the other the archcommunist. They became heroes of the competing systems during the Cold War. West Germany put Fugger on a postage stamp and East Germany put Müntzer on a five-mark bill.

Most of the peasant leaders focused on local matters. Müntzer thought globally and took to the road to export his brand of communist millennialism. He preached to crowds in Frankfurt and Hanover and Nuremberg. After creating a ruckus in Fulda, he spent time behind bars. If his disciples hadn't begged him to come home, Müntzer might have stayed in southern Germany and picked up followers in Augsburg. He was fiery, emotional and so convincing that Luther's protector, Frederick the Wise, refused to muzzle him. After hearing him, Frederick no longer knew whom to believe, Müntzer or Luther.

Luther now had a rival, one with a competing and compelling vision of his own. Luther saw Müntzer as an enemy to his own agenda of reforming the church through a strict adherence to Scripture. He and Müntzer agreed that usury and indulgences were criminal, and that Germany needed to break from Rome. But while Luther argued that the Bible, not the pope, had the final word, Müntzer declared that God spoke directly to select individuals, including himself. Müntzer's supporters jeered Luther, eyed him with menace and rang cowbells to drown out his sermons. With his reform movement threatened from below, Luther cast aside his preference for peaceful measures. He became an unwitting ally of Fugger by encouraging the lords to do whatever it took to obliterate the peasants. "Crush them, strangle them and skewer them, in secret places and in the sight of men, even as one would strike dead a mad dog," Luther wrote. "Strike them all and God will know His own." For his part, Müntzer egged on the peasants. "Attack, attack, while the iron is hot," he said.

Truchsess was too busy in western Germany to pursue Müntzer in the east. The task fell to a group of princes that included Fugger's client and pen pal, Duke George of Brandenburg. George joined the dukes of Hesse and Brunswick to attack Müntzer in Mühlhausen, a small city Müntzer had seized and sought to run as a communist utopia. Anticipating trouble, Müntzer cast a cannon and readied for battle. The dukes chased Müntzer and 8,000 followers to a hill above the town. The peasants circled their wagons. Aware of where events were heading, a priest in the peasant camp suggested Müntzer surrender. Müntzer ordered his beheading.

Müntzer tried to keep up spirits. He delivered a rousing speech referencing Gideon, David and other biblical heroes who overcame the odds. He led his people in a hymn, "Now beseech we the Holy Ghost." A rainbow appeared. Müntzer declared it a sign of divine favor. When the deadline passed, the dukes opened fire and destroyed the wagons. The peasants scattered and the dukes killed thousands as they fled. Müntzer disguised himself in a headdress and hid in a hay loft. A servant discovered him and turned him over after finding his knapsack stuffed with incriminating papers. The dukes shoved splinters under Müntzer's fingernails and locked him in a tower as they pondered how to kill him. Müntzer wrote a letter in the tower admitting to having "seductively and rebelliously preached many opinions, delusions and errors . . . against the ordinances of the universal Christian church." The next day, the dukes hauled Müntzer from the tower and Duke George, as committed a Catholic as Fugger, scolded Müntzer for having taken a wife. Priests, he reminded Müntzer, shouldn't marry. After beheading Müntzer, the executioner put his head on a pole and impaled the body. Müntzer would bother Fugger no more.

❧

The rebels pursued bigger targets as more peasants joined the cause. Stuttgart, Frankfurt, Mainz and Strasbourg were less prepared than Weissenhorn and surrendered. It was only a matter of time before the peasants tried for Augsburg. The city was the biggest in Swabia and had everything the peasants needed: gold, weapons and booty.

But Augsburg was ready. Any internal threat had disappeared with the execution of the two Barefoot rebels. The executions had robbed the movement of its will. And like Weissenhorn, Augsburg had hired reinforcements just in case. A peasant band arrived at the gates one day and demanded surrender. They stared up at the soldiers posted on the crenellated stonework. The soldiers told them to scram and that was that. Life in Augsburg went on. Matthaus Schwarz, Fugger's dapper bookkeeper, adapted by making a nifty reversible cloak that let him travel during the Peasants' War and perform his audits without fear. He wore red in town to look sharp and green in the country to blend in.

Truchsess passed Augsburg enroute to a climactic showdown in Boblingen, outside Stuttgart, where he confronted the Memmingen peasants who had started it all. They had 12,000 men. Truchsess had 11,000. The combined figures were huge, similar to those at Pavia. The peasants had thirty-three cannons. Truchsess had even more cannons and vastly superior organization. He installed himself at Böblingen Castle as the peasants took a defensive position behind wet ground. The battle began in mid-morning and was soon a bloodbath. Truchsess chased the peasants into the plains, where he mowed them down by the score. It was all over in a few hours. As the peasants fled, Truchsess sent his cavalry in pursuit. The horsemen spared no one. One witness said peasant bodies lined the road for miles.

Böblingen marked a turning point and the rest of the war was a mop-up. Two events are worth noting because they illuminate the savagery that Fugger sponsored. One was the capture of Rohrbach, the executioner of the emperor's son-in-law. Truchsess chained him to an elm tree with a six-foot leash, surrounded the tree with dry branches and set them on fire. He and his men watched as Rohrbach hopped, squirmed and roasted to death. The other event was the final battle. The last and largest peasant army numbered 23,000 and had concentrated near the Swiss border in Kempten. Truchsess, who was in Ingolstadt, passed Augsburg on his way there. He arrived with inferior numbers and tilted the odds by bribing two of the peasant commanders. The traitors ordered the peasants to leave their safe zone behind a swamp and mass in an open field. Truchsess cut them down by the thousands. Like so many of his other investments, Fugger's bet on Truchsess had paid off. Calm returned to southern Germany. As for the goods stranded after the Frankfurt trade fair in a warehouse, they made it to Augsburg without trouble.

⚜

At this point, the drama shifted to Austria, where another of Engel's powerful and tenacious figures emerges. Archduke Ferdinand called the peasant leader Michael Gaismair "the chief agitator, ringleader and commander" of the Austrian rebels. Gaismair called himself "neither a brigrand nor a murderer," but a "pious and honest man who fought for the sake of the Gospel."

Gaismair was the son of a mine owner. He hated Fugger and the rest of the elite. He noted that Jesus preached a message of love and compassion but society's leaders—men who should have been setting an example and living the Gospel—exploited the common man like the Caesars in ancient Rome. Gaismair combined a popular touch with organizational skills and years of practical, bureaucratic experience. Backed by a people's army of peasants and miners, he forced Ferdinand to consider a new constitution for Tyrol. The constitution contained a special provision about Fugger. It stripped away his mining leases, gave the state his belongings and demanded that he be punished for enriching himself on the backs of the poor.

Gaismair entered the fray at the urging of Fugger's miners. The miners had been radicalized by two priests working the area. The first, Jacob Strauss, had fallen under Müntzer's spell. The pope may have sanctioned lending, but to Strauss and his muse Müntzer, it remained a damnable offense. From the pulpit, Strauss declared Fugger the greatest offender. He didn't mention his name, but there was no question about whom he spoke. "I know very well what I'm saying," Strauss preached. "It is unfortunately the case that many great and mighty principalities are burdened right now to the point that, for each penny per year that the prince receives, an important archusurer gets ten. I don't have to name that land destroyer because he is well known to the whole world."

The other priest, Urbanus Rhegius, was the one Fugger and his friends had chased from Augsburg only to invite back as an alternative to Schilling, the Barefoot monk who inspired the Augsburg uprising. Rhegius landed in Schwaz after leaving Augsburg. The miners were already angry at Fugger before Rhegius got there; they claimed Fugger owed them 40,000 florins in back pay and blamed him for inflation. Rhegius stirred the pot. In early 1525, the miners stopped work and blocked the roads out of Schwaz. When Fugger's pit bosses ordered them back to work, they responded as if they had been asked to fetch snails. They sacked the Fugger offices in City Hall where Fugger's men, on the ground floor of an ancient castle, ran the Tyrolean mint. The miners refused to pick up their tools unless Fugger raised wages and restored back pay.

Innsbruck was less than a day's walk from Schwaz. Archduke Ferdinand feared the miners would come for him. Instead, a mob went south to Brixen, the city where Fugger's client, Melchior von Meckau, had served as bishop. They destroyed the abbey, mocked the old-school priests and chased them from the city. With the bishop on the run, the mob aimed their venom at his secretary, who happened to be Gaismair. Gaismair refused to open the iron doors of the bishop's palace and the attackers rammed the door with such force that the marks remain visible. But the door held and, the next day, in a strange reversal, the peasants named Gaismair their leader.

Gaismair and his supporters terrified the archduke. The duke agreed to their demand to convene a diet and discuss the grievances and Gaismair's draft of a new constitution. At previous diets, only nobles, priests and rich merchants attended. A terrified Ferdinand now made an exception and not only let in the peasants but gave them the largest voice in the proceedings. Gaismair expanded the Memmingen Articles to sixty-two items, including one that blasted Fugger and other bankers for price gouging, diluting the currency and driving independent miners to ruin. Bankers used their money "to spill human blood," it declared. As a result, "the whole world is burdened with their unchristian usury, whereby they amass their princely fortunes."

Ferdinand successfully killed Gaismair's most radical demands—those abolishing the nobility and political power of the clergy. But he stood by as the diet affirmed thirty of the articles outright and another nineteen with modifications. Some of the demands were uncontroversial, such as the introduction of "a good heavy coinage as in the days of Duke Sigmund." Others—price controls, restrictions on moneylending and the redistribution of private property—tried to turn back the clock on economic development. As for the article aimed at Fugger, the diet affirmed and expanded it. The peasants had achieved what the Tyrolean Council had been unable to accomplish. They had gotten the archduke to agree to emasculate Fugger.

But they only won the battle. The meeting was still in session when Ferdinand learned that Truchsess had defeated the German peasants and stood ready to fight in Austria. With that, Ferdinand recovered his roar. He broke up the diet, renounced the articles, chased Gaismair to Switzerland and put a bounty on his head. From encampments in the woods near Zurich, Gaismair pinned his hopes on the Schwaz miners, believing they were the most radical element of society and the most likely to fight to the last. Ferdinand bought them off with concessions. The miners picked up their tools and went back to work. Gaismair became a pawn in future wars between the Habsburgs and Venice. He mounted two armed attacks on Tyrol, but nothing came of them. He survived more than a hundred attempts on his life until, in 1532, two Spanish adventurers tracked him to an apartment in Padua. They snuck in and stabbed him in the heart. They cut off his head for evidence.

Truchsess had an easy time in Austria and only dirtied his hands when he rescued a certain Count Dietrichstein. Fugger knew Dietrichstein from the Congress of Vienna where Fugger gave him a gift to win his favor. When the peasants of central Austria rebelled, Dietrichstein went on a savage killing spree. He sliced the breasts off peasant women and cut babies from their wombs. A peasant army in Tyrol surprised him in the town of Schlamding where Dietrichstein surrendered in return for his life. Truchsess liberated him from a peasant jail and avenged his capture by setting fire to the city. When the peasants, including women and children, tried to flee, soldiers tossed them back into the flames. That finished the peasant revolt in Austria. A satisfied Ferdinand named Truchsess governor of Württemburg and gave him several estates. Fugger, his Austrian mines again secure, turned to other concerns.

❧

In the eventful year of 1525, Fugger faced an even greater challenge than mutinous peasants. A growth had appeared on his body just under the navel. It caused him horrible pain. His doctor, the noted physician Dr. Adolph Occo, recommended an operation.

Medicine was still in an age when physicians were more advisors than practitioners. Trained in the ideas of the ancient Greeks, they thought good health resulted from the right mix of black bile, yellow bile, phlegm and blood—the four humors. They might recommend leeches or vomiting, but they rarely touched patients and left surgery to the people most adept with sharp blades—barbers.

It would be another three hundred years before anyone thought to sterilize surgical instruments. Operations often resulted in death from infections. Fugger's brother Ulrich had died after an operation. Fugger was not going to risk the same fate. He refused surgery. By the time Hungary rebelled, Fugger could no longer get out of bed. A fever left him weak and unable to eat. He battled through the pain and proved himself as tough as ever.

❧

Fugger needed to be tough for what happened next. While the Peasants' War bled itself to death in Germany and Austria, Hungary faced a fresh and vigorous rebellion. King Louis, the Habsburg puppet on the Hungarian throne, had committed the all-too-common error of watering down the currency to balance his budget. The ensuing inflation was more than the people could take. Employers, including Fugger, paid their workers in pennies. Before Louis, the pennies gleamed with silver. Now they were black with iron. Food and other essentials doubled in price while wages stayed put. The public blamed Fugger and Alexi Thurzo, one of the sons of Johannes Thurzo. Alexi was both Fugger's partner and the treasurer of Hungary.

Miners at Fugger's mine in Neusohl demanded higher pay to keep up with their rising expenses. They downed their tools and threatened to flood the mines and loot the warehouses if Fugger refused them. Fugger's agent at the mine, Hans Ploss, negotiated with the miners, but two weeks of talks failed to get them back to work. Copying a tactic of the Swabian League, Ploss softened up the rebels with promises. He brought in 500 soldiers a few weeks later, presumably with Fugger's consent. The soldiers achieved their ends without firing a shot. By pounding on drums and parading around the town square with their guns, the soldiers intimidated the miners into giving up their demands.

Outbreaks flared across Hungary. Zápolya, the rich landowner who had "enthroned" the peasant leader Dozsa, blamed the incompetence of Louis and the Habsburg loyalists who surrounded him. At a meeting of Hungarian nobility, Zapolya forced Bishop Zalkanus, one of the most powerful people in the country, to resign. Louis remained king, but Zapolya appointed the top councilors and personally replaced Archduke Ferdinand as the puppet master of King Louis.

The crisis came to a head when mobs under Zapolya's control swarmed an elite district in Buda and arrested Hans Alber, Fugger's top lieutenant in Hungary. They hauled him to the city's castle and made him sign an agreement handing over the Hungarian mines— the crown jewels of the Fugger enterprise—to the state. Fugger had spent a lifetime creating his Hungarian business. More than anything he ever did, it embodied his organizational, financial and political genius. It created his fortune. At the point of death, Alber gave it away.

Alber's deputy, a man named Hans Dernschwamm, didn't know what had happened to his boss. All he knew is that the mob had busted into the bishop's palace a few doors down from Fugger House and set it on fire and were now coming his way. He gathered gunpowder and muskets, hauled his arsenal to the roof, and took aim. Zápolya had been encouraging the mob to loot and destroy. When he saw the guns on the roof, he feared a slaughter and ordered the rebels home.

Dernschwamm had won himself time. Knowing the mob would return, he took all the money in the safe—about 40,000 florins— and deposited it with the pope's Hungarian office. That carried its own risks, but the cash was safer with the pope than with him. Next, Dernschwamm ordered his best horseman to ride to the Neusohl mine with instructions to haul Neusohl's cash over the Polish border to Cracow. He ordered his people to leave and go to Cracow, too. They would be safe there.

He was preparing his own getaway when he first learned that Alber had surrendered the mines to King Louis. He considered flooding the mines as a parting gift to the king, but decided to keep them dry in the belief Fugger would eventually get them back. Dernschwamm, as able and loyal an employee as a boss could want, left Buda after doing all he could. The mob took Fugger House unopposed. With Dernschwamm out of the way, Louis took over the mines and ordered the operators to send him the profits.

In a letter to his Cracow agent, Fugger again blamed Luther. "The new priests are telling people to disobey the law. That's what the peasants wanted, to ignore their lords." He despaired. "I don't know what is going to happen," he wrote. In a letter to Duke George, Fugger compared King Louis to the peasants. He wrote that Louis only turned on him because he owed him money.

Fugger may have been uncertain, but he wasn't paralyzed. He immediately rallied his network. Pope Clement wrote Louis to praise Fugger and demand that Louis give Fugger his property back. The Swabian League threatened Hungary with invasion. Maximilian announced a boycott of Hungarian products. The duke of Bavaria followed suit, as did the duke of the Palatinate. Even Louis's brother, King Sigismund of Poland, agreed to boycott Hungarian products until Louis returned Fugger's mines.

Economic sanctions as weapons of war go back at least 2,400 years, when Athens hit its neighbor Megara with a trade embargo. But the boycott against Hungary was on a scale rarely witnessed and was about as stark an example of crony capitalism as could be. All of those bringing pressure on Louis were Fugger customers. By doing favors for Fugger, the boycotters could look forward to getting the favors returned.

The boycott wasn't the only reason for Louis to consider surrender. States are often ill-suited to run businesses and Hungary was no exception. Without the expertise of Fugger's mining engineers, the mines lost money. The men Louis sent to run the mines knew nothing about mining. They found the workers unmanageable and were at sea with the pumps and furnaces. It didn't help that

Dernschwamm issued sabotage directives to Fugger loyalists still at the mines. The sabotage, the boycott and the mismanagement overwhelmed Louis. Mines that made enormous profits for Fugger lost money under Louis.

Still, Louis held on. To justify the seizure in the face of the international pressure to return the mines, he forced his captive, Alber, to sign a second document. This one denied that Louis owed Fugger anything and instead claimed that Fugger owed Louis the considerable sum of 200,000 florins. Louis nonetheless agreed to return some valuables to Fugger and asked to open discussions about more loans, but he insisted on keeping the mines and the equipment. He also demanded Fugger drop his claims. Louis's proposal was a nonstarter; it offered Fugger almost nothing. As Fugger told Duke George, "The proposal is worthless and is completely dead."

Fugger continued to work every angle to reclaim his mines. He reached out to Zápolya, sending him a diamond ring and extending greetings to his wife and daughter. Recognizing his own unpopularity, he tried to shift blame away from himself by fingering Alexi Thurzo as the engineer of the currency debasement. In November, imperial representatives joined with councilors from Bavaria and Palatinate in Buda to negotiate with Louis. They hoped for compromise. Louis refused to yield.

⚜

Süleyman the Magnificent, the sultan of Turkey, was in his pleasure gardens in Adrianople when he got word of trouble back home. Süleyman's elite fighters, the Janissaries, had revolted. The revolt strengthened Fugger's hand.

Süleyman was the most feared man in Europe. The great grandson of Mehmed II the Conqueror, the sultan who took Constantinople, Süleyman was determined to extend his reach into the heart of Europe. In 1521, 300,000 of Süleyman's men had marched on the once-invincible citadel Belgrade, a fortress Mehmed himself had failed to take. Süleyman won it after a seven-day siege. The victory gave Turkey control of Hungary's southern flank. Süleyman only stopped there because of distractions elsewhere in the vast Ottoman Empire. Then came Pavia and Charles's stunning capture of King Francis. Süleyman now faced in Charles V a man as powerful as himself. From the time that Mehmed took Constantinople, popes had been calling for a crusade to win it back. The kings of Europe were individually too weak and divided to answer the call. Charles was the first one strong enough to fight the sultan on his own.

The Janissaries were children of Christian slaves, raised as soldiers. The sultan paid them in war loot. If there was no war, there was no pay. Tradition promised them a major campaign—one offering abundant opportunity for plunder—every three years. They demanded Süleyman attack Charles before Charles attacked them. They wanted a quick strike on Buda followed by a march on Vienna. When Süleyman dashed off to Adrianople to think about it, the Janissaries lost patience and rebelled. Adrianople, near the Greek border, had a harem, cedar groves and hunting grounds caressed by a gentle breeze. It was the sultan's favorite place on earth. But after the Janissaries revolted, he had no time for pleasure. He rushed back to Constantinople where he executed the Janissary leader but promised to attack Buda.

Louis desperately needed money to build his defenses. With his biggest source of funding—the copper mines—in shambles, he blinked and offered to give Fugger back his concessions in return for a loan of 150,000 florins. Fugger wasn't willing to compromise. He demanded Louis make good on all the metal he had stolen from Fugger's warehouses and pay the costs for bringing the mines back to order. Fugger told Louis he wasn't picky about the form of payment. Cash, silk, land or jewels would do just so long as they made him whole. He also demanded more privileges. The mining rights, he pointed out, barely covered the costs. Louis would have to offer him more—another mine, some land or a tariff reduction—if he wanted a loan. Louis thought Fugger asked too much. Despite the advancing Turks, he gambled that he could survive without Fugger. He rejected Fugger's offer.

⚜

The letters, contracts and ledgers that make up Fugger's historical trail reveal much about Fugger's commercial activities but little about his personal relationships. We think he and his wife had a frosty relationship, but we don't know for sure. We know Fugger could be jovial with customers and hard on his nephews. But we only know pieces of the story. One of these pieces, however, is revealing; it involves Johannes Zink, Fugger's one-time man in Rome. An incident that took place about the time of Fugger's fight with King Louis shows Fugger to be inflexible if not heartless.

After Fugger sent his nephew Anton to Rome to replace Zink, Zink returned to Augsburg ill and in debt. There was no reason for him to have money troubles. Not only had Fugger paid him handsomely, but Zink, through a mix of purchases and bribes, had acquired enough church offices to make himself rich. But Zink was never satisfied. Wanting to become even richer, he often borrowed money and inevitably lost it in failed schemes.

As the crisis in Hungary raged, Zink's family begged Fugger to see Zink before it was too late. Maybe Fugger felt sentimental toward Zink and wanted to say good-bye. Or maybe he wanted to extract some final intelligence about Rome. In any case, Fugger appeared at Zink's bedside and Zink asked him for help. He told Fugger that his family would lose everything if he died before paying off his debts.

Fugger himself was Zink's biggest creditor. Instead of directly asking Fugger to cancel his obligations, Zink took his house key and tried to force it into Fugger's hand. The meaning would have been clear to contemporaries. If Fugger accepted the keys, he accepted Zink's obligations. Fugger brushed off the keys with such warmth and friendliness that Zink died believing Fugger would protect his interests. Zink's family was shocked when, shortly after Zink died, a bailiff showed up demanding immediate payment of the debt. The Zinks had no income other than what came in from a single church office owned by Zink's son. The matter went to court and the court ruled in Fugger's favor. Fugger confiscated the claim to the church office and presumably resold it. Fugger may have genuinely liked Zink. But a deal was a deal.

12

❧

THE DRUMS GO SILENT

On a December morning in 1525, a small crowd gathered in the chapel in the Fugger Palace and waited for the news. The group included Fugger's nephews, two notaries and some nonfamily members that served as witnesses. Fugger, now deathly ill, was resting in a room next door. After everyone arrived, a door opened and a servant wheeled him in. One of the notaries looked down at words written on paper. Fugger had revised his will and the notary was about to read it. He was about to inform the audience how Fugger had divided the world's greatest fortune. Christmas was three days away. For some, it was coming early.

This was the second draft of the will. Fugger had written the first one four years earlier at the time of Worms. He was feeling his age when the diet convened and had sent his nephew Ulrich, his most likely heir apparent, in his place. Now four years later, Fugger was still alive, but Ulrich was dead. He had passed away at age thirty-five. Ulrich's death forced Fugger to change the will and map out a new plan for succession.

The notary started to read. He began with a surprise. Unlike the first will, the new version included something for Fugger's most trusted employees. It named ten people in Fugger's inner circle and ordered that the nephews look out for them and provide for their retirement. Before, Fugger's attitude was that he paid the staff a fair wage and they deserved no more. He had softened in the interim. The crowd then learned that the new will retained the parts from the original about priests reading masses in Fugger's name and the estate paying peasants to pray for Fugger's salvation. It also underlined Fugger's attachment to the Fuggerei housing project by pledging gifts to all its residents—one florin for families with children and half a florin for those without.

Next came the question of who would control the money. Fugger's nephew Ulrich was dead but Ulrich's brother Hieronymus, the other son of Ulrich the Elder, was still healthy. He was one candidate. The others were the sons of George Fugger, Raymund and Anton. Under the old will, Hieronymus would have gotten Ulrich's share. But Fugger had been watching Hieronymus and decided he was incompetent. In the new will, Fugger reported that Hieronymus "was not especially useful in the family business nor in the business he took on himself. One supposes that he would not enjoy this sort of work." Confirmation of his inadequacy came the following year when Hieronymus got drunk at a wedding and cut the hair off a servant girl. Fugger awarded him shares for a third of the business and forbid him from selling them. He insisted that his stake would go to

Raymund and Anton when he died. This was significant because it affected not only Hieronymus but all the other heirs of Ulrich the Elder. Fugger gave them token amounts. Otherwise, he left them out in the cold. He wanted George's boys, and only them, to carry on the Fugger business and care for the fortune.

Fugger wrote that Anton and Raymund were the ones who had "so far helped me in business." He assigned them different roles. Raymund was often sick and, in Fugger's mind, physically unequipped for the rigors of commerce, so Fugger assigned him the task of running the fiefdoms. He became overseer of Weissenhorn, Kirchberg and the other holdings. Fugger gave the business itself, the largest commercial establishment in the world, to Anton. Fugger made the appointments sound like punishments. They would inherit the "burden, inconvenience and toil" of management.

Anton, thirty-two years old, was four years younger than Raymund, but Fugger liked what he saw. Fugger had trained Anton by sending him on the road and letting him get to know the people and the issues in the regional offices. Anton distinguished himself early when he successfully negotiated a sensitive deal over a Polish gold mine. In Buda, he showed his talent again by spotting a self-dealing agent and firing him. Anton also had a wild side that almost spoiled his career. Once, while on assignment in Rome, he borrowed some money and fell into debt. With the help of an uncle, he recovered the money before Fugger found out. He warned a friend to say nothing: "It will do no good to write about it." The episode sobered him. He succeeded Zink as the lead manager in Rome and successfully worked his Vatican connections to persuade the pope to join the Hungarian boycott.

In the will, Fugger gave his nieces 5,000 florins each, an increase of 1,800 florins from the first will. He never gave any thought to giving them assets. He believed the business and fiefdoms could more easily function with fewer, not more, decision makers. Nor did he want women, including his wife, Sybille, involved in management. His grandmother and mother emerged as first-rate businesspeople after their husbands died. But Fugger wanted men to make all the decisions.

In the first will, Fugger was generous to Sybille. He awarded her the house where the two of them lived before they moved to the palace. This was a sentimental offering. The bigger award was the spectacular neighboring property complete with a garden, chapel and tournament grounds for at-home jousting. The house was newly renovated and stuffed with furniture, tapestries and bejeweled decorations. He ordered the nephews to pay the taxes on the homes and maintain the garden. The old will returned Sybille's 5,000 florins dowry, gave her 5,000 florins in a lump sum for her to keep invested in the business at a 5 percent interest rate and gave her 800 florins a year for expenses. In describing his award to her of the couple's silver plate and jewelry, Fugger added a personal note about a "big diamond and large ruby panel that I recently gave her." Sybille had a full closet. Fugger directed her to keep her best dresses but give the rest to other family members. He also gave her the marital bed. The bed had special meaning for Fugger. He noted how they had slept "by and with" each other in the bed. When she died, Fugger wanted her placed beside him in the Fugger Chapel at St. Anne's.

Now, four years later, Fugger was angry at Sybille and she lost ground. Her family had gone over to Luther and Sybille was leaning that way herself. Fugger may also have known about her affair with Conrad Rehlinger. In the new will, he didn't throw her out into the street. He let her keep her dowry and the silver, but only gave her one house and it wasn't the newly renovated one with the garden and tournament grounds but a more modest one. He canceled the 800-florin annuity and the 5,000-florin lump sum in favor of a 20,000-florin lump sum that would fall to 10,000 florins if she remarried. He let her keep their bed but struck out references to her wardrobe and her right to burial in the Fugger Chapel. Sybille's reaction to the changes was not recorded.

After the reading of the will, Fugger still had two issues to discuss with Anton. The first was Hungary. Under no circumstances, Fugger urged Anton, should he accept anything but full restitution. King Louis would soon be desperate, he told him. Just be patient. As the sultan inched closer, Louis would come around.

The second issue concerned Fugger's burial. St. Anne had fallen into the Lutheran camp when the priest Urbanus Rhegius, after his time in Schwaz, came back to Augsburg and took up a post there. Rhegius tried to be a diplomat; he still offered communion in the old form for traditionalists and in the new form for followers of Luther. Fugger hated the compromise. To him, Rhegius was as bad as Luther. As Fugger lay dying, he told Anton to find him a more suitable burial site. Anton persuaded him that St. Anne, despite Rhegius, remained true to Rome. It was a lie, but it solved the problem of where to lay Fugger's bones.

As this was going on, Archduke Ferdinand visited Augsburg for a meeting with the local nobility. A parade heralded his arrival. In the eight years since the imperial election, Ferdinand, now twenty-three, had come to know and respect Fugger. The Peasants' War had brought them closer and the archduke understood the importance Fugger played in the Habsburg rise. He knew that Fugger only had a few days to live. As the parade marched past City Hall and toward the Fugger Palace, he ordered the trumpets and drums to stop. Wrote Sender, the Augsburg chronicler: "He didn't want to cause inconvenience." Ferdinand's aides exhibited less dignity than their lord. During the Augsburg stay, the aides came to Fugger's side and wheedled a small loan from him.

December 28 was Fugger's last day of work. In his final business decision, he rejected a loan request from Duke Albrecht of Prussia. Albrecht had recently resigned his post as Grand Master of the Teutonic Knights, a Catholic order, to become a Lutheran. The loan was financially solid, but Fugger drew the line at lending to converts. The next day, Fugger fell into a deep sleep "as if," wrote Sender, "he was dead." Dr. Occo shooed away visitors. Others stayed away by choice. When the end came, Fugger's nephews and wife Sybille were elsewhere. Fugger died at 4 a.m. on December 30, 1525, at the age of sixty-six. The only ones with him were a nurse and a priest. The exact cause of death is unknown, but it may have been a prostate infection.

Sender berated himself for missing the signs. A mysterious black rainbow had appeared over Augsburg a couple of months earlier. In hindsight, he writes, the meaning was obvious. The Lord was heralding the death of Augsburg's greatest citizen. There was no other explanation. His chronicle and other sources are mum about Fugger's funeral, so we can only guess at the details. We can assume it lasted all day, that horses drew the hearse and that twelve pallbearers, dressed in black, carried the coffin to the crypt. The only reference to the actual event appears in the fashion book of Matthaus Schwarz. He is mum about the funeral itself, other than that he wore black. The accompanying illustration shows him and no one else.

Sender seems to have missed Fugger more than anyone. He wrote what amounted to a eulogy in his chronicle: "The name of Jacob Fugger and his nephews are known in all kingdoms and countries and in the fields. Emperors, kings, princes and lords sent their greetings to him. The pope greeted him as a son. The Cardinals stood for him. All the businessmen of the world described him as enlightened. He was an ornament for all of Germany."

Sender saved his criticism for Sybille, telling a story of how Sybille bolted from "the home of her blessed husband"—taking along jewels, cash and a maid—to live with the "old man," Rehlinger. Sybille's relatives, in a chronicle of their own, claimed that Fugger's nephews forced her and Rehlinger to marry using "violence and by armed force." That way, they would only have to pay her 10,000 florins instead of 20,000 florins. Even then, the nephews refused to pay. The dispute went to court and Fugger's will prevailed. The nephews paid her only 10,000 florins.

⚜

When Fugger was in his thirties, he had proclaimed his intent to earn a profit as long as he could. He fulfilled the vow by working until the last. More remarkable is that Fugger died solvent. He had played a high-stakes game and, despite numerous assaults, won. Jacques Coeur, the French banker who played the same game, lost everything and died in exile. The Florentine bankers who reigned supreme in the fifteenth century—the Bardi, the Peruzzi and others—fared no better. They fell under the weight of loans to the English kings. Even the Medici only had a brief turn as a financial force. The family was a model of financial strength under Cosimo, but his grandson Lorenzo the Magnificent cared more about state-craft and the arts than business. The firm liquidated two years after Lorenzo's death under the weight of debt. As we've seen, even some Fuggers had flopped. Jacob Fugger's cousin Lucas went bankrupt after lending to the very client, Maximilian of Habsburg, who made Jacob Fugger's career. Fugger's rival Hochstetter was still in business after the Peasants' War, but his luck ran out in 1529 after he tried to take the Maestrazgos for himself and corner the mercury market. Faced with liquidation, he begged "my dear cousin" Anton Fugger for a bailout. Anton refused and Hochstetter went to debtor's prison. Anton was among the creditors and took Hochstetter's castle in Burgwalden, his house in Schwaz and a smelter in Jenbach.

Fugger survived because of a dull but common-sense approach to financial planning. Despite the massive, unsecured loan to Charles V, he had squirreled away enormous sums—putting much of it in real estate—and took fewer risks as he grew older. Yet he continued to earn a strong return as shown in a balance sheet his accountants compiled shortly after his death.

The balance sheet of 1527 is the most important document for understanding Jacob Fugger. For this reason, it's worth considering the nature of the thing. While a balance sheet might seem dull and indecipherable, it is remarkably revealing because it records every activity of an enterprise from the moment of inception. It is like a beach whose shape changes with every wave. Each transaction—every payment to a contractor, every weekly pay stub, every cashed check—adds or reduces the whole. A balance sheet is history condensed to a few lines and a single page. It is the document banks should look at, but often don't, before making a loan. It is the document that prompted Goethe, the great Romantic writer, to declare,

"Double-entry bookkeeping is one of the most beautiful discoveries of the human spirit." He understood how a balance sheet turns the mere recording of receipts and expenses—the stuff of income, cash flow and other accounting statements—into something infinitely more informative.

If someone asked Fugger to name his greatest achievement, he might cite the imperial election or the Fuggerei. Or he could cite the balance sheet of the firm Jacob Fugger & Nephews. It is a summary of a career that, although reduced to numbers, tells a story about kings and queens; popes and loved ones; overseas adventures and shifting fortunes; resource plays and enough real estate to merit the attention of mapmakers. It is the story of his life.

The balance sheet of 1525, Fugger's final year, has been lost like most of Fugger's papers. The 1527 balance sheet offers a fair approximation. On the left side of the page are the assets or the things Fugger owned. The biggest items were loans. Ferdinand owed him 651,000 florins on loans backed by the mines of Tyrol. Charles and the Kingdom of Spain owed him 500,000, backed by the mercury mines of the Maestrazgos. The king of Portugal owed him 18,000. The viceroy of Naples, which was under Ferdinand's control, owed him 15,000. Kasimir of Brandenburg owed him 2,000.

The next largest item, 380,000 florins, was inventory. This was the copper and textiles in the Fugger warehouses. Then came real estate at 150,000 florins. Breaking it down, it valued Weissenhorn and the other Fugger estates at 70,000, the Augsburg properties at 57,000, the Antwerp office at 15,000 and the Rome office at 6,000. It valued Fugger's mines at 270,000, presumably based on the price Fugger paid rather than the value of the ore in the ground. Other assets—cash plus various loans and investments—came to another million.

There was nothing like the Securities & Exchange Commission to keep him honest. Nor were there fixed rules for how to do things like value assets and recognize revenue. Fugger could prepare the books any way he pleased. He took a path of prudence. He wrote off worthless assets and classified others as doubtful. Among those in the doubtful category were 260,000 florins' worth of loans to Hungary, a 113,200-florin loan to Alexi Thurzo and a 20,958-florin loan to Pope Leo X, the pope who sanctioned moneylending. Leo had died but Fugger held a ring as collateral, so there was still a chance of collection if Leo's family wanted the ring back.

On the other side of the page were the liabilities. These were what Fuggers owed to others. The Fuggers owed 340,000 florins to creditors in Spain, 186,000 to other creditors and 290,000 to depositors. These amounts were manageable and indicate that the most striking aspect of the 1527 balance sheet was neither the assets nor the liabilities but the difference between the two. The difference was the equity or what the business was worth. It can be equated with the value of Fugger's personal fortune at the time of his death. His nephews had shares in the business, but he controlled the business completely and had full authority to direct how the money was spent. When he talks in his epitaph about being "second to none in the acquisition of extraordinary wealth," he is referring to the equity. It came to 2.02 million florins. Maybe another businessman before Fugger was worth more than a million in a standard European currency but, if so, none ever put it on paper. If one believes the accounting statements of the Medici, the Medici family, or at least its bank, was never worth more than 56,000 florins. Fugger can claim to be the first millionaire for this reason.

Comparisons between the 1527 balance sheet and earlier ones

indicate his investment return. In 1494, when Jacob became a partner, the firm had equity of 54,385 florins. By 1511, it had grown to 196,791 for a return of 8 percent a year. By 1427, it reached 2.02 million for an annual return between 1511 to 1527 of 16 percent. It's tempting to think that the returns increased in the latter period because Fugger had full control while, in the first term, returns were diluted because he had to share decision making with his brothers. Once liberated from interference, he was free to invest as only he could. But the improved returns are more of a case of Fugger reaping profits from earlier investments. Fugger's total return over the entire thirty-three years was 12 percent. He might have made even more if had taken more risk but, as the balance sheets indicate, he became cautious in the latter phase of his career. With his equity and the cash coming in from his mines, he could have, in modern terms, put his balance sheet to work by borrowing more money and investing it. But what would he have done with the money? Lucrative investment ideas were in short supply, particularly for someone who had to find big opportunities in order to make a difference in his fortune. Besides, he valued wealth preservation above wealth accumulation as he grew older. He wanted the firm to remain standing for generations even if the Habsburgs defaulted. The wisdom of this became clear after his death when Anton made a bad bet on tin, trying but failing to corner the market by monopolizing production in Bohemia and Saxony. The mistake cost nearly 500,000 florins, but the firm survived. No other business in Europe could have withstood a blow like that.

⚜

Fugger was dead but his business kept going. In a development that might have surprised him, it reached its greatest height after his death. Its balance sheet grew bigger, it opened offices in more cities, it became more international and more sophisticated, and retained its influence in world affairs. The Fugger company lasted another hundred years and wrapped up its affairs only because Fugger family members lost interest and preferred to live as country squires rather than businessmen. Some became art patrons and built libraries. Two went bankrupt and took day jobs. Another built a castle larger than the Fugger Palace.

Because his business lived on, a summary of the two generations after Fugger is needed to complete his story. The longevity of the business reflects the strong foundation Fugger created as well as the rarity of his skills and character. Some of his successors had talent but none in the same degree. Nor did they have his conviction, his steely temperament and his ambition. How could they? Great men like Fugger are statistical flukes. But even lesser men can shape history and, in the generations that followed, subsequent Fuggers influenced the major events of the day.

For a time, his nephew Anton Fugger did everything right. The tin fiasco excluded, he was careful and avoided becoming more entangled with the Habsburgs. In his first significant act, he settled with King Louis of Hungary and got the mines back. Louis blinked because, just like Fugger predicted, he needed cash to fight the sultan. After receiving encouragement from France, Süleyman and the Janissaries were now racing across the plains to Buda. Anton loaned Louis 50,000 florins. A Fugger agent later noted that a figure four times as high would have made no difference; the Turks were simply too formidable. Louis took the field himself and the Turks killed him at the Battle of Mohacs. His death made Ferdinand lord of Hungary or at least the areas the Turks failed to control. The Habsburg parts included Neusohl and the other Fugger mines. The relationship between the Fuggers and the Thurzos had soured with the Hungarian uprising in 1525. The Thurzos owed so much money to the Fuggers that Anton went to court to get it back. He settled after the Thurzos surrendered the 50 percent stake in the Fugger-Thurzo partnership to him. Anton retained Alexi as an agent. The Turkish threat eventually became more than Anton could tolerate. He surrendered his Hungarian leases to another Augsburger, Matthias Manlich, who later went bankrupt.

At first, Anton steered a cautious course and let other bankers finance Emperor Charles. Charles had confined his prisoner, King Francis, to a palace in Madrid. Francis promised to give Charles the duchy of Burgundy if he let him go free. After Francis surrendered two of his sons as a security pledge, Charles let him go. Francis renounced the agreement as soon as he crossed the Pyrenees and, with the pope and Henry VIII as allies, declared war on the Habsburgs to chase them out of Italy. Anton refused to fund Charles and Charles managed on money he found elsewhere. This had calamitous consequences. The Habsburg mercenaries went unpaid and, determined to find compensation, they sacked Rome, stole its treasures and killed thousands of defenders. Had the mercenaries been Catholics, they might have spared Rome the worst of the abuses. But many were Lutheran and they let loose their rage in Vatican City. The pope escaped from his palace through a secret passage. Charles was not a party to the sacking, but the episode, more than any other, shaped his reputation in history.

Anton reengaged in 1530 after Charles tried to lessen his own workload by transferring his duties as king of Germany to Ferdinand. Anton financed the handover by bribing the electors with 275,000 florins. This was good business for Anton because he received a claim to the prodigious Neapolitan tax revenues, additional contracts in Schwaz and another chunk of Habsburg real estate.

The election paved the way for what could have potentially been the most exciting chapter in the family's already remarkable history. After Fugger underwrote Ferdinand's election, Charles returned the favor by making Anton a tempting offer—the chance to colonize Peru and Chile. Pizarro had defeated the Incas in 1532 and Charles needed someone to exploit the potential of the Andes. The plan would have made the Fuggers lords over much of South America. Anton agreed but changed his mind before doing anything about it. Meanwhile, the Welsers accepted a similar deal for Venezuela. It generated only losses. The Welser episode is best remembered for a slave voyage in 1528 that brought 4,000 Africans to the colony. Two years later, Charles visited Augsburg and stayed with Anton in the Fugger Palace where he ennobled Anton, Raymund and Hieronymus. They, like their uncle Jacob, could now call themselves counts. And like Jacob, they never did. During the same visit, Anton supposedly burned some imperial documents that obliged Charles to pay off a debt. A Carl Becker painting from 1866 shows Charles seated in a throne as Anton tosses the notes into a fireplace. The piece hangs in the National Gallery in Berlin and the story has become an accepted part of Fugger lore. The story is based on facts. Anton voided some obligations in 1546. Unknown is the value of the burned notes or why Anton did it. It may have been to avoid having to loan Charles even more money.

Anton continued to earn large profits on Schwaz and in Spain.

In 1538, he put down 224,000 ducats for a five-year lease for Mae-strazgos and earned a profit on the deal of 152,000 ducats. He added offices in London, Madrid, Lisbon and Florence, taking the branch count up to seventy. He trafficked in gold from the Ameri-cas and India. The balance sheet of 1546 shows a business that had never been stronger. With assets of 7 billion florins and liabilities of only 2 billion, the capital came to 5 billion, indicating a 7 percent annual return over the nineteen years since Jacob's death. This was a solid but unspectacular return. But in Anton's defense, he battled the law of large numbers. It's easier to grow off a small base than a big one. Jacob had already created the biggest business on earth. Anton had put even more distance between the Fuggers and the others. That alone was remarkable.

Germans, including several electors, rushed to become Protestant in these years. The Fuggers and the Habsburgs stayed true to the old faith, convinced that Luther had it wrong. Raymund Fugger was unsparing when it came to Luther. "He shit on the Gospels," he said. Anton's life became more complicated as tension between the Catho-lics and Protestants escalated. In 1546, the Lutheran princes joined to fight the Habsburgs and claim all of Germany for the new faith. Charles, backed by Anton, defeated the Protestants in one of the great conflicts of the Reformation, the Schmalkaldic War. Charles pressed his luck in the aftermath and tried to force his opponents to return to Catholicism. The Protestants, led by the elector duke Maurice of Saxony, fought back and threatened to bring the hostilities to Augs-burg unless Anton loaned as generously to them as he loaned to the Habsburgs. Anton lied and said he had nothing to give.

The strain of being Europe's most powerful banker wore on Anton in a way that it never did on his robust uncle. He had never asked to lead the business. Fugger turned it over to Anton only because the death of his older cousin Ulrich created a vacancy. He complained of exhaustion and ill heath, and considered liquidating the company's assets, paying off the debts and distributing the wealth among family members. His own sons were too young to take over and his nephews eschewed the responsibility. In his will of 1550, Anton wrote that he would "end and retire" the enterprise.

He might have liquidated immediately if not for the war with the Protestants and the danger to himself and Augsburg. Charles had spent all he had and then some on the war. Anton and other bankers turned him down when he asked for more money. "It seems as if the merchants were agreed together to serve me no longer," Charles said. "I find neither in Augsburg nor elsewhere any man who will lend to me, howsoever large a profit offered him." But the war trudged on and Maurice, backed now with French gold, took over one Habsburg stronghold after another. He chased Charles to Innsbruck where, high in the mountains, Charles was safe but had neither money nor troops. Feeling utterly trapped, the emperor wrote a personal note to Anton, asking him to come to the Tyrolean capital to discuss financing: "This is what I now most greatly desire."

Loyalty and the chance to win generous terms compelled Anton to make the trip. As the negotiations slogged forward, Maurice closed in on Innsbruck. The emperor and his court fled to Villach, hard on the Italian border, joined by Anton. Villach was a pleasant walk to the Fuggerau factory, but Anton had no time for strolls because Charles had already opened surrender negotiations with Maurice.

What follows is a key moment in the story. Mercenaries stood by awaiting Anton's decision. If Anton opened his purse and paid them, Charles could put enough men on the field to chase Maurice back to

Saxony and save at least a part of Germany for Catholicism. If Anton refused, the Protestants would take all of Germany. Anton, sixty-one and exhausted by business, was facing a choice as momentous as the one his uncle Jacob faced when deciding who to support in the 1519 imperial election. Like his uncle, Anton stayed true to the Habsburgs and made an enormous loan of 400,000 florins. Charles and his mercenaries routed Maurice and forced him back to his castle. Northern Germany stayed Protestant and southern Germany Catholic, and so it remains to the present.

Anton managed to sell some assets and dole out the proceeds to his family. By 1553, he had distributed 2 million florins. This was as much as the firm's entire value when Jacob Fugger died and 40 percent of its capital at its peak under Anton seven years earlier. Jacob would never have undertaken such a liquidation, partial or otherwise. He could not bear to shrink the business. But it was the right decision for Anton because it sheltered the family's fortune from the possibility of a Habsburg bankruptcy. Anton continued to discuss a total liquidation but, when a boom gripped Europe in the 1550s, he couldn't resist and he made more loans. The volume of American gold flowing into Europe reached 330 tons a year in the 1540s and tripled over the next ten years. Confident that the supply was limitless and the boom would last, he and other financiers lent freely and borrowed money to make even more loans. Trouble came in 1554 when Spain delayed an interest payment. Anton needed the money to pay a loan. In a panic, he ordered his agent in Antwerp, Matthaus Oertel, to pay whatever interest rate it took to raise money and avoid default "for my credit stands thereon." The Fugger name was strong and a single missed payment could destroy it. Anton knew this: "I think as much on men's mockery as on the money itself."

Despite the warning shot, Anton remained ebullient as New World gold continued to land on European shores. He gave Oertel free rein to lend money in his name and, after Charles's son Philip replaced Charles on the Spanish throne, Oertel loaned Philip 1.5 million florins in anticipation of quick repayment. An installment of 800,000 florins worth of American gold was on its way to Antwerp to repay Anton when Philip ordered the convoy to turn around. He needed the money for a war he was fighting with France. He apologized to Anton but said he had no choice. Anton, in a fury, fired Oertel: "The devil thank you for this agency." But he only had himself and his greed to blame. Anton again faced default. "The creditors are many," he wrote. "A man might shudder to think of them." He paid his bills by going deeper into debt. His greatest fear came in 1557 when Spain defaulted. The crash pushed a number of Augsburg financiers into bankruptcy. By all rights, Anton should have joined them. But he was too big to fail. Philip thought he might need Anton again, so he suspended the claims against him. Other bankers, under court order, held fire sales to raise money and satisfy creditors. Anton continued as if nothing had happened.

Approaching seventy, Anton was ill and needed someone to take over. His eldest nephew, Hans Jacob, refused. Another nephew, George, told Anton "he could not do the work and would rather live in peace." With nowhere else to turn, he went back to Hans Jacob and forced him to step up against his wishes and run the business "until everything be recovered and until trading runs out and comes to an end." Anton died in 1560 and, when personal debts forced Hans Jacob into bankruptcy in 1563, Anton's eldest son, only thirty-four, took over.

The balance sheet from that year shows capital of 663,229

florins. This was still considerable but only an eighth of the peak level. The Genoese and the traders of the Antwerp Boerse had by now surpassed the Fuggers as Europe's leading financiers. The family seemed headed for oblivion. Then a strange thing happened. Markus Fugger, who studied ancient languages and wrote a book on horse breeding, had an aptitude for business that would have impressed his granduncle. He closed unprofitable operations, struck favorable deals on the Spanish mercury mines and used new methods to boost ore production. His efforts combined with inflation to push the firm's capital back to prior levels. Markus distributed most of it to family members.

The Fuggers numbered several dozen when Markus died in 1595. The money Anton and Markus gave them ensured that none of them—nor their children nor their children's children—would ever have to work. Some of the Fuggers worked anyway and used their money to build successful businesses of their own. Others retired and enjoyed quiet lives as members of the landed gentry, living on the estates Jacob Fugger had bought from Maximilian in more adventurous times. In 1620, the Fuggers began using the noble titles Charles had conferred on their forefathers. Jacob and Anton had never used titles because they feared rebuke. The new generation of Fuggers, who were old money by now, didn't care. The Spanish business of the Fuggers, the rump of the enterprise Jacob created, fell into bankruptcy in 1637 but it no longer mattered. The Fugger counts and countesses already had their money. They moved on. Thus the firm of Jacob Fugger & Nephews didn't die as much as fade away.

Epilogue

Three hundred B-17 bombers took off from England for Augsburg on February 24, 1944. They targeted the Messerschmidt operation outside the city and faced little resistance as they dropped 4,300 bombs during a daylight raid on Europe's largest aircraft factory. Twice as many bombers returned that night. This time, they had a different target: civilians. The mission belonged to a plan, realized a year later to its horrific extreme in the firebombing of Dresden, to bomb cities until Germany begged for mercy. Hitler had a soft spot for Augsburg. He dreamed of building on the city's legacy by investing in its industry and creating a "City of German Businessmen." He planned to convert the Fugger Palace into a museum of trade.

If Hitler still had those hopes before the raid, he abandoned them afterwards. Bombers leveled the city. They knocked the top off the Perlach Tower and destroyed City Hall. The Fugger Palace, then a warehouse, went up in flames. The Fugger Chapel at St. Anne survived, but fires badly damaged the crypt and the Dürer designs. The Fuggerei fared worse. The settlement was occupied when the raid came. One resident died when he prematurely left the on-site shelter. Others survived but their homes were gone.

The experience of the Fuggerei mirrored that of the entire city. Only 730 Augsburgers died in the raid but, like the residents of the Fuggerei, the bombs left survivors homeless. Fires set by phosphorus bombs burned through the night. When the flames finally died, Augsburg was in ruins. Augsburg native Bertolt Brecht captured the scene when he said the doors were closed, but the roofs were open.

On the day after the bombing, three prominent Fugger descendants signed a pledge to rebuild the Fuggerei out of their own funds. They worried that if they didn't, their name would be forgotten. These Fuggers, seventeen generations after Jacob Fugger, were nowhere near as rich as their ancestors, but they still enjoyed income on land Jacob acquired centuries earlier. In rebuilding the complex, they got materials from the American occupying forces and followed the original plans except with better plumbing. They increased the number of units from 106 to 140.

One of the three, Josef Ernst Count Fugger von Glott, later took part in the Stauffenberg plot to kill Hitler. He agreed to lead the German state of Bavaria if the plotters succeeded. The Nazis easily identified him and the other conspirators after the attempt failed. The Gestapo found Fugger at his castle in Kirchheim. They hung Stauffenberg and most of the others, using piano wire to ensure slow strangulation. But they let Fugger live. After the war, the Americans released him from a Nazi prison and he served in Germany's first postwar parliament.

While the Fuggers rebuilt the Fuggerei, other Augsburgers rebuilt the city center as best they could. It now looks much like it did in Fugger's time, but the similarity goes no deeper than the facades. At the Fugger Palace, only the entrance and the Damenhof courtyard, now a café where tourists jump into the fountain with bare feet for pictures, look like they did in Fugger's day. Lawyers, dentists and accountants have offices in the rooms where the Fuggers dined with emperors and a Vatican emissary interrogated Luther. The house where Fugger's brothers lived and worked is a department store. A bay window on the second floor sticks out from the shoe department. Done up in Renaissance style, it marks the spot of Fugger's Golden Counting Room. Nearby, a Nuremberg insurance company operates the Prince Fugger Private Bank that its literature says "combines the principle and visionary energy" of its famous founder. The family owns a small stake for the sake of continuity. Augsburg goes by the nickname Fuggerstadt or Fugger City. There are references to Fugger everywhere. In the old town, there is a statue of Hans Fugger, one of Fugger's grandnephews and a great patron of the arts. The Fuggerei has a bust of Jacob.

Weissenhorn also calls itself Fuggerstadt. The stately Fugger headquarters, on the same square as the city hall, recently underwent a renovation. A mural above a gate to the old city shows Fugger's administrator rebuffing the peasants who tried to take the city in 1525. A bookstore across the street brims with Fugger souvenirs and books, including a coffee-table version of Fugger's last will and testament and fictionalized romances about Fugger's life with Sybille. Jacob is a wedding night rapist in Thomas Mielke's potboiler *Jacob the Rich*: "Jacob's rage consumed him. With a cry, he threw the young woman to her side, ripped the night clothes off her young and beautifully freckled body and forced himself inside." On a neighboring shelf is Hilary Mantel's Man Booker Prize-winning *Bring Up the Bodies*. In a scene introducing Thomas Cromwell's young assistants, Cromwell's son Gregory wonders at their handbags, the same whimsical bags favored by Fugger's bookkeeper Matthaus Schwarz. "This season young men carry their effects in soft pale leather bags, in imitation of the agents for the Fugger bank, who travel all over Europe and set the fashion. The bags are heart-shaped and so to him it always looks as they are going wooing, but they swear they are not." In Arnoldstein, Austria, a local businessman built a tower over the ruins of the Fuggerau factory in 1864 to make lead pellets, the kind used in shotgun shells. It now stands empty. There are few traces of Fugger here. The city's Fugger Street runs through an industrial park. A plaque by the monastery mentions that Fugger bought the site of the Fuggerau in 1495, but the nearby 1495 Café that blasts Deep Purple and Foreigner for the lunch crowd has nothing to do with him. The name honors the date when the local brewery made its first batch.

The Fuggers themselves are a scattered bunch who preserve Jacob Fugger's memory by financing the Fuggerei. Count Alexander Fugger-Babenhausen runs the foundation that oversees the housing project and other family projects. After graduating from Harvard, he worked for Morgan Stanley and the private equity firm Texas Pacific Group. He and the others are descended from Jacob's brothers, not Jacob himself. Jacob's only direct descendants come through his illegitimate daughter, Mechtild Belz. At the author's request, genealogists looked for living direct descendants of Jacob and found six.

They are members of a noble family, the Leutrum von Ertingens, from the Stuttgart area. One of them is a banker like his distant ancestor. Five centuries have passed since Mechtild. There could be dozens if not hundreds of others who are descended from her, but they are hard to find because records on most commoners don't go back that far. The genealogists only found the Leutrum von Ertingens because bluebloods are fascinated by family records and keep good accounts.

Another mystery is the fate of the Burgundian Treasure, the jewels the Swiss salesmen sold Fugger. Fugger is believed to have sold the Little Feather to Maximilian for 30,000 florins. It never surfaced again. In 1545, Anton Fugger sold Henry VIII the Three Brothers and some other pieces for 60,000 pounds. The Tudors had the Three Brothers until 1623 when James I sent it off to Spain for his son Charles to present as a wedding gift. It disappeared after that. The Burgundian pieces are believed to no longer exist in their original forms. More likely is the possibility that the owners removed the stones from their settings and sold them individually. The images of all four jewels are preserved. The sketches the salesmen brought Fugger are on display at the Historical Museum in Basel.

In 1530, the pope gave Charles V the imperial crown, the crown that Maximilian repeatedly fought to attain. Charles was the last emperor to wear it. Future emperors saw no value in the crown itself and never bothered making the trek to Rome. Napoleon abolished the Holy Roman Empire in 1806, but the Habsburgs remained European power players for centuries. The eighteenth-century empress Maria Theresa was the only female to lead the Habsburgs. She had a forty-year reign and sixteen children, including Marie Antoinette. In 1864, a Habsburg archduke named Maximilian in honor of his illustrious ancestor left Austria for a tragic three-year run as king of Mexico. Republican rebels, led by Benito Juarez and aided by Washington, who objected to European meddling in the Americas, executed him in front of a firing squad. Archduke Franz Ferdinand became the best-known Habsburg when his assassination in Sarajevo in 1914 sparked World War I. More recently, Otto von Habsburg was crown prince of Austria until World War I brought an end to the monarchy. He served as a German representative to the European Parliament before dying in 2011 at age ninety-eight.

Fugger hoped he had settled the usury controversy in his lifetime, but it came roaring back in 1560 when Jesuit reformers came to Augsburg and tried to abolish lending by refusing to absolve moneylenders. "Real usury is here openly committed . . . whatever objections are made by certain men skilled at law," said Peter Canisius, a Jesuit priest whom Rome later canonized. Ursula Fugger, Fugger's pious grandniece, asked the Jesuits "about the usurious contracts in which our family is not a little entangled." They told her Rome was investigating. The Vatican was in a bind because Lutherans allowed lending and Augsburg might abandon Catholicism if Rome ruled against it. Twenty-one years after the Jesuits sought a ruling, Pope Gregory VIII affirmed Pope Leo's approval of lending and the Jesuits agreed to let the matter go. Today, Christians have gotten over their qualms about moneylending, but Muslims still consider interest charges usurious and Islamic banks get around the restrictions with ruses similar to those used by lenders like Fugger during the Renaissance.

⚜

This book began with the assertion that Fugger was the most powerful businessman of all time. It is an easy claim to make because the competition barely compares. Sure, others made a mark. Before Fugger, Cosimo de' Medici, who was a banker first and a statesman second, ruled Florence and used his influence to keep France and the Holy Roman Empire out of Northern Italy. After Fugger, Samuel Oppenheimer served the Habsburgs under the official designation of "Court Jew," raising money from other Jews to save Vienna from the Turks in 1683 and the Palatinate from Louis XIV in 1688. In more recent times, Francis Baring advised British prime ministers, and, in the United States, J. P. Morgan stopped the Panic of 1907.

Of all the businessmen in history, Nathan Rothschild came closest to matching Fugger's influence and his life and career echoed Fugger's own. Like Fugger, Rothschild came from a family of ten children. He worked in partnership with his brothers and, although not the oldest, rose to lead the family business because of his intelligence and daring. Rothschild began in Germany as a wholesaler of textiles and, like Fugger, left the rag trade for banking. His customers, like Fugger's, borrowed to fight the French. Rothschild financed Wellington at Waterloo and later arranged a 5-million-pound loan to Prussia. He loaned to the Habsburgs. They ennobled him with the title "baron." Rothschild, like Fugger, never used the title but his heirs did. In another coincidence, Rothschild had the lease for the Maestrazgos mercury mines in Spain. The mines still dominated global mercury production in the eighteenth century. Rothschild, again like Fugger, exploited an informational edge. In the most famous episode of his life, he made a killing after his agents alerted him to Wellington's victory at Waterloo an hour before other investors knew. Curiously, the two differed on a fundamental point.

Fugger swore by double-entry bookkeeping. Rothschild never bothered with it until late in life and his sloppy approach to record keeping drove his brothers crazy. Rothschild might have made even more money if he had kept clean books like Fugger.

To say Rothschild and history's other great financiers lacked Fugger's influence in no way diminishes their accomplishments. It's just that Fugger lived at a unique moment where one man could make all the difference. Governments still live beyond their means. They need financing more than ever. But instead of raising money from individuals who risk personal fortunes, they borrow from insurance companies and pension funds that share the risk of government default with taxpayers. The world no longer needs a Fugger because we, as holders of whole life insurance policies and IRAs, have all in a sense become Fuggers.

A writer for *Rolling Stone* memorably described Goldman Sachs in 2010 as a "giant vampire squid." The founder of the German socialist party, Ferdinand Lassalle, used similar language to describe Fugger.

> *Now everyone is in the bankers' hands*
> *They are the true kings in these days!*
> *It looks as if a mammoth suction gear*
> *At Augsburg has been set at work, and*
> *Its tentacles around the land has strung*
> *And all the gold afloat pumps into its chest*

There is no question that Fugger was voracious and that he squeezed workers, bullied his family, fought Luther and funded wars against his own people in the name of social order. But Fugger also created jobs, satisfied consumer demands and spurred progress just like others engaged in the furiously creative give-and-take of capitalism. The spirit that drove him is the same spirit that moves people to develop drugs and vaccines, build skyscrapers and invent more powerful computers. In socialist East Germany, the land of Müntzer, people drove Trabants, plastic death traps barely updated over their thirty-year production run. In capitalist West Germany, in the land of Fugger, they drove Volkswagens, not to mention BMWs, Mercedes and Porsches. The cars not only went fast but competed with each other on fuel efficiency, safety, reliability and value. The lure of profits drove the competitive battle, and the creativity fostered by the battle made the cars better every year and put tens of thousands of people to work. The idea that money spurred initiative would have been obvious to Fugger. He was a champion of free enterprise and unfettered capital markets, a crusader for economic and personal freedom, and a warrior for capitalism at a make-or-break moment in its development. To condemn Fugger for his ambition is to deny the vital forces unlocked in the Renaissance and to dismiss what drives humanity forward.

In the Bavarian city of Regensburg, on a hill overlooking the Danube, is a building that looks like the Parthenon. This is Walhalla, a German hall of fame named after the resting place of the Norse gods. The induction ceremonies are a mirror of German opinion. At the first ceremony in 1842, King Ludwig I filled Walhalla with kings and generals including Maximilian and peasant hunter George von Truchsess. Hitler set the tone for the *Anschluss* in 1937 by ordering the inclusion of Austrian composer Anton Bruckner. He watched as officials pulled a Nazi flag off a marble bust. Regensburg is fifty miles from the Czech border. In 1967, a year before the Prague

Spring, Walhalla thumbed its nose at the nearby communists by welcoming its first and only businessman. Jacob Fugger proclaimed in his epitaph that he was "second to none in the acquisition of extraordinary wealth" and deserved to rank among the immortals. It took nearly five hundred years, but when officials pulled the sheet off his bust and welcomed Fugger into the hall of German gods, he had finally made it.

Afterword

I first heard the name Jacob Fugger in freshman history when the professor introduced us to the Diet of Worms, the epic and hilariously named confrontation between Emperor Charles V and Martin Luther. After becoming a regular visitor to Germany, I heard Fugger's name so often that I became curious. Who was this guy Jacob the Rich, whom Germans praised as the greatest businessman who ever lived? Who was this "German Rockefeller?"

After one of my visits, I decided to do some research but found nothing at my local library. A search on Amazon turned up only one title in English, a 1931 translation of historian Jacob Strieder's *Jacob Fugger the Rich*. I later came to love this quirky and provocative book, but I initially found it challenging for its lack of context and absence of a story line. As I struggled with it, an idea hit me.

Someone should write a book in English that makes Fugger's story accessible to the general reader. Thinking back to an old editor who once reminded me that I was a reporter and shouldn't suggest stories for others to do that I could do myself, I realized that someone was me.

I thought it would be easy. One of my first journalism jobs was preparing entries for the Forbes Richest List. I saw my Fugger book as a Richest List entry only longer. I was dead wrong about that, but my naïveté served me well because I would have abandoned the project if not for that miscalculation. I submitted the final manuscript seven years after that first visit to the library. Much of the work was drudgery. I spent a crazy amount of time reading books in German with the help of a translation app, mostly wedged between fellow commuters on Metro North. But I also had a lot of fun. I scrambled up the steps of a knight's castle near Saarbrücken, peered into the crypts of the Burgundian dukes in Dijon, handled antique torture instruments in Ghent and drank beer along riverbanks in the Carpathians. I got to know Augsburg almost like an insider. I met fascinating people, including several devoted academics and even a few ascot-wearing aristocrats.

A major source for this book was the work of Götz Freiherr von Pölnitz, who once ran the Fugger archives, the family-sponsored research facility in Dillingen, near Augsburg. Pölnitz wrote sixteen books on Jacob Fugger and his nephews. He built on the works of Strieder, Max Jansen, Aloys Schulte and Richard Ehrenberg to create, among other books, the 662-page doorstop *Jakob Fugger* and its 669-page companion volume of notes. The work says just about everything that ever needs to be said about Fugger and is a masterpiece of research. Unfortunately, it has never been translated into

English and even scholars find it wordy and difficult. Günter Ogger, a popular German writer of business books, wonderfully synthesized Pölnitz in the 1978 German bestseller about the Fugger clan, *Kauf dir einen Kaiser*. I relied on Ogger to make sense of Pölnitz. Another enormously helpful book was Mark Häberlein's *The Fuggers of Augsburg*, which appeared in German in 2006 and in English in 2012. Häberlein, a professor at the University of Bamberg, graciously answered questions and helped develop my own thoughts about Fugger. University of Augsburg's Rolf Kiessling and Johannes Burkhardt, University of Pennsylvania's Thomas Max Safley and University of Zurich's Bernd Roeck took time to educate me on Renaissance Augsburg. Columbia University's Martha Howell and Innsbruck University's Heinz Noflatscher illuminated other aspects of the period. Count Alexander Fugger-Babenhausen opened the Fugger Archives to me and Franz Karg, the director, showed me the city and pointed me to the right sources.

The argument that Jacob was the most influential businessman in history is not my own. James Westfall Thompson, a University of Chicago professor for thirty-seven years and one-time president of the American Historical Association, made the assertion in his 1931 book *Economic and Social History of Europe in the Later Middle Ages*. After examining the facts, it became clear to me that Thompson was right and that his assertion, more than any other, explained why Fugger was worth getting to know. For the argument that Fugger was the richest person in history, I used methodology I came across in a 2007 front-page story in the *New York Times*. The piece, based on a 1996 book by Michael Klepper and Robert Gunther, compared a person's net worth with the size of the economy in which he operated and named John D. Rockefeller as the richest American of all time. The method is flawed. As a friend cleverly pointed out, the richest man by this standard was the biblical Adam, who with his partner Eve possessed all global wealth. But I liked this method because it equalizes for differences in economic landscapes across time. To measure Fugger by his worth in gold, a method that has the virtue of adjusting for inflation, chops him down to a mere $50 million, making him no wealthier than, say, a successful real estate developer or a multilocation car dealer. That's not right either.

Special thanks go to retired Colgate University professor Dirk Hoffmann. Dirk taught me German more than thirty years ago and, for this book, helped me decipher Pölnitz, Fugger's letters to Duke George, and the significance of Ulrich von Hutten, among other things. Dirk also provided valuable feedback on the many drafts of this book. His fingerprints cover the pages. Maureen Manning, Jane Reed and the rest of the staff at the University Club library in New York tracked down as many as four books a day for me. I could never have finished the book without their heavy lifting. Priscilla Painton at Simon & Schuster immediately recognized why Fugger's story was worth telling and understood what I was trying to say before I did. Her sharp pencil saved this book from being unreadable mush. David Kuhn was everything an agent should be. Bob Goldfarb and my colleagues at Ruane, Cunniff & Goldfarb provoked me with well-considered questions.

My reader circle of John Bensche, Robert Clymer, Bill Griffin, Doug Lavin, Terence Pare, Robin Rogers, Art Steinmetz, Julia Steinmetz and Martin Uhle read early drafts and provided terrific feedback. Tobias Dose, Regine Wosnitza and my cousin Robert Richter helped with the research. Catherine Minear and Claudia and Andre Castaybert helped with the French. All errors are all mine.

Notes

Pilgrimage to Jerusalem in the Year 1494 (Manchester: University Press, 1907), 29.

8   *"Here wealth flows like water in a fountain."* Crowley, *City of Fortune*, 273.

10   *"If Augsburg is the daughter"* Philippe Erlanger, *The Age of Courts and Kings: Manners and Morals,* 1558–1715 (Garden City, 1970), 90.

13   *"His name is great"* Leopold von Ranke, *History of the Latin and Teutonic Nations* (London: G. Bell & Sons, 1887), 101.

13   *"oon of the myghtyest Princez"* Richard Vaughan, *Charles the Bold: The Last Valois Duke of Burgundy* (Woodbridge, UK: Boydell, 2002), 47.

15   *"respectability, truthfulness"* Pölnitz, *Jakob Fugger,* 14.

17   *Owing to scarcity* Solem Geir. *The Historical Price of Silver.* http:// blog.elliottwavetechnician.com/2010/06/historical-price-of-silver -from.html. Accessed October 20, 2012.

18   *"It is noteworthy"* Vaughan, *Charles the Bold* , 91.

24   *"Happiness is to forget"* Andrew Wheatcroft, *The Habsburgs: Embodying Empire* (London, 1996), 80.

CHAPTER 2: PARTNERS

27   "It cost more than" Janssen, *Anfänge der Fugger*, vol. 2, 61.

28   *Approaching Vienna at the head* R. W. Seton-Watson, *Maximilian I: Holy Roman Emperor*, (London: Constable, 1902), 29.

28   *He became a father* Dan Fagin, *Toms River: A Story of Science and Salvation* (New York, 2013).

29   *"No business can fall apart"* Léon Schick, *Jacob Fugger* (Paris, 1957), 273.

30   *"for the furtherance"* Günther Ogger, *Kauf dir einen Kaiser: Die Geschichte der Fugger* (Munich: Droemer-Knaur, 19798), 42.

33   *Miners barricaded* Gerhard Benecke, *Maximilian I* (London, 1982), 87.

34   *Fugger's letters preceded* Victor Klarwill, *The Fugger News-Letters* (New York, 1926), xiv.

35 *In the summer of 1495* Ranke, *History*, 97.

36 *"I know not which to admire most"* Seton-Watson, *Maximilian I*, 14.

41 *"achieved nothing but"* Pölnitz, *Jacob Fugger*, 72.

CHAPTER 3: THE THREE BROTHERS

48 *"In the year 1498"* Inscription on Fugger wedding portrait, Dirk Hoffman, trans.

49 *"overweening pride"* Mark Häberlein, *The Fuggers of Augsburg (1367–1650)* (Charlottesville: University of Virginia Press, 2012), 177.

51 *"Although Gossembrot is dead"* Pölnitz, *Jakob Fugger*, 134.

51 *"She had gold jewelry"* Clemens Sender, *Die Chroniken der Schwäbischen Städte* (Leipzig:, 1894), 169.

55 *"It gives us Augsburgers"* Donald Lach, *Asia in the Making of Modern Europe* (Chicago, 1994), 162.

57 *"A great Lord came"* Franz Huemmerich, *Die Erste Deutsche Handelsfahrt nach Indien, 1505/1506: Ein Unternehmen der Welser, Fugger und Anderer* Augsburger sowie Nürnberger Häuser (Munich: 1902), 62.

59 *"If the captains went ashore"* Cross, op. cit., 253.

60 *"He has advisors who are"* Pölnitz, vol. 2, 126.

61 *"From our treasury"* Pölnitz, *Jacob Fugger*, 175.

63 *"Thou art our duke"* Ranke, *History*, 93.

64 *Joanna tried to shore up* Bethany Aram, *Juana the Mad* (Baltimore, 2006), 93.

67 *"This he is and will ever be"* Ernest Belfort Bax, *German Society at the Close of the Middle Ages* (London, 1894), 83.

68 *"His majesty wants"* Pölnitz, *Jakob Fugger*, 182.

69 *"Reasonable people know this"* Pölnitz, *Jakob Fugger*, 192.

71 *Fugger served seven popes* Aloys Schulte, *Die Fugger in Rom: 1459–1523* (Leipzig, 1904), 216.

73 *"God must help"* Pölnitz, *Jakob Fugger*, 209.

CHAPTER 4: BANK RUN

82 *"When I go to bed"* Ogger, *Kauf dir einen Kaiser*, 106.

CHAPTER 5: THE NORTHERN SEAS

85 *The attack was the work* Götz von Pölnitz, *Fugger und Hanse* (Tübingen, 1953), 16.

87 *They stretched others on altars* E. Gee Nash, *The Hansa* (New York, 1995), 110.

87 *Fugger kept his activities* Philippe Dollinger, *The German Hansa* (Stanford, 1970), 423.

89 *"valid, reasonable"* Pölnitz, *Fugger und Hanse*, 293

90 *"A captain ought to endeavor"* Niccolò Machiavelli. *The Prince and Other Works by Nicollò Machiavelli.* http://www.gutenberg.org /files/1232/1232-h/1232-h.htm.

91 *"Your good father"* William Coxe (New York, 1971), 362.

94 *"There are fountains"* Antonio de Beatis, *The Travel Journals of Antonio de Beatis* (London, 1979), 67.

95 *"The marble floor was slippery"* Erlanger, *Age of Courts*, 91.

95 *"We were permitted to see two rooms"* Häberlein, *Fuggers of Augsburg*, 149.

96 *Fugger informed the gathering* Strieder, *Jacob Fugger*, 69.

CHAPTER 6: USURY

107 *"Wretched usurers"* Plutarch, www.platonic-philosophy.org. Accessed June 13, 2013.

110 *"Usury means nothing else"* Thomas Storck, "Is Usury Still a Sin?" *The Distributist Review,* January 30, 2012.

112 *enthronement* Bax, *German Society*, 82.

115 *"We cannot do this"* Strieder, *Jacob Fugger* , 200.

116 *"Ask God for my health"* Wiesflecker, *Maximilian I* , 190.

118 *"disadvantage, expletives and ridicule"* Pölnitz, *Jakob Fugger*, 89.

120 *"strange and difficult"* Pölnitz, *Jakob Fugger*, 334.

CHAPTER 7: THE PENNY IN THE COFFER

124 *"God has given us"* Chamberlin, E. R., *The Bad Popes* (New York, 1969), 210.

125 *"How very profitable"* Chamberlin, *The Bad Popes*, 223.

127 *"God himself could not"* Russel Tarr and Keith Randell, *Access to History: Luther and the German Reformation 1517–55*, 3rd ed. (London, 2008).

128 *"As the penny in the coffer"* Bainton, *Here I Stand*, 61.

128 *Frederick's business was relics* Roland Bainton, *Here I Stand* (Peabody, MA 1950), 53.

129 *"The indulgences, which merchants extol"* http://www.spurgeon.org /~phil/history/95theses.htm.

130 *"Father in Christ"* Bainton, *Here I Stand*, 67.

CHAPTER 8: THE ELECTION

133 *The St. Moritz dispute* Benjamin Scheller, *Memoria an der Zeitwende: Die Stiftungen Jakobs Fuggers des Reichen vor und waehrend der Reformation* (Berlin, 2004), 105.

134 *Years later, one of the servants* Pölnitz, vol. 2,, 380.

136 *"These little men"* Pölnitz, op. cit., 340.

137 *"Rarely will three people share"* Schick, *Jacob Fugger*, 235.

137 *"I don't know what"* Häberlein, *Fuggers of Augsburg*, 126.

143 *"The reason that moves me"* R. J. Knecht, *Francis I* (Cambridge, UK, 1982), 72.

144 *"If I only had to deal with the virtuous"* Knecht, *Francis I*, 72.

145 *"These Fuggers are among the greatest"* Beatis, *Travel Journals*, 67.

146 *"a devilish man"* Schick, *Jacob Fugger*, 172.

150 *"Now I must die"* Reston Jr., *Defenders of the Faith*, 23.

CHAPTER 9: VICTORY

156 *"He accomplishes so many"* Pölnitz, *Jakob Fugger*, 427.

157 *"If we had done that"* Schick, *Jacob Fugger*, 173.

158 *"preferred to be a powerful duke"* J. Haller, *The Epochs of German History* (New York, 1930), 101.

159 *"German tongue"* Jervis Wegg, *Richard Pace* (New York, 1932), 146.

161 *"My voice and vote"* The Golden Bull of Charles IV, 1356.

162 *"When the king's highness"* Scarisbrick, J. J., *Henry VIII* (Berkeley and Los Angeles, 1968).

163 *"We should consider"* Deutsche Reichsakten (Gotha, Germany: 1893), 872.

164 *"There is more at the back of his head"* Jack Beeching, *The Galleys at Lepanto* (New York, 1983).

165 *"Spain is not well"* Pölnitz, Jakob Fugger, 449.

165 *"There is no one"* Stephen Haliczer, *The Comuneros of Castile* (Madison, WI, 1981), 164.

167 *"The brothers Ulrich, George and Jacob"* Scheller, *Memoria an der Zeitwende*, 156.

169 *"Commerce is hard on the conscience"* Scheller, *Memoria an der Zeitwende*, 152.

169 *"to honor and love God"* Pölnitz, *Jakob Fugger*, 350.

CHAPTER 10: THE WIND OF FREEDOM

172 *The wind of freedom stirs* http://www.stanford.edu/dept/pres-provost/president/speeches/951005dieluft.html. Accessed March 12, 2012.

173 *"acorns from whence issued"* Peter Ball, *The Devil's Doctor: Paracelsus and the World of Renaissance Magic and Science* (New York, 2006), 224.

174 *"The Fuggers have earned"* Schulte, *Die Fugger in Rom*, 110.

176 *"You do not steal"* Victor Chauffeur-Kestner, *Ulrich Von Hutten: Imperial Poet and Orator* (Edinburgh, 1863), 129.

177 *"You see what Hutten wants"* David-Friedrich Strauss, *Ulrich von Hutten: His Life and Times* (London, 1874), 259.

178 *"Nine of ten"* James Reston Jr., *Defenders of the Faith* (New York, 2009), 53.

183   *"What has impelled thee"* Bax, *German Society*, 183.

184   *"empty windbags"* Strauss, *Ulrich von Hutten*, 204.

189   *"Most Serene, All-Powerful"* Strieder, *Jacob Fugger*, 140.

190   *"In no way will I allow"* Pölnitz, *Jakob Fugger*, 547.

196   *"no unseemly nor criminal"* Ogger, *Kauf dir einen Kaiser*, 210.

CHAPTER 11: PEASANTS

198   *"It is high time to remind the German people"* Frederick Engels, *The Peasants War in Germany*, 3rd Ed. (New York: International Publishers, 2006), xvi.

199   *"common riffraff"* Pölnitz, *Jakob Fugger*, 581.

200   *"We inform you that"* Tom Scott and Bob Scribner, eds., *The German Peasants' War: A History in Documents* (Amherst, NY, 1991), 153.

204   *"A more drunken"* Bax, Ernest Belfort, *The Peasants' War in Germany* (London, 1899), 164.

204   *"I have been informed otherwise"* Bax, *Peasants' War*, 195.

204   *"the initiator"* Pölnitz, *Jakob Fugger Zeitungen und Briefe an die Fürsten des Hauses Wettin in der Frühzeit Karls V. 1519–1525. Nachrichten von der Akademie der Wissenscgaft in Göttingen* (Göttingen, 1941).

205   *"In a golden chariot"* Bax, *Peasants' War*, 130.

205   *"The crime must be chastised"* Bax, *Peasants' War*, 195.

206   *Not knowing when* Scott, *German Peasants' War*, 259.

206   *"First I must undo"* Bax, *Peasants' War*, 190.

208   *"Crush them, strangle them"* Bax, *Peasants' War*, 279.

209   *"seductively and rebelliously"* Bax, *Peasants' War*, 268.

211   *"the chief agitator, ringleader and commander"* Walter Klassen, *Michael Gaismair: Revolutionary and Reformer* (Leiden: E. J. Brill, 1978), 88.

212   *"I know very well"* James M. Stayer, *The German Peasants' War* (London, 1991), 48.

213   *"a good heavy coinage"* Scott, *German Peasants' War*, 268.

218   *"The new priests"* Pölnitz, *Jakob Fugger*, 159.

219   *"The proposal is"* Ogger, *Kauf dir einen Kaiser*, 159.

CHAPTER 12: THE DRUMS GO SILENT

225 *"burden, inconvenience and toil"* Pölnitz, *Jakob Fugger*, 642.

228 *"He didn't want to cause"* Sender, *Die Chroniken*, 167.

228 *"as if he was dead"* Sender, *Die Chroniken*, 170.

229 *"violence and by armed force"* Häberlein, *Fuggers of Augsburg*, 183.

230 *"my dear cousin"* Häberlein, *Fuggers of Augsburg*, 73.

231 *"Double-entry bookkeeping"* J. W. Goethe, *Wilhelm Meister's Apprenticeship*, bk. 1.

232 *The Fuggers owed 340,000* Richard Ehrenberg, *Capital and Finance in the Age of the Renaissance* (London, 1923).

237 *"He shit on the gospels"* Häberlein, *Fuggers of Augsburg*, 183.

238 *"It seems as if the merchants"* Ehrenberg, *Capital and Finance*, 107.

239 *"my credit stands"* Ehrenberg, *Capital and Finance*, 110.

239 *"I think as much"* Ehrenberg, *Capital and Finance*, 110.

240 *"The creditors are many"* Ehrenberg, Capital and Finance, 115.

240 *"he could not do the work"* Häberlein, Fuggers of Augsburg, 94.

EPILOGUE

244 *In rebuilding the complex* Gregor Nagler, *Das Wegwerfen ist ja ein Irrglaube* (Berlin, 2009).

245 *"combines the principle"* https://www.fuggerbank-infoportal.de /about/history.php. Accessed October 8, 2013.

246 *"Jacob's rage consumed him"* Thomas Mielke, *Jakob der Reiche* (Cologne, 2012), 236.

246 *"This season young men"* Hilary Mantel, *Bring Up the Bodies* (New York, 2012), 52.

249 *Like Fugger, Rothschild came* Schick, Jacob Fugger, 13.

250 *Rothschild never bothered* Niall Ferguson, *The House of Rothschild* (New York, 1998), 103.

250 *"Now everyone is in"* Ferdinand Lassalle, *Franz von Sickingen* (New York, 1904), 25.

Bibliography

Ackroyd, Peter. *Venice: Pure City*. New York: Doubleday, 2009.

Adamski, Margarete. *Herrieden Kloster, Stift und Stadt im Mittelalter bis zur Eroberung durch Ludwig den Bayern im Jahre 1316*. Kallmünz über Regensburg: Buchdruckerei Michael Lassleben, 1954.

Andrean, Linda. *Juana the Mad: Queen of a World Empire*. Minneapolis: University of Minnesota Center for Austrian Studies, 2012.

Aram, Bethany. *Juana the Mad*. Baltimore, Maryland: Johns Hopkins, 2006.

Bainton, Roland. *Here I Stand*. Peabody, MA: Hendrickson Publishers, 1950.

Ball, Philip. The *Devil's Doctor: Paracelsus and the World of Renaissance Magic and Science*. New York: Farrar, Straus and Giroux, 2006.

Barstow, Anne. *Witchcraze. A New History of European Witch Hunts*. New York: HarperCollins, 1995.

Baum, Wilhelm. *Sigmund der Münzreiche: Zur Geschichte Tyrols und der habsburgischen Länder im Spätmittelalter.* Bozen, Austria: Athesia, 1987.

Baumgartner, Frederic J. *France in the Sixteenth Century.* New York: St. Martin's Press, 1995.

Bax, Ernest Belfort. *The Peasants' War in Germany 1525–1526.* London: Swan Sonnenschein, 1899.

Bax, Ernest Belfort. *German Society at the Close of the Middle Ages.* London: Swan Sonnenschein, 1894.

Beatis, Antonio de. *The Travel Journals of Antonio de Beatis.* London: Hakluyt Society, 1979,

Beeching, Jack. *The Galleys at Lepanto.* New York: Charles Scribner's Sons, 1983.

Benecke, Gerhard. *Maximilian I (1459–1519).* London: Routledge & Kegan Paul, 1982.

Blickle, Peter. *The Revolution of 1525.* Baltimore: Johns Hopkins University Press, 1985.

Black, Jeremy. *A Brief History of Slavery.* Philadelphia: Running Press Book Publishers, 2011.

Blanchard, Ian. *The International Economy in the "Age of the Discoveries," 1470–1570.* Stuttgart: Franz Steiner Verrlag, 2009.

Blockmans, Wim. *Emperor Charles V: 1500–1558.* London: Arnold, 2002.

Brotton, Jerry. *The Renaissance Bazaar: From the Silk Road to Michelangelo,* Oxford: Oxford University Press, 2002.

Brandi, Karl. *The Emperor Charles V.* London: Jonathan Cape, 1939.

Brant, Sebastian. *The Ship of Fools.* New York: Dover Publications, 1944.

Bryce, James. *The Holy Roman Empire.* Oxford: T. & G. Shrimpton, 1864.

Chamberlin, E. R. *The Bad Popes.* New York: Dorset, 1969.

Chauffeur-Kestner, Victor. *Ulrich Von Hutten: Imperial Poet and Orator.* Edinburg: T. & T. Clark, 1863.

Cliff, Nigel. *Holy War: How Vasco da Gama's Epic Voyages Turned the Tide in a Centuries-Old Clash of Civilizations.* New York: HarperCollins, 2011.

Cosman, Madeleine Pelner. *Medieval Holidays and Festivals*. New York: Charles Scribner's Sons, 1981.

Coxe, William. *The History of the House of Austria*, Vol. 1. New York: Arno Press, 1971.

Crowley, Roger. *Empires of the Sea*. New York: Random House, 2009.

Crowley, Roger. *City of Fortune: How Venice Rules the Seas*. New York: Random House, 2013.

Dauser, Regina and Magnus Ferber. *Die Fugger und Welser*. Augsburg: Verlagsgemeinschaft Augsburg, 2010.

Denucé, Jean. Magellan. *La question des Moluques et la première circumnavigation du globe*. Academie Royale de Belgique. Memoires. Vol. 4. 1908–1911.

Deutsche Reichsakten. Gotha, Germany: F. A. Perthes, 1893.

Dollinger, Philippe. *The German Hansa*. Palo Alto, California: Stanford University Press,. 1970.

Donavin, Georgiana, Carol Poster, and Richard Utz, eds. *Medieval Forms of Argument*. Eugene, Oregon: Wipf and Stock Publishers, 2002.

Duby, Georges. *The Early Growth of the European Economy*. Ithaca, New York: Cornell University Press, 1973.

Eberhard Unger, Eike. *Die Fugger in Hall i. T.* Tübingen: J.C.B. Mohr, 1967.

Ehrenberg, Richard. *Capital and Finance in the Age of the Renaissance*. New York: Harcourt, Brace. 1923.

Erlanger, Philippe. *The Age of Courts and Kings: Manners and Morals*, 1558–1715. Garden City: Anchor Books, 1970.

Erlichman, Howard. *Conquest, Tribute and Trade: The Quest for Precious Metals and the Birth of Globalization*. Amherst, NY: Prometheus Books, 2010.

Fagin, Dan. *Toms River: A Story of Science and Salvation*. New York: Random House, 2013.

Ferguson, Niall. *The House of Rothschild*. New York: Penguin, 1998.

Flynn, Thomas. *Men of Wealth: The Story of Twelve Significant Fortunes from the Renaissance to the Present Day*. New York: Simon & Schuster, 1941.

Frey, Albert Romer. *A Dictionary of Numismatic Names.* New York: American Numismatic Society, 1917.

Freytag, Gustav. *Pictures of German Life in the XVth, XVIth, and XVIIth Centuries,* Vol. 1. London: Chapman and Hall, 1862.

Frisch, Werner. *Ulrich von Württemberg: Herzog und Henker.* Erfurt: Sutton Verlag, 2011.

Gaiser, Horst. *Jakob Fugger und Lamparter: Wandmalerei, uneheliche Kinder, Zinsstreit. Bayern, Schwaben und das Reich.* Festschrift für Pankraz Fried zum 75 Geburtstag. Augsburg: Peter Fassl, 2007.

Garlepp, Hans-Hermann. *Der Bauernkrieg von 1525 um Biberach a.d. Riss.* Frankfurt: Verlag Peter Lang, 1987.

Geffcken, Peter. *Jakob Fuggers frühe Jahre, Jakob Fugger (1459–1525): Sein Leben in Bildern.* Augsburg, 2009.

Geir, Solem. The Historical Price of Silver. http://blog.elliottwave technician.com/2010/06/historical-price-of-silver-from.html.

Gies, Frances. *The Knight in History.* New York: Harper & Row, 1984.

Gies, Joseph and Frances. *Life in a Medieval City.* New York: Harper & Row, 1969.

Gies, Joseph and Frances. *Merchants and Moneymen: The Commercial Revolution, 1000–1500.* New York: Thomas Y. Crowell, 1972.

Gladwell, Malcolm. *Outliers: The Story of Success.* New York: Little, Brown, 2008.

Goertz, Hans-Juergen, ed. *Profiles of Radical Reformers: Biographical Sketches from Thomas Muentzer to Paracelsus.* Kitchener, Ontario: Herald Press, 1982.

Greenfield, Kent Roberts. *Sumptuary Laws of Nuremberg.* Baltimore: Johns Hopkins University Press, 1918.

Greif, B. *Tagebuch des Lucas Rem aus den Jahren 1494–154*1. Augsburg: J. N. Hartmann'schen Buchdruckerei, 1861.

Groebner, Valentin. *Liquid Assets, Dangerous Gifts, Presents and Politics at the End of the Middle Ages.* Philadelphia: University of Pennsylvania Press, 2002.

Häberlein, Mark. *The Fuggers of Augsburg.* (1367–1650). Charlottesville, VA: University of Virginia Press, 2012.

Haebler, Konrad. *Die Geschichte der Fuggerschen Handlung in Spanien.* Weimar: Verlag von Emil Felber, 1897.

Haliczer, Stephen. *The Comuneros of Castile.* Madison, Wisconsin: University of Wisconsin Press, 1981.

Haller, J. *The Epochs of German History.* New York: Harcourt, Brace, 1930.

Heal, Bridget and Grell, Ole Peter. *The Impact of the European Reformation: Princes, clergy and people.* Burlington, VT: Ashgate Publishing, 2008.

Herberger, Theodor. *Conrad Peutinger in seinem Verhaltnisse zum Kaiser Maximilian I.* Augsburg: F. Butsch, 1851.

Howell, Martha. *Commerce before Capitalism in Europe, 1300–1600.* New York: Cambridge University Press, 2010.

Howell, Martha C. *The Marriage Exchange.* Chicago: University of Chicago Press, 1998.

Hümmerich, Franz. *Die Erste Deutsche Handelsfahrt nach Indien, 1505/1506: Ein Unternehmen der Welser, Fugger und Andere.* Munich: Verlag von R. Oldenburg, 1902.

Huizinga, Johan. *The Autumn of the Middle Ages.* Chicago: University of Chicago Press, 1996.

Hunt, Edwin S. *The Medieval Super Companies: A Study of the Peruzzi Company of Florence.* Cambridge: Cambridge University Press, 1994.

James, Pierre. *The Murderous Paradise: German Nationalism and the Holocaust.* Greenwood Publishing Group, 2001.

Jansen, Max. *Die Anfänge der Fugger.* Leipzig: Verlag von Duncker & Humboldt, 1907.

Jansen, Max. *Jakob Fugger.* Leipzig: Verlag von Duncker & Humboldt, 1910.

Jardine, Lisa. *Worldly Goods: A New History of the Renaissance.* New York: W.W. Norton, 1996.

Johnson, Paul. *A History of the Jews*. New York: Harper & Row, 1987.

Klassen, Walter. Michael Gaismair: *Revolutionary and Reformer*. Leiden: E. J. Brill, 1978.

Kellenbenz, Hermann. *The Rise of the European Economy: An Economics History of Continental Europe: 1500–1750*. New York: Holmes & Meier Publishers, 1976.

Kerridge, Eric. *Usury, Interest and the Reformation*. Aldershot, UK: Ashgate, 2002.

Kiessling, Rolf. *Bürgurliche Gesellschaft und Kirche in Augsburg im Spätmittelalter*. Augsburg: Verlag H. Mühlberger, 1971.

Klarwill, Victor. *The Fugger News-Letters*. New York: G.P. Putnam's Sons,. 1926.

Klepper, Michael and Gunther, Robert. *The Wealthy 100*. Secaucus, NJ: Carol Publishing, 1996.

Knecht, R. J. *Francis I*. Cambridge: Cambridge University Press. 1982.

Kramer, Heinrich, and James Sprenger. *The Malleus Maleficarum*. New York: Dover Publications, 1971.

Kraus, Victor. *Maximilian I: Vertraulicher Briefwechsel mit Sigmund Prueschenk Freiherrn zu Stettenburg*. Innsbruck: Verlag der Wagner'schen Universitaets-Buchhandlung, 1875.

Krondl, Michael. *The Taste of Conquest: The Rise and Fall of the Three Great Cities of Spice*. New York: Ballantine Books, 2007.

Lach, Donald. *Asia in the Making of Modern Europe*. Chicago: University of Chicago Press,1994.

Lassalle, Ferdinand. *Franz von Sickingen*. New York: New York Labor News Company, 1904.

Lehrer, Steven. *Explorers of the Body: Dramatic Breakthroughs in Medicine from Ancient Times*. New York: Doubleday, 1979.

Lieb, Norbert. *Die Fugger und die Kunst*. Munich: Verlag Schnell & Steiner, 1952.

Luther, Martin. *The 95 Theses*. http://www.spurgeon.org/~phil/history/95theses.htm. Accessed September 12, 2012.

Lutz, Heinrich. *Conrad Peutinger; Beitraege zu einer politischen Biographie.* Augsburg: Verlag Die Brigg, 1958

Machiavelli, Nicolo. *The Prince and Other Works by Niccolò Machiavelli.* Translated by W. K. Marriott. http://www.gutenberg.org/files /1232/1232-h/1232-h.htm

Maltby, William. *The Reign of Charles V: 1500–1558.* New York: Palgrave, 2002.

Mantel, Hilary. *Bring Up the Bodies.* New York: Henry Holt, 2012.

Martin, Marty. *Martin Luther.* London: Penguin, 2004.

Mathew, K. S. *Indo-Portuguese Trade and the Fuggers of Germany.* New Dehli: Mahohar, 1997.

Matthews, George. *News and Rumor in Renaissance Europe: The Fugger Newsletters.* New York: Capricorn Books, 1959.

McNally, Raymond T., and Radu Florescu. *In Search of Dracula.* New York: Warner, 1973.

Midelfort, H. C. Erik. *Witch Hunting in Southwestern Germany 1562–1684.* Stanford, CA Stanford University Press, 1972.

Mielke, Thomas. *Jakob der Reiche.* Cologne: Emons, 2012.

Miskimin, Harry A. *The Economy of Later Renaissance Europe 1460-1600.* Cambridge: Cambridge University Press, 1977.

Mollat, Michel and Wolff, Philippe. *The Popular Revolutions of the Late Middle Ages.* London: George Allen & Unwin, 1973.

Moore, T. Sturge. *Albert Durer.* Bibliobazaar. www.bibliobazzar.com /opensource.

Moxey, Keith. *Peasants, Warriors and Wives: Popular Imagery of Reformation.* Chicago: University of Chicago Press,1989.

Nash, E. Gee. *The Hansa.* New York: Barnes & Noble Books, 1995.

Nagler, Gregor. *Raimund Von Doblhoff und der Wiederaufbauder Fuggerei, der Fuggerhaüser, der Fuggerkapelle und des Neuen Baues in Augsburg.* Berlin: Dietrich Reimer Verlag, 2009. As found in Werner Lutz, *Raimund von Doblhoff 1914–1993.*

———. *Das Wegwerfen ist ja ein Irrglaube: Doblhoff, Raimund von,*

Architekt zwischen Rekonstruktion und Innovation. Edited by Werner Lutz. Berlin: Dietrich Reimer Verlag, 2009.

Newett, M. Margaret. *Canon Pietro Casola's Pilgrimage to Jerusalem in the Year 1494*. Manchester: University of Manchester Publications, 1907.

Noonan, John. *The Scholastic Analysis of Usury*. Cambridge, Mass.: Harvard University Press,. 1957.

Oberman, Heiko. *Masters of the Reformation: The Emergence of a New Intellectual Climate in Europe*. Cambridge: Cambridge University Press, 1981.

Ogger, Günther. *Kauf dir einen Kaiser: Die Geschichte der Fugger*. Munich: Knaur Taschenberg Verlag, 1979.

Palme, Rudolf. *Pits and Ore and Tallow Candles. A Short History of Mining at Schwaz*. Schwaz: Berenkamp Verlag, 1993.

Payne, Robert. *Leonardo*. Garden City: Doubleday, 1978.

Pirenne, Henri. *Medieval Cities: Their Origins and the Revival of Trade*. Princeton, NJ: Princeton University Press, 1969.

Pölnitz, Götz von. *Die Fugger*. Tübingen: J.C.B. Mohr, 1999.

Pölnitz, Götz von. *Jakob Fugger*. Tübingen: J.C.B. Mohr, 1949.

Pölnitz, Götz von. *Fugger und Hanse*. Tübingen: J.C.B. Mohr, 1953.

Pölnitz, Götz von. *Jakob Fugger Zeitungen und Briefe an die Fürsten des Hauses Wettin in der Frühzeit Karls V. 1519–1525. Nachrichten von der Akademie der Wissenscgaft in Göttingen. Göttingen*: Vanderhoeck & Ruprecht, 1941.

Ranke, Leopold von. *The History of the Latin and Teutonic Nations*. London: George Bell and Sons, 1887.

Ranke, Leopold von. *The History of the Reformation in Germany*, Vols. 1–2. New York: Frederick Ungar Publishing Co., 1966.

Redlich, Otto Reinhardt. *Der Reichstag von Nürnberg 1522–1523*. Leipzig: Gustav Fock,1887.

Reston, James Jr. *Defenders of the Faith*. New York: Penguin, 2009.

Reyerson, Katherine L. *Jacques Coeur: Entrepreneur and King's Bursar*. New York: Pearson Longman, 2005.

Robbins, Rossell. *The Encyclopedia of Witchcraft and Demonology*. New York: Crown Publishers, 1959.

Robertson, William. *The History of the Reign of the Emperor Charles*. Vol, 2. London. W. and W. Strahan, 1769.

Roeck, Bernd. *Geschichte Augsburg*. Munich: Verlag C.H. Beck, 2005.

Roover, Raymond de. *The Rise and Decline of the Medici Bank 1397–1494*. New York: Norton, 1966.

Roper, Lyndal. *The Holy Household: Women and Morals in Reformation Augsburg*. Oxford. Claredon Press, 1989.

Rublack, Ulinka. *Dressing Up*. Oxford: Oxford University Press, 2010.

Safley, Thomas Max. *Charity and Economy in the Orphanages of Early Modern Augsburg*. New Jersey: Humanities Press, 1997.

Scarisbrick, J. J. *Henry VIII*. Berkeley; Los Angeles: University of California Press, 1968.

Scheller, Benjamin. *Memoria an der Zeitwende: Die Stiftungen Jakobs Fuggers des Reichen vor und waehrend der Reformation*. Berlin: Akademic Verlag, 2004.

Scott, Tom, and Bob Scribner, eds. *The German Peasants' War: A History in Documents*. Amherst, NY: Humanity Books, 1991.

Schad, Martha. *Die Frauen des Hauses Fugger von der Lilie*. Augsburg: J.C.B. Mohr, 1989.

Schulte, Aloys. *Die Fugger in Rom: 1495–1523*. Leipzig: Verlag von Duncker & Humblot, 1904.

Sender, Clemens. *Die Chroniken der Schwaebischen Staedte*. Leipzig. Verlag von S. Hirzel, 1894.

Seton-Watson, R.W. *Maximilian I, Holy Roman Emperor*. London: Archibald Constable & Co, 1902.

Schick, Léon. *Jacob Fugger*. Paris: S.E.V.P.E.N, 1957.

Sider, Sandra. *Handbook to Life in Renaissance Europe*. New York: Facts on File, 2005.

Sigerist, Henry. *Four Treaties of Theophrastus Von Hohenheim, called Paracelsus*. Baltimore: Johns Hopkins Press, 1941.

Simnacher, Georg. *Die Fuggertestamante des 16. Jahrhunderts.* Weissen-horn: Anton H. Konrad Verlag, 1994.

Spufford, Peter. *Handbook of Medieval Exchange.* London: Royal Histori-cal Society, 1986.

Spufford, Peter. *Power and Profit: The Merchant in Medieval Europe.* New York: Thames and Hudson. 2002.

Stahl, Alan. *Zecca: The Mint of Venice in the Middle Ages.* Baltimore: Johns Hopkins University Press, 2000.

Stayer, James M. *The German Peasants' War.* London: McGill-Queen's University Press, 1991.

Strauss, David-Friedrich. *Ulrich Von Hutten, His Life and Times.* London: Daldy, Isbister,. 1874.

Strauss, Gerhard. *Manifestations of Discontent in Germany on the Eve of the Reformation.* Bloomington: Indiana University Press, 1971.

Strieder, Jacob. *Jacob Fugger the Rich: Merchant and Banker of Augsburg, 1459–1525.* New York: Archon Books, 1966.

Storck, Thomas. "Is Usury Still a Sin?" *The Distributist Review*, January 30, 2012.

Sugar, Peter. *A History of Hungary.* Bloomington: University of Indiana Press, 1994.

Tanner, Marcus. *The Raven King: Matthew Corvinus and the Fate of his Lost Library.* New Haven: Yale University Press, 2008.

Tarr, Russel, and Keith Randell. *Access to History: Luther and the German Reformation 1517–55* [Third Edition]. London: Hodder Education, 2008.

Thausing, Moritz. *Albert Dürer: His Life and Works.* London: John Mur-ray, 1882.

Todd, Walker. *Progress and Property Rights: From the Magna Carta to the Constitution.* Great Barrington: American Institute for Economic Research, 2009.

Unger, Miles. *Machiavelli.* New York: Simon & Schuster, 2011.

Unger, Miles. *Magnifico: The Brilliant Life and Violent Times of Lorenzo de' Medici.* New York: Simon & Schuster, 2008.

Van der Wee, Herman. *The Growth of the Antwerp Market and the European Economy*. The Hague: Martinus Nijhoff, 1963.

Vaughan, Richard. *Charles the Bold: The Last Valois Duke of Burgundy*. Woodbridge, UK: Boydell, 2002.

Wehr, Gerhard. *Thomas Muentzer*. Hamburg: Rowolt, 1972.

Wegg, Jervis. *Richard Pace*. New York: Barnes & Noble, 1932.

Wellman, Sam. *Frederick the Wise: Seen and Unseen Lives of Martin Luther's Protector*. Lexington, KY: Wild Centuries Press, 2011.

Wheatcroft, Andrew. *The Habsburgs: Embodying Empire*. London: Penguin Books, 1996.

Wiesflecker, Hermann. Maximilian I: *Die Fundamente des habsburgischen Weltreiches*. Vienna: Verlag fuer Geschichte und Politik, 1991.

Whiteway, R.S. *The Rise of Portuguese Power in India: 1497–1550*. New Delhi: Asian Educational Services. 2007.

Wood, Diana. *Medieval Economic Thought*. Cambridge: Cambridge University Press, 2002.

Worden, Skip. *Godliness and Greed: Shifting Christian Thought on Profit and Wealth*. Lanham, MD: Lexington Books, 2010.

Wurm, Johann Peter. *Johannes Eck und der Oberdeutsche Zinsstreit, 1513–1515*. Münster: Aschendorffsche Verlagsbuchhandlung, 1997.

Zimmerling, Dieter. *Die Hanse: Handelsmacht im Zeichen der Kogge*. Duesseldorf: Econ Verlag, 1984.

Zimmermann, Wilhelm. *Der Grosser Deutscher Bauernkrieg von 1525*. Berlin: Dietz, 1952.

Zimmern, Helen. *The Hansa Towns*. New York: G.P. Putnam & Sons, 1889.

Index

About the Author

GREG STEINMETZ grew up in Cleveland, Ohio, and spent fifteen years as a journalist for publications including the *Sarasota Herald-Tribune*, the *Houston Chronicle*, *Newsday* and *The Wall Street Journal*, where he served as the Berlin bureau chief and later the London bureau chief. He currently works as a securities analyst for a money management firm in New York. He is a graduate of Colgate University and has a master's degree from Northwestern's Medill School of Journalism. He has three children and lives in Larchmont, New York.